Luke

AMERICA'S PIONEER ACES

A Historic Perspective on the First Pursuit Group's Remarkable Anomalies: Frank Luke, Jr. and Eddie Rickenbacker, and Their Times

by
James H. Farmer

Foreword
by

Frederic C. Blesse, M/Gen. USAF (Ret.)

"Rick"

BAC
Publishers, Inc.

America's Pioneer Aces – A Historic Perspective on the First Pursuit Group's Remarkable Anomalies: Frank Luke, Jr. and Eddie Rickenbacker, and Their Times.

Cover painting and chapter drawings by James H. Farmer.

Cover design by Robert Burke

Printed in the United States of America.

Published by: BAC Publishers, Inc.
                  1749 W. 13th St.
                  Upland, CA 91786

Library of Congress Control Number
                  2003106505

First Edition 2003

ISBN 0-9655730-1-X

*Dedicated to my best friend, my love
and life partner, my wife Calane.*

TABLE OF CONTENTS

A heritage of excellence, then Major Frederick C. "Boots" Blesse with his boyhood hero and fellow ace, Captain Eddie Rickenbacker at a 1953 Richmond, Virginia air show Photo courtesy Gen. Blesse.

FOREWORD

Captain Eddie Rickenbacker was my boyhood hero and my role model. At a very early age I made up my mind I wanted to be like him, become an ace and be a positive force of some kind in the aviation world.

I was the leading ace when I returned from Korea in 1952 and through a quirk of fate was thrown together for about an hour with "Captain Eddie" at an air show in Richmond, Virginia. That hour with him was the high point of my military career. We talked about World War One and compared the tactics they used fighting the Germans with the tactics we used fighting against the Russians and Chinese in Korea. A few days after our meeting I received several photos from Captain Rickenbacker taken of the two of us shaking hands before my Sabre and a Spad painted in his wartime markings. In his generous cover letter he asked if I would mind autographing one of the enclosed photos for his collection. He asked for *my* autograph, and I would have pushed a golf ball from Virginia to Washington with my nose for the same favor!

In reading this well documented account by Jim Farmer of the experiences of these early American aces you have to be impressed, no, shocked by the daring actions of these men. They flew alone much of the time attacking four, six even eight enemy aircraft shooting down one or two, scattering the remaining aircraft before withdrawing to the safety of their own lines.

Mr. Farmer has produced a thoughtful, insightful chronicle in his documentation of the lives and actions of these American Aces. They were men of incredible bravery and their exploits helped us formulate the tactics we used in World War Two, Korea and Vietnam.

Frederick C. Blesse,
M/Gen. USAF (Ret.)

VIII

ACKNOWLEDGEMENTS

Such an effort is never possible without a network in depth of knowledgeable friends and advisors. This was never more true than during the writing of *America's Pioneer Aces!* Truly invaluable was the research prowess of the remarkable Gary Fisk. No less important was the sage counsel and generous, long-practiced editorial skills of Art Ronnie. So, too, were hard to come by photographs dug out by David Menard of the USAF Museum, Research Division and Fred Freeman. Rare photos of the Luke family itself were provided by Luke family relative, R. G. Schipf. Equally priceless was the generous time of Phoenix family heir, Don Luke. Nor should the able efforts of Luke AFB's Public Affairs Office, as well as the Office of the Historian of Tyndall AFB, and Vic Johnston, 1st FW Public Affairs at Langley AFB go without a note of sincere appreciation.

No less important was the spirited encouragement and generous time, freely given, by Major General Frederick C. "Boots" Blesse, USAF (Ret.).

Sincere thanks also go to Peter M. Bowers, Walter Boyne, "Frau" Mary Ann Campbell, Tom Cassidy, Jennie Ethell Chancey, Stan Cohen, Larry Davis, Tom Doherty, Carolyn Grote of the Arizona Historical Society, Jim Hare, Lee Hauenstein, Meyers Jacobsen, Phil Jelinek, Bill Larkins, Frank Lawson, Tom Maloney, Peter Mersky, John D. Mullins, Leo Opdyke, Walter V. Powell, Dic Shepard, former Luke AFB historian Bob Sullivan, Dan Taylor, Barrett Tillman, John Underwood, Duncan Wilmore, Grandville Woodard, H. Hugh Wynne and my scriptwriting partner, John Cassidy, who put me onto the scent in the first place.

This author's exploration of various historic sites in France would not have been as rewarding as it truly was without the counsel and expertise of traveling companion/fellow historian/author Art Ronnie and the wonderful people of France. Most notably in the latter category are Lt. Col. Andre Donzeau of the French Army (R.) and Murvaux resident Bruno Alberti. Thank you, gentlemen!

Sincere appreciation also goes to my life's partner, Calane, and our daughter Christa who have endured too many absent hours.

x

INTRODUCTION

This book is the result of background research gathered over a more than twenty-year period for a feature screenplay on American World War One ace Frank Luke, Jr. Growing up steeped in the aviation literature of World War Two and Korea, it came as something of a revelation in 1978 when fellow writer and film historian John Cassidy introduced this writer to the remarkable legend and world of the famed Arizona Balloon Buster, Frank Luke.

John and this writer had spent much of our college years and adult lives delving into aviation and dramatic film history. Between the two of us, we've written four books on the subjects, not to mention an additional some 200 national and international magazine articles by this writer.

We'd also tried our hand at a couple of episodic aviation-related television scripts, one of which was produced – with another person's name on the show! But that's another story best told over a couple of drinks.

It was during these dark days that John had first brought Luke into the picture. Why not try our hand at a feature script on the great Frank Luke?

And why not?

We, of course, had not been the first, or the last to discover the story's screen merits. As early as 1929, Hollywood had taken notice of Norman S. Hall's *Balloon Buster* pulp-styled biography of Luke. World War One and early film historian Hugh Wynne had shared with this writer the recollections of the early film stunt fliers. They had told of pre-production preparations during the early 1930s, possibly by RKO Studios, and the proposed use of locally available original SE-5s and SE-5 stand-ins for the ultimately shelved project. So too had some talk circulated in the late 1960s of a feature project, to be based on Arch Whitehouse's later

Luke biography, *Hun Killer,* amid the growing popularity of such "anti-establishment" characters. And still today, as this is being written, internet rumors abound of a feature Luke film project titled *Twenty-One* under development, variously, at Paramount and Fox Studios. And still another feature-length Luke script is being shopped in cyberspace under the title *Wolves of the Sky*!

Whatever the facts of the matter, it is a remarkable, if sadly true footnote on the some 75-year history of the feature aviation film that a picture has yet to be produced on the true wartime life of a WWI American flier. And though Twentieth-Century Fox produced the 1945 feature *Captain Eddie,* the World War One phase of Eddie Rickenbacker's life in this romantic "bio-pic" occupied little more than a minute of screen time! Blink too long and audiences missed the film's star, Fred MacMurray, at the controls of Hollywood stunt flier Paul Mantz's Spad VII downing a Travel Aire "Fokker!"

The absence of such films from Hollywood's long history of air films gave even more weight to the suggestion of a Luke script. And what a character-driven story it is! Talk about a universal theme. It is a story of "Everyman," no – of the "ugly duckling" overcoming remarkable odds to emerge tragically triumphant.

There would be action, air action, aplenty. And like *Rocky*, which had just come out in 1976 to rave critical and popular acclaim, the Luke story would be a soul-searching picture personifying the desire to achieve recognition, to prove one's worth, whatever the odds and obstacles. Unlike *Rocky,* however, the odds were truly monumental: life itself.

The more this writer dug into the historical facts of the US Air Service, circa 1918, the more promising the story appeared. Air Service Colonel Billy Mitchell, as the founders of the famed Lafayette Escadrille before him, had determined to stock his pool of flying cadets with the best and brightest the nation had to offer. So it was that young men from some of the most prominent and wealthiest northeastern families, including a former president's son, headed to flying schools across the country and Canada. Many already had professional degrees from some of the most important schools of higher learning in the nation, among them: Harvard, Yale and Princeton.

How was it then that someone like Frank Luke, our high school educated "ugly duckling," springing, as he had, from blue-collar German immigrant stock, could hope to compete with such a distinguished crowd? But succeed he did – beyond everyone's wildest dreams! Luke was, and remains, the type of gifted underdog character with which audiences quickly and naturally identify.

One could even see the "logline," that all important single opening pitch line Hollywood loves so well, that conveys the essence of our story:

"A real-life examination of the ultimate price one immigrant's son pays for acceptance into the most exclusive club of American 'silver-spoon' combatants of World War One's Western Front."

Yet, there is a deeper resonance here, something profoundly democratic, uniquely American about the story. For all the obstacles, there existed a fluid, uniquely mobile American social order at play here. Something first observed a century earlier by the remarkable French sociologist Alexis de Tocqueville. There was, and remains, a certain grudging tolerance of diversity, perhaps even more important today, which left, and still leaves, the door ajar for *anyone* with the intelligence and guts to go for the brass ring.

Beyond that, however, is the mythic mystique of the *Gunfighter Nation* to which American sociologist Richard Slotkin has spoken so eloquently in more recent years. In his epic work, *Gunfighter Nation,* Slotkin defines myths as "stories drawn from a society's history that have acquired through persistent usage the power of symbolizing that society's ideology and of dramatizing its moral consciousness." He goes on to say that "when history is translated into myth the complexities of social and historical experiences are simplified and compressed into the action of representative individuals or "heroes." The narrative of the hero's action exemplifies and tests the political and/or moral validity of a particular approach to the use of human powers in the material world.

The heroes of myth embody something like the full range of ideological contradictions around which the life of the culture revolves and their adventure suggests the range of possible resolutions that the culture's lore provides."

As those mythic frontier tales of such heroes as James Fenimore Cooper's Hawkeye, Daniel Boone, Davey Crockett and the penny-dreadfuls suggest, traditional heroes "regress" to a more basic, or "primitive" condition of life, stripping away the "false values of the 'metropolis'" in order to enact a "new purified social contact." "By resisting the physical threats," while at the same time taking for his own the spiritual and intellectual prowess of his enemy, the hero is able to overcome his opponent thereby vindicating "both [his] own moral character and the power of the values [he] symbolizes."

By cutting through the negative superficiality of his metropolitan social order, the hero brings to focus those values recognized by the society at large as most essential for its survival.

So too does the simplistic, yet disturbingly complex persona of Frank Luke cut through the social order of his day to lay bare his enemies and in the process prove his ultimate worth. And as perplexing and troublesome as was Luke's behavior for his superiors, so it was all the more so for his enemies. German flight commanders were to find, to their surprise, his brand of aggressive, uniquely New World "rugged individualism" provided no end of trouble in the air. As one unnamed German Air Force intelligence officer observed after the war, American pilots "fought more like Indians than soldiers [upsetting] all our training by dashing in single-handed against our [tight, highly disciplined] formations." Many, if not most, of the American aerial victories in the First World War historically were scored on such "lone-wolf" or "voluntary patrols" after or before a day's regularly assigned operation.

To be sure, it was, and remains, a uniquely American tale.

And so it was that John Cassidy and this writer began to dig and to write. Script drafts began to flow forth, one revision after another over the years. There unfortunately, however, was no getting around the historic fact that both Luke and his equally humble partner, Joe Wehner, are dead by the end of act three. Something of a "downer," to say the least! As *Top Gun's* "Maverick" and "Goose" needed an "Iceman," so too did Frank and Joe need their own foil or benchmark – and an uplifting, living victor by film's end. In this case, it was another immigrant son, Eddie Rickenbacker, who was soon introduced to our evolving screenplay, and research files.

In the end, history's remarkable true tale of our "commoner Everymen" not only proves the equal of their well-heeled peers, but they soar to unequaled heights. Of the 130 fliers who passed through the rolls of the 27th and 94th Pursuit Squadrons during WWI, these three blue-collar immigrant sons, Luke, Wehner and Rickenbacker, would claim fully forty per cent of the two squadrons' entire wartime score! Though the price was high (two would not survive the war), so too were the rewards: two would receive their parents' adopted nation's highest honor, the Congressional Medal of Honor. Additionally, the lone survivor would successfully and astutely convert his hard-earned wartime fame into a remarkably successful postwar career, truly a Horatio Alger tale of fame and fortune, that is the "American Dream" incarnate.

So it was that in looking for a universal Everyman theme to engage an audience in the year 2000 with a fact-based dramatization set in 1918, the screenwriters turned their focus to the "underdog" backgrounds of three primarily poor immigrant sons. So too does this theme permeate this background document, leaving us with the question: "Why do the exceptions often become the exceptional?"

Today such military air arms as the Swedish and U.S. Air Forces pride themselves in having created entry level screening exams which eliminate the vast percentage of applicants ill-suited to the demands of military flying. Such tests, especially in Sweden, have drastically lowered washout rates and made more cost effective their already costly flight training programs. Still today, however, as man regularly ventures into space, if only in orbit about our frail planet, there remains no real measure to identify who, once in the cockpit, will ultimately become – should future history and technology permit – our next top scoring aces.

So it is that *America's Pioneer Aces* is the story principally of this country's two top scoring WWI aces, Frank Luke and Eddie Rickenbacker. It is the documented journey of background exploration into the origins of U.S. involvement into history's first major airwar, as well as the physical, social and technical environment that was their world. Should the case for the place of the "common man" in those relatively simplistic turn-of-the-century times be too often stressed, the writer asks the reader's forbearance. And should his dramatist's eye and fresh-found amazement, particularly with the primitive technical and physical challenges of the day, show through on occasion it is with sincere apologies.

Jim Farmer,
February 2003

XVIII

Chapter One

A GENTLEMAN'S GAME?
The First World War's American Aviators

Among the first Americans to see action at the front in the Great War of 1914-1918 were that handful of young men who joined the famed French Foreign Legion. Many fought in the trenches. A small number, however, decided they wanted to fly and transferred to the French Air Service during the first year of the war. These first American volunteers, once trained, were individually dispersed to escadrilles (air squadrons) throughout the service, flying a variety of missions and aircraft types.

It was Norman Prince[1], the pioneering American aviator and Harvard son of a wealthy Massachusetts family who first proposed the idea of an all-American squadron to fly and fight on behalf of the embattled French. Though at the time frowned upon by the neutrality-obsessed and Democratic administration of President Woodrow Wilson, it was a move whole-heartedly endorsed by a large faction of the country's moneyed Republican leadership and highly vocal former president, Theodore "Teddy" Roosevelt. Prince, soon joined in his efforts by Dr. Edmund Gros, one of the key leaders of the American Ambulance Service in France and an early advocate of America's role in the air, began actively and successfully lobbying the French government upon his arrival in Paris in the Spring of 1915. The pair was handsomely backed and financed in their efforts by railroad magnate William K. Vanderbilt and banker J.P. Morgan.

The small group was soon joined by William Thaw, the Yale son of a wealthy Pittsburgh family; Elliott Cowdin, the Harvard son of a moneyed Long Island family; Frazier Curtis, James J. Bach, and notorious prevaricator Bert Hall. Thaw, Bach and Hall had seen service in the French Foreign Legion before transferring to the air service in December 1914. Prince, Cowdin and Curtis had joined the French Air Service in March 1915 and were sent to Pau, the Prince family's second home for more than a decade, for flight training.

On 15 March 1915 the predominantly American-piloted flying unit was formally organized under the command of French Capitaine Georges Thenault and designated that April "N.124." As was the French custom, the unit's designator prefix: "N" stood for Nieuport, the make of chasse, or pursuit airplane assigned to the squadron. On 20 April, N.124 was moved to the front under the control of the French VII Armée.

For political purposes, the squadron was known to the press as the Escadrille Americaine (The American Squadron). That November, however, after formal German protest pointing to the United States' official and continuing neutrality in the conflict, the name was first changed to a rather nondescript Escadrille de Volontaires (Squadron of the Volunteers). On 6 December 1916 Dr. Gros offered the inspired final handle for N.124: L' Escadrille Lafayette, the Lafayette Escadrille. With an eye toward keeping the American-manned air unit in the press and before the American public, Dr. Gros had brilliantly pulled a gallant French name from his homeland's proud revolutionary history. The unit now show-cased the name of the famed French general who so gallantly helped direct the American colonies to victory in their war of independence from Britain. And while inspiring just the right note of purpose, America's brave young men now returned the favor. The title made no specific mention of direct, if unofficial U.S. citizen involvement in the conflict.

Of this "Valiant 38" Americans who served with the Lafayette Escadrille, nearly half came from prominent northeastern families.

Fully 11 of these Yankee fliers were millionaire's sons, 23 more came from upper and upper-middle-class families. The fliers' median age of 26 was some five years higher than the average wartime pilot. So too was the educational background remarkably higher than the average wartime doughboy by a wide margin. Fully 30 of the 38 fliers came to the Lafayette Escadrille with college degrees, 25 of these from noted eastern colleges – including nine from Harvard. Their young prewar careers had ranged from architects, engineers, pre-med students, adventurers and one professional polo champion to the poor son of a Baptist minister.

The reasons for the disproportionately high percentage of representation from the upper rungs of the societal ladder among America's early wartime fliers are many. First, of course, and quite simply, many of these young men had the independent means and freedom to travel to Europe. Secondly, many were from families who had substantial investments at stake in France and willingly supported the cause, even if their nation's administration did not. Third, Dr. Gros was looking for America's best and brightest, to equal and hopefully to best the finest young warriors the aristocracies of the European combatants were fielding for their air forces. The American college campus, then heavily populated, if not dominated by sons of privilege, became a logical hunting ground.

But were such men the whole answer, the only answer?

On 18 May 1916 Kiffen Rockwell of Ashville, North Carolina – a graduate of the famed Virginia Military Institute (VMI) and Washington and Lee College – scored the Escadrille's and America's first aerial victory of the war. Within weeks, the squadron's exploits had spread across the Atlantic, generating a flood of American volunteers and a ground-swell of popular national support.

Soon there were more American volunteers for flight training than could be handled by a single squadron. The Lafayette Flying Corps came into being to handle the overload. And in the end, the original Lafayette Escadrille had well served its most important function, generating American popular support and increasingly strong political support for the allied cause.

But of these "Valiant 38," 11 would not survive the war; and before being disbanded in February of 1918, the Lafayette Escadrille had amassed a rather pedestrian 39 aerial victories. None of this unit's widely heralded and high-priced 'livestock' had amassed more than three kills, save one. And that one had dropped out of school as a young teenager to help support his family and later to see the world. His name was Gervais Raoul Lufbery, and his lone official score of 16 had accounted for nearly half of his Escadrille's victories.

Clearly, there was more to the making of a successful fighter pilot than social standing and higher education, but the message would be slow in coming.

As late as the summer of 1915 the British had assumed that "gentlemen weekend fliers" would continue to keep the Royal Flying Corps well supplied with aviators. And as late as 1917 Sefton Brancker, the British Director General of Military Aeronautics, continued to equate the pilot class with that of a cavalry officer. "Flying," he suggested, "is perhaps a little easier than riding a horse because you sit in a comfortable armchair in a quiet machine instead of a slippery saddle on a very lively horse."[2]

"From such assumptions," points out historian Denis Winter, "it follows that almost any *gentleman* was acceptable for training."[3] And, to be sure, a number of the war's most celebrated fliers came from the ranks of the cavalry, among them, Canada's Billy Bishop and Germany's Werner Voss and Manfred von Richthofen.

Though class distinctions were certainly less rigid within American society – the elite, the moneyed, higher educated elements of society recruited and drawn to flying were no less obvious when the United States finally entered the war.

THE YANKS ARE COMING

After the Germans announced a return to unrestricted submarine warfare on the Atlantic in January of 1917 and the public revelation of Germany's notorious Zimmermann Telegram to Mexico promising aid in the restoration of their former territories in Texas,

The Lafayette Escadrille's sole air ace, Raoul Lufbery, is seen here at the controls of his French Nieuport Scout preparing for another sortie from the squadron's aerodrome at Cachy. Though he became a triple-ace with N.123, officially downing 16 enemy airplanes, Lufbery was anything but a model poster child for the Escadrille Lafayette!

New Mexico and Arizona, President Wilson finally went before Congress. On 2 April he asked for a declaration of war against Germany and the Central Powers.

Four days later, the United States officially entered the war.

Though the American declaration couldn't have come at a better time for beleaguered Allied air services, then withering under the German aerial onslaught of 'Bloody April,' relief would not be soon in coming. For considerably more problematical than the expansion of its Army and world-class Navy would be the creation – from virtually nothing – of a world-class air service. By the summer of 1918 U.S. Army Signal Corps chief Brigadier George Squier's rash assertion the previous spring that the nation would build "an army in the air, regiments and brigades of winged cavalry on gas driven flying horses" had become a national joke of politically embarrassing proportions; the nation's first year goal of 22,000 aircraft remained nowhere in sight. Indeed, by war's end not a single combat land plane of original American design would have reached the front.[4]

No less challenging for the United States was the demand for pilots. In the Spring of 1917 the aviation section of the Army Signal Corps boasted but 26 'fully trained' pilots – none of which had so much as seen a 'modern' warplane. In fact, in the face of growing congressional opposition party protests, the Wilson administration had purposely and repeatedly forbid military expansion since 1914 for fear of inciting the German government – an ocean away.

Neither the nation's infant aircraft industry nor the Signal Corps pilot training program was immediately up to the volume demanded of a world war. To organize the country's massive air training program, Squier selected Yale University history professor and Air Guard flier, Dr. Hiram Bingham. Bingham established a training program composed of three major components: ground school, primary flight training and advanced flight training. The ground school phase would ultimately be offered through eight campuses of the nation's university system.

Less immediate, however, would be the creation of the Army's primary flight training program. On 5 August 1917, Major Henry H. "Hap" Arnold was appointed head of the Airfield Selection Board. Within a month the sites for most of the war's new airfields had been selected. Most of these would be in operation by Christmas. Many of the fields were to become legendary in the history of U.S. military aviation. Among the airfields opened during World War One were Kelly and Brooks Fields near San Antonio, Texas; Talliaferro Field near Fort Worth; Love Field, Dallas; Call Field, Wichita Falls; Rich Field, Waco; and Ellington Field, Houston, all in Texas. Branching out around the country, Scott Field, Belleville, and Chanute Field, Rantoul were both in Illinois. Selfridge Field was established in Mt. Clemens, Michigan; Wilbur Wright Field, Dayton, Ohio; Langley Field, Virginia; March Field, Riverside, and Mather Field, Sacramento, both in California; and Post Field, Fort Sill, Oklahoma.

During the summer of 1917, however, and despite a construction rate pushed to a "furious pace," these new fields remained months away from operation. In the meantime, Canada had agreed to provide primary flying facilities during the summer months in

When in Rome ... At Issoudun in France, what today might be called the schools basic flight trainer was the early Nieuport Scout. Note the "V" wing strut, which often contributed to lower wing twisting and occasional structural failure. The United States purchased 705 of these so-called Nieuport "Vee-Strutters," series 17 throught 27, for their French-based flight training program.

exchange for the use of American fields during the winter. While Canadian facilities began to make up some of America's shortfall in primary flight instruction, General Pershing ordered another 100 cadets per month to Europe beginning 1 July, to get their primary instruction at the hands of our new Allies. Unfavorable fall weather on the continent, however, made the effort all but futile.

It was decided early on that the advanced portion of the flight training program would take place overseas in France, England and Italy. There were neither advanced aircraft types nor American instructors with the requisite combat experience for such a program in the United States.

By the Armistice, the United States had constructed nine Aviation Instruction Centers (AIC) in France, England and Italy. Seven of these AICs, however, were located in France – the largest and most renowned being the expansive facility whose headquarters was located in Central France, some six miles outside the city of Issoudun. Designed in large measure by U.S. Training Division head Colonel W.G. Kilner, the complex, designated as the Third AIC, was composed of three primary flight training fields clustered around the school headquarters with another seven satellite fields dedicated to advanced pursuit flight training.

So important was the chasse, or pursuit program, to World War One aviation that the Fourth AIC at Avord and the Sixth AIC at Pau and the Ninth AIC in England – nearly half of the nine AICs constructed – were dedicated to producing fighter pilots. The Seventh AIC in Clermont-Ferrand, France and the Eighth AIC in Foggia, Italy, were concerned with bombardment, while the First AIC in the Paris area and the Fifth AIC in Bron, France, trained aircraft mechanics. The Second AIC at Tours, France, was a primary flight instruction facility until January 1918 when it converted over to observation training.

THE AIRMEN

While aircraft and flight training facilities were in decidedly short supply during the first months after the United States entry into the war, there was no shortage of American volunteers for the Air Service. The romanticized tales of the airwar in Europe, with such "Knights of the Sky" as France's George Guynemer, England's Albert Ball, "Mick" Mannock and Jimmy McCudden, Canada's "Billy" Bishop, and America's own Lafayette Escadrille, observed World War air historian James J. Hudson, "fired the imagination of American youth."[5]

By the Armistice, some 40,000 Americans had volunteered for flight training. Of these, approximately 15,000 actually entered the primary flying schools in the United States, 8,688 ultimately receiving their Reserve Military Aviator (RMA) ratings. With another 2,000 American aviators trained in Europe, the United States had more than 10,000 pilots at its disposal by November 1918. Ultimately, it was these fresh, enthusiastic aircrews who became America's most important contribution to the Allied air campaign.

But, what kind of man was the U.S. Air Service looking for?

The U.S. Army's largest overseas Aviation Instruction Center (AIC) was located near Issoudun in Central France. The massive complex, officially known as the Third AIC, consisted of three primary and seven satellite flight training fields.

Certainly, individuals of superior intelligence and athletic ability would be desirable. A college background, such as those of so many of the Lafayette Escadrille fliers, was to be encouraged. But to find such highly-educated young men, in the vast numbers required by a world war, in the United States of 1917 where Americans with at least two years of college then made up but 2.2 percent of the population, would prove problematical at best.[6] Clearly, however, this was the kind of flying candidate then Major Billy Mitchell, as head of the Signal Corps aviation section, was looking for as early as the Fall of 1916. In an effort to help silence the issue of military preparedness during his run for reelection and a second term, President Wilson had conservatively approved the formation of a 500-pilot aerial reserve corps. But it was Mitchell who established the recruitment guidelines for the flying cadets. The men were to be "between the ages of 21 and 27, with a college education or its equivalent."[7] By the declaration of war less than a year later, the top age would further have been lowered to 25.

Happily, by the arrival of the war in April 1917, fortune was

As early as the fall of 1916 Major William "Billy" Mitchell, as head of the Signal Corps' Aviation Section, suggested pilot cadets should be "between the ages of 21 and 27, with a college education or its equivalent." At that time in American history a college education was a privilege generally limited to society's upper class - their numbers strictly limited.

shining on the selection process as scores and hundreds of well-heeled, college-educated young men volunteered for the Air Service. And, to be sure, a significant portion of those first American Air Service pilots reaching the front in the spring of 1918 did, indeed, have impressive educational credentials. Early confirmation of Dr. Bingham and the air training program appeared to have arrived with remarkable speed on 14 April 1918, on the first official day of U.S. Air Service (USAS) operations at the front. On that opening day, Harvard graduate Douglas Campbell and Yale alum Alan Winslow of the 94th Aero Squadron downed the first two German aircraft of the war to rave press accountings. Yet by that July nearly half, 38 of 80, of these highly select young men of the 94th's parent and pioneering 1st Pursuit Group had been lost in the fierce fighting over Chateau-Thierry. Their ranks, however, would soon be restocked with new, often less celebrated Americans from the replacement pool. And though the vast numbers required by war's attrition dictated that many of their backgrounds would lack the social and educational luster of their earlier cohorts, an extraordinary, if ill defined potential nonetheless, resided in a number of their rough-hewn 1918 contenders. Just where these unseen seeds of aerial greatness lay hidden, and in whom, remained unanswered for the Allies' newest combatant nation – the United States. But they would flower in their own time – and then often within the most unexpected individuals.

Chapter One
Insert No. 1

GERVAIS RAOUL LUFBERY

For all the famed Lafayette Escadrille pilots' oft celebrated advanced college degrees and social prominence, the unit's top scorer, and indeed only ace, was school dropout/adventurer Raoul Lufbery. And while a couple of the squadron's 38 members left the organization with one, two or three confirmed victories, Lufbery's remarkable official score of 16, some sources say 17, was in itself deceptive. A number of fellow fliers after the war suggested his actual record of aerial kills was closer to 70!

When asked by one flier if his long list of unconfirmed engagements didn't bother him, he was said to have replied, "What the hell do I care? I know I got them."

Raoul Lufbery was born in Clermont-Ferrand, France, on 21 March 1885, the youngest son of New York chemist/researcher and stamp collector Edward Lufbery. His mother, Annette, had died within a year of his birth. By 1890, Raoul's remarried father had moved with his new wife, Marie, back to the United States, leaving the five-year-old Raoul and his two older brothers to be raised by French relatives. As would Eddie Rickenbacker, the 16-year-old Raoul dropped out of school around 1910 and, with his brother Charles, began to work in a chocolate factory to help support the family.

Raoul's wanderlust, however, had gotten the better of him by 1904 when he left France. Supporting himself with odd jobs, he traveled through North Africa, Turkey, the Balkans and Germany. In 1906 he headed for the United States and Wallingford, Connecticut, to see his father, who was, as it turned out, on his way to Europe. Raoul remained in Wallingford for the next two years supporting himself as a maker of casket handles.

Around 1908 the youth again hit the road and the high seas,

going first to Cuba, then New Orleans and San Francisco before joining the U.S. Army where he served two years in the Philippines. While in the Army, Raoul became a naturalized U.S. citizen, but for the remainder of his life he would continue to see himself as a Frenchman. While in the Army, Raoul also distinguished himself as the top rifle marksman in his regiment.

After two years and an honorable discharge, Lufbery headed first for Japan, then China and on to India where, in 1912 Calcutta, he was befriended by French exhibition pilot Marc Pourpe. The intelligent, quick-study Lufbery had soon learned all there was to know about the rotary-powered Bleriot and had become Pourpe's personal mechanic. Together, the pair toured China and Egypt.

During the summer of 1914, Pourpe and Lufbery returned to France to re-equip and prepare for a new Asian tour. When war broke out that August, the two volunteered for the French Air Service. On 2 December 1914 Pourpe was killed in a failed landing attempt in fog. Raoul Lufbery, his devoted mechanic, would blame the mishap on the Germans.

Volunteering for flight training himself, Raoul was assigned to the Voisin-equipped bombing squadron Escadrille V.B. 106 in October 1915. In May 1916 Lufbery requested retraining as a chasse or pursuit pilot. Though Raoul Lufbery was nearly washed out for failing to master the aerobatic regimen, his determination won out and later that month he was assigned to the new Nieuport-equipped Escadrille Americaine.

As Rickenbaker after him, Corporal Lufbery's maintenance expertise, close attention to his Lewis machine gun and ammunition was to pay handsome dividends. On 30 July 1916, the recently promoted Sergeant Lufbery earned his first confirmed aerial victory. A second enemy would fall the following day, with a third official kill by the end of the week. A fourth victory over an Aviatik was scored on 8 August.

Soon, the Lafayette Escadrille commander, Captain Georges Thenault, was calling Lufbery a "superman." On 12 October, Raoul was the first American flier to become an ace when he downed a Roland C.II.

Never a social mixer, the quiet-spoken, often sullen Lufbery was a natural loner, preferring voluntary, or "lone-wolf" patrols over formation assignments. Rather than fight Lufbery's natural inclinations, Thenault channeled them for the squadron's good by making him the unit's lone top cover man, shadowing and forewarning his squadron mates of enemy attack.

On 24 October 1917 Raoul Lufbery was made a sous-lieutenant, with Bill Thaw, the only other N.124 pilot to earn an officer's commission during his tenure with the Lafayette Escadrille. By 2 December 1917, Lufbery was officially a triple ace with 16 kills to his credit. Lufbery's score would not be surpassed by another American until the September 1918 rampage of Arizonan Frank Luke, Jr.

Not bad for an impoverished teen dropout!

Chapter One
Insert No. 2

PROFILE OF A SUCCESSFUL
AMERICAN GREAT WAR PILOT

The July 1983 issue of *World War I Aeroplanes* reprinted the results of a mid-1970s study of those "recurring sets of qualities" which characterized 40 veteran World War One fliers who had survived the conflict. The results had originally been published in *Focus,* the medical journal of the Harvard Medical Area. The report outlined the conclusions of Dr. Thomas Hackett, then an Eban S. Draper Professor of Psychiatry and Chief of the Department at Massachusetts General Hospital. With Dr. Edwin Cassem, Associate Professor of Psychiatry, Hackett had, in 1969, developed the Hackett-Cassem Denial Scale.

PERSONALITY AND BACKGROUND
CHARACTERISTICS

Among Dr. Hackett's conclusions, such aerial survivors typically had:

1. Strong psychological denial mechanisms. That is they "consciously or unconsciously repudiated part or all of the total available meaning of a [life threatening] event to allay fear and anxiety.
2. They possessed a strong sense of optimism. "Many maintained an attitude of invulnerability. These pilots saw themselves as indestructible. They found the prospect of flying exciting – until they began to see most of their friends shot down. Even then, they rarely thought they themselves would be hit."
3. They possessed a strong sense of humor. It was another device that further reduced their sense of fear or worry "in times of

great stress, as in combat."

4. Almost all were non-introspective. "They liked to talk about things, like politics, [rather than] about their own psychology or that of others."

5. All knew how to relax. That is, they knew how to escape, how to have fun.

6. "All took risks throughout their lives, yet they worked to minimize the degree of risk and only took chances under optimal conditions. They wouldn't take foolish risks" – neither during the war nor later when considering postwar business ventures.

7. "All were [the] eldest sons of middle – or upper income families which had not been split by divorce. Twenty-four of those interviewed strongly identified with their fathers."

8. "Seventy-five percent were college graduates or in college when they entered the Air [Service] during World War One. All of the pilots went on to work as lawyers, businessmen, professors, or other white collar professions."

9. "All were athletic, they played contact sports as young adults."

10. "All were Republicans." – when interviewed during the mid-1970s.

Chapter Two

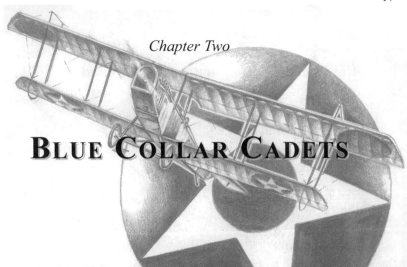

BLUE COLLAR CADETS

The iron door of the dusty jail swung open with audible complaint, The smiling, remorseless youth was brought into the sheriff's coldly functional office and bid seated. There the teenager's older brother Edwin, then a Phoenix deputy, tore into his junior sibling for yet his latest adventure the other side of the law.

"Folks don't take kindly to stealing or careless gunplay in these parts. It isn't, after all, your first run in with the sheriff. You weren't suspended from the school football team or expelled from Phoenix High itself without good cause.

"When are you going to learn, Frank!"

The Arizona son could only offer a mischievous twinkle and that infuriatingly infectious smile.

———

An American aero squadron composed entirely of former professional racecar drivers? Ridiculous, thought the Army staffer fingered to dispose of the well-meaning, if absurd proposition. He took full measure of the earnest six-foot-two Columbus, Ohio, native before him, before returning to the written proposal lying on his overburdened desk. Why, none of these drivers have more than a high school education! The least qualified of these was perhaps the gentleman seated before him in the expensive suit. He hadn't even finished the seventh grade and at 27 was already over the age limit for Air Service flying cadets. Perhaps even more important, as a gifted mechanic, he knew too much about the frail inner workings of the internal combustion engine – a decidedly debilitating psychological factor for a flier who must come to rely upon his engine as life itself.

After the ground-bound officer politely put forth the United States Air Service's grounds for rejecting his proposal as well as his personal services, it was the celebrated race driver's turn to shake his head with unfathomable incredulity.

———

"The most unexpected people make good pilots and very often the most promising ones never attain more than mediocrity in the air..."[1]

So declared England's Sefton Brancker, Director General of Military Aeronautics, in a 1916 address before his nation's Aeronautical Society. Nowhere would this emerging fact of aerial warfare be more true than within the American Air Service. Of the 114 American aces, pilots with five or more aerial victories – or aerial kills – to their credit by war's end, less than a third, 34, are known to have had at least some college background – an educational factor originally carrying considerable weight with USAS recruiters. Interestingly, of the nine American wartime fliers who attained the rarified status of double ace or better (10 or more victories), the top three scorers, all American "Ace of Aces" at one time or another, had no better than a high school education.

What then, if not a youth below the age of 25 and high education credentials, made for a superior combat flier? Depending upon the nationality, some would call it "tener," "ganas," "avoir," "desire," "spirit," or simply "grit." Whatever the word or term and regardless of circumstance or background, the Great War quickly and cruelly separated those who had that all too elusive element, or combination of elements, from those who did not.

A SELF-MADE MAN

The man who came to be known as Edward Vernon Rickenbacker came into this world on 8 October 1890 simply as Edward Rickenbacher – no middle name and no Anglicized second 'k' to replace the 'h' in his family name. He was born far from the materiality and socially privileged elite of the eastern United States. An Ivy League higher education was not a part of his birthright.

Rather, young Eddie was the third child of eight born to the Columbus, Ohio working class family of William and Elizabeth Rickenbacher. The undersized youth's parents had emigrated from Switzerland, his father entering the country as a common laborer, his mother as a housemaid.

What moneys brought into the household by William and Elizabeth, who took in laundry after marriage, were managed with evangelistic fervor. In 1893, William moved his growing family into a four-room house, which he'd built with his own hands, at 1334 East Livingston Avenue in the blue collar section of

Army Sergeant Eddie Rickenbacker first served in France as an Army driver for ranking U.S. Officers - most notably and fortuitously, Colonel William "Billy" Mitchell, head of U.S. air operations on the Western Front.

Columbus. Most of the family's food was raised on their 50 by 200-foot lot. The children's milk was provided by the family goat; the eggs were supplied by their yard's chickens.

Despite his deceptively diminutive size, young Eddie was a tough kid, a street fighter and natural born leader who headed up the local Horse Head gang. He was also a practiced thief who routinely cashed in his haul of portable goods with a local fence.

Eddie's early years sorely tried the patience of his reverent Swiss Calvinist mother who feared reform school might be in her adventuresome son's future.

Nor had Eddie's early years in public school helped tame his bent for trouble. Never hesitating to enter a fight when challenged, Eddie had more to defend than his shabby hand-me-down clothes or mismatched shoes. Before his parents had become comfortable with their new country's tongue, German was the household, as well as young Eddie's, first language. He'd entered school with what he later called "an atrocious accent." He regularly fought through the school yard and surrounding streets going to and leaving school.   He was variously called "Whitey," "Towhead," "Dutchy," or simply "Kraut" by the neighborhood kids.

"Learned men," writes Rickenbacker biographer Finis Farr, "tell us that experiences of this sort have something to do with making juvenile delinquents."[2]

There were, however, numerous evolving elements of character and environment going into the makeup of the young Rickenbacher. Certainly not the least of these was the strong spiritual influence of his mother, to whom he was devoted until death, and with whom he shared nightly the reading of the family's German-language Bible. Rick's strong positive mental attitudes, which he consciously developed as he matured, possessed significant spiritual overtones.

And then there was his natural art abilities, which Eddie and his teachers discovered at an early age. The young Rickenbacher loved to draw. These superior gifts, as revealed through his rendering, painting, and later sculpture, offered a portent of things to come. Recent right-brain studies suggest there is a strong correlation between such spatial-relationship abilities as those exhibited in drawing and the related arts and the natural skills so important to motoring and piloting. Indeed, as strange as it may seem, many a celebrated military pilot has possessed such artistic skills in abundance![3]

Finally, Eddie's father William passed on to his young son a love of tools and machines. He also instilled a strong work ethic that warned against procrastination and leaving a job half-done or trusting to chance. As the years passed, a maturing Eddie would begin to perceive an amalgamation of his art skills with those of the machine age, recognizing the functional beauty of a well designed and crafted piece of machinery – be it a 70-mile-per-hour Duesenberg automobile or a French-made Spad pursuit plane.

But perhaps the most valuable gift Eddie received from his father was his positive sense of wonder as the new Machine Age continued to unfold about them.

In 1904, the year after the Wright Brothers' first flight, William told his son: "Eddie, you're a lucky boy to be born when you were. There are a lot of new things in the making, and you ought to be ready to have a hand in them."[4]

It was an outlook that was to frame Rickenbacher's view of the world for the rest of his days, right into the dawning of the Jet Age.

In August 1904, at the age of 12, Eddie's childhood effectively came to an abrupt end with the death of his father. Contrary to the sanitized account told in Rickenbacker's own autobiography and in the 1945 biographical feature film *Captain Eddie,* the senior Rickenbacher did not succumb to an industrial accident, but rather was murdered on the job. Columbus was experiencing an unrelenting hot spell on 22 July. Tempers were short. William, who was laying cement sidewalks seven blocks from his home, got into a verbal altercation with an African-American man later identified as William Gaines. The confrontation soon escalated to the point where Gaines struck the senior Rickenbacher unconscious with a spirit level. Rickenbacher lingered in the hospital for the next week before going into a coma and finally passing away on 5 August.

Convicted of manslaughter, Gaines would serve ten years in

prison.

Facing financial reality, Elizabeth, now a widow with seven children and little money, reluctantly consented to Eddie's dropping out of the seventh grade so that he might help support the family with a full-time job. Lying about his age, Eddie found work at a glass factory working a 12-hour night shift, six days a week. After his shift and the four-mile round trip walk to and from work each day, Eddie still had his day's chores to do. Looking back on this period of his life years later, Rickenbacker would recall there never was a day when he was not tired.

The new responsibilities quickly matured Eddie's thinking. There was little time for mischief now that he worked in a man's world, putting food on the family table. Keeping his eyes open, never doubting something better was lying just a couple of blocks away, he began to look for better paying day jobs closer to home. Eddie took a job at a steel-casting plant for three months and then moved on to a brewery, setting pins after hours at a local bowling alley. He then went to work for the Zender Monument Company where he put his artistic skills to work personally carving and engraving a headstone for his father's grave.

Eddie's thoughts of becoming, as he put it, a "great sculptor" in the vein of Michelangelo, however, were short-lived, given the hazards of breathing marble dust all day and the immediate lure of "gasoline alley" and the thriving young automobile industry which was then headquartered in Columbus.

After six months working in the machine shops of the Pennsylvania Railroad, Rick got a job at the Evans Auto Garage. The year was 1905. The young Rickenbacher learned all he could before moving on to work with pioneering auto builder Lee Frayer at the Frayer-Miller auto plant.

Frayer soon took the quick learning, fatherless boy under his wing, promoting him from janitor to the engineering department. Rick continued with his after-hours studies, keeping up with a cor-respondence course in mechanical engineering he'd begun while still working at the Evans Garage.

Rickenbacher also got his first taste of auto racing with Lee

Rickenbacker, who'd taken part in the first Indianapolis 500-Mile Race in 1911, had become famed automotive designer Fred Duesenberg's auto race team leader. By 1915 Eddie was earning $60,000 annually - a monetary value approaching some $1 million dollars in the currency of the year 2000. That is annual, untaxed income!

Frayer in the September 1906 Vanderbilt Cup Race. He served as Frayer's onboard race mechanic. In 1907, the respected automotive engineer asked Eddie to join him when Clinton D. Firestone hired Frayer as the Columbus Buggy Company's new chief engineer and general manager. Eddie, who was then 17 years old, was put in charge of the 15-man experimental department shortly after Frayer's arrival. Quickly coming to know the inner workings of the new two-cylinder Firestone-Columbus motor car with the gifted insight of an uptown New York surgeon, Eddie was sent into the field as a company representative to troubleshoot local maintenance and engineering problems. He also found himself promoting regional sales.

By March 1910, at the age of 19, Eddie was assigned to the North-Central states and promoted to branch manager. With a growing appreciation for the importance of public promotion, as well as a fascination for the new sport, Eddie began a new weekend career of dirt track racing with a personally modified version of his company's product. Unlike other drivers, who trusted their fate to chance, Eddie made a point of driving the track the day *before* each race until he knew the course like the engine of his car. During the summer of 1910 he raced throughout Nebraska and Iowa. And though he was making a handsome $150 a month as a branch manager, he discovered himself clearing $1,500 – nearly a year's income - during one two-day race period alone!

On 30 May 1911, Eddie took part in his first Indianapolis 500-mile race. And though he lost, he was finding it harder to return to the mundane chore of selling cars. During the summer of 1912, Eddie resigned his lucrative position to sign on as a three-dollar-a-day mechanic working for the brilliant automotive designer, Fred Duesenberg. By 1913, Eddie had moved his way up to becoming Duesenberg's auto race team leader. That summer, under Eddie's aggressive leadership, the team won $12,500 at the Sioux City races. Eddie had now entered the big leagues of professional auto racing, enjoying and enduring all the fame, monetary rewards and physical risks that came with the elevated public position. Sports writers were calling him the "Speedy Swiss," "The Dutch Demon," "The Big Teuton," and "The Baron." In 1915 Eddie branched out on his own, leading his own race team to glory and, for Rick, his most profitable year ever as a racecar driver. That year Rickenbacher personally earned $60,000; an amount certainly approaching, if not surpassing the million dollar mark in year 2000 dollars! Less welcome that year, as time would prove, would be a Los Angeles sports columnist's creative fiction about Eddie's background, calling him "Baron Edward von Rickenbacher," the dispossessed son of a Prussian nobleman.

The Allies' Great War had been raging in Europe against Germany and the Central Powers for two years when Eddie, drawn by visions of foreign travel, agreed to join Englishman Louis Coatalen's Sunbeam Motor Works racing team in England to prepare for the 1917 racing season in the United States. To the native-born American's great surprise, he was detained on his ship when it arrived in Liverpool in December 1916. The reason? "Von Rickenbacher" was suspected by British intelligence agents of being a German spy! After a couple of days, Coatalen was able to get Eddie to London under tight secret service scrutiny. Rickenbacher remained in England for two months working with the Sunbeam racing team. During this period he visited the famed Brooklands Speedway track which had been turned over to the Royal Flying Corps for use as a flight-training field. So impressed was Rick with the blooded veteran RFC flight instructors he talked to that he determined he would fly for his country should it come into the war.

He did not have long to wait.

On 3 February 1917, after Germany declared unrestricted submarine warfare, the Central Powers gave Americans abroad five days to leave Europe. Eddie promptly returned to the United States where, at his own expense, he went on a cross-country speaking tour warning of Germany's intent. So strong was Rickenbacher's opposition to Germany that he formally changed his family name, replacing the 'h' with a second anglicizing 'k.' He would also, over the years, add the middle name of "Vernon," to lend an air of sophistication to his evolving, carefully-crafted, upwardly mobile persona. And though he would forever respond to the well known "Eddie," his friends knew to call him "Rick." "Eddie," the mature Rickenbacker felt, was more properly the familiar nickname of a preteen youngster.

On his return to the United States, Rick had more on his mind than his "personal handle." He envisioned an American aero squadron made up entirely of "mature men of proven swift reflexes" – that is, racecar drivers. The Signal Corps chief, General George Squier, assigned a staff officer to let the famed racecar driver down gently. In the unsettling process, however, Rick learned that not only was his idea rejected, but that he himself at the "advanced" age of 27 was too old by two years to be accepted into the air cadet program. Nor did he have the required formal education.

Rickenbacker was stunned by his government's response. He

determined he would find a way into the air service, but for the moment all he could do was wait and see what developed.

Again, he did not have long to wait.

In May 1917, a month after America's entry into the war, Rickenbacker received a call from one of his longtime racing fans, Army Major Burgess Lewis. General Pershing and his advance staff were preparing to leave New York within three days for Europe. Lewis asked the Columbus native if he would like to come along as a staff driver. Within two days Rick had turned over his Mercedes-equipped race team to his crew chief and arrived in New York to be fitted for the uniform of a freshly minted, if untrained, army sergeant.

Once in the combat zone, Rickenbacker hoped to somehow find a way around the "ridiculous regulations" that were keeping him out of the air. Contrary to popular belief, Rickenbacker never was General Pershing's personal driver. He was, however, frequently requested to drive for Colonel William "Billy" Mitchell, head of the U.S. air operations on the Western Front. Among the trips Eddie took with Mitchell was to inspect the wheat fields near the village of Issoudun, the future site of the famed and extensive ten-field complex, officially to be known as the Third Aviation Instruction Center.

Throughout this period, Rickenbacker's renown as a professional racecar driver continued to pay dividends. William S. Nye, head of the U.S. Secret Service, was one of those fans. He warned Rick that he was still under surveillance by counterintelligence, and would continue to be during his first months in combat. Another fan, former New York banker James Miller, asked Rick to serve under him as the engineering officer of the new Issoudun complex. Rick's face lit up. He agreed to take on the position, adding, however, that he felt such an *officer* should know how to fly.

Standing in good stead with Billy Mitchell, the necessary orders were cut within days – pending a physical. Once again luck was on Rick's side as the examining physician was yet another of his racing fans. The doctor officially recorded Rickenbacker's birth date as 8 October 1892 so that he could fall within the maximum twenty-five year old age requirement.

Early in September 1917, Rick arrived at the French primary flying school at Tours. After gaining ground handling experience with non-flying clipped-wing Morane-Saulniers, Rickenbacker soloed in the pusher-type Caudron biplane. The course lasted 17 days. After 25 hours of flight time, Rick emerged as an officer and pilot in the U.S. Air Service.

Returning to Issoudun by the end of the month, Rick dove into his new responsibilities as the field's engineering officer. There he organized the repair shops, spare parts and transportation departments. In time, Major Carl "Tooey" Spaatz replaced Miller as field commander. With Rickenbacker, Spaatz was one of five of the field's staff officers to possess Germanic family names. Collectively, the newly arriving American cadets called them the "five German spies."

By January 1918, some one thousand cadets, honor graduates of stateside ground schools, had been "rewarded for good work and high qualities" by being sent directly to France for primary flight training. Among the cadets were future members of the 94th and 95th Aero Squadrons.

It was soon discovered, however, there was no room in the country's already overcrowded primary flight school system for new students. The group was diverted to the mud hole of the as yet uncompleted advanced flying school at Issoudun. There they performed manual labor and construction duties in an effort to get that facility up and running. At Issoudun the cadets soon became known as "The Million Dollar Guard," since each American was paid $100 a month and it was calculated that it would take ten months for these high-priced laborers to find postings at primary flight schools. Tensions, needless to say, between the cadet-laborers and their commanding officers ran high.

"The new group [of American cadets]," recalled Rickenbacker, "had good reasons to object to me personally. Its members were all young men of good family; recruited from Ivy League universities... they came in expecting to find a flying school in full operation. Instead they found a mud hole and a tough Swiss-German engineer with a grammar-school education and the grubbiest of chores for them to perform."[5]

Adding to the tension as the weeks passed, those students of less sterling backgrounds and academic prowess, such as Frank Luke, who'd remained in the United States to take their primary flight training began arriving in France as commissioned officers. In an effort to correct the injustice, "The Million Dollar Guard" was awarded their commissions before primary flight training. Should they later wash out, their ranks reverted to that of an enlisted man.

As Rickenbacker's demanding schedule permitted, he stole time to sit in on ground school lectures and continued to build flying hours on his own away from the field and official eyes. Over the months Rick gained experience and command of the 23, 18 and 15-meter Nieuports. By February 1918 Rickenbacker had so worn down Spaatz with his continual requests for combat duty that he was transferred to the aerial gunnery school at Cazeau in Southern France.

Next stop: the front.

Frank Luke, Jr. at the controls of his Nieuport trainer, possibly at the gunnery school at Cazeau in Southern France.

The Arizona Hellion

As a young man he was called "arrogant as Lucifer," "self-centered," "belligerent," "a hell raiser," and later: "absolutely fearless," "that mad flier," "the greatest fighting aviator the world has known." Yet he would never see the inside of an Ivy League college. He had, however, been expelled, if only briefly, from his high school and had seen, if only briefly, the inside of the local jail. Nor had he enjoyed growing up with the social privileges of a moneyed Eastern family, though what privileges that did exist surpassed those of the young Rickenbacher. And, most certainly Frank Luke Jr. did not fulfill the idealized model of the shave-tail cadet officially put forth by the U.S. Air Service recruiting office. Yet when all was said and done, Frank Luke, Jr. had few equals in the air.

It was a singularly remarkable, if brief life whose heritage led directly back to Prussia.

Frank's paternal grandfather, Lorenz Lueck, was born in the Ruhr Valley in 1821. In November 1853 he was married by a Catholic priest to Regina Rosenberg in Dahlhausen. Frank Lueck, the third of the couple's four children, was born in 1859. Sometime between 1860 and 1862 the Lueck family moved to the United States. As thousands of their countrymen had before them and as thousands did after, the family left behind political and economic oppressions and a series of regional wars for the promise of a better life. The Luecks moved into a poor working class district in New York.

Lorenz's limited resources as a basket maker were stretched thin supporting his family of six. At the height of the American Civil War, Lorenz decided to join the Union Army in the place of a Frederic Russell, thereby earning a most welcome government bonus. On 12 December 1862 Lorenz joined Company B of the 14th New York Cavalry. The unit was one of a number of New York regiments made up of recently emigrated German-Americans.

As a member of the North's Army of the Tennessee, Lorenz's unit took part in the July 1873 Battle of Vicksburg. Five months later the senior Lueck was honorably discharged in New Orleans on 27 December 1863. He was 38 years old. Lorenz had been physically disqualified by "phthisis," a chronic bronchial condition for which he had been hospitalized in New Orleans for some time.

Making his way back to New York, Lorenz and Regina had their fifth and final child in 1866. It was also in postwar New York that the Old World family name of Lueck was Anglicized to become "Luke."

According to Norman S. Hall's account in his 1928 biography of Luke, *The Balloon Buster,* Lorenz had a nameless brother who served as a "commissioner representing Arizona in Vienna, Austria."[6] In April 1873, the financially strapped Lorenz agreed to permit the brother, upon his return from Europe, to take his son, Frank Luke Sr., with him out West to Prescott, in what was then the Territory of Arizona.

According to contemporary Luke family chronicler and first cousin of Frank Luke Jr., Robert Schipf, Charles Lueck (or Luke) took both Lorenz's elder son John and Frank Sr., age 14, with him to Arizona in 1873. The purpose of Charles' business remains unclear to Schipf.[7]

Returning to Hall's account, the aviator's father, Frank Sr., received an appointment to the United States Military Academy at West Point in 1877. Poor vision, however, disqualified the senior Frank Luke. By 1880 Frank Senior had made his way to Phoenix. There he married Otillia Liebenow in 1884. Otillia, born in Brooklyn, New York, in 1867, was also the daughter of German emigrant parents.

Before her death in 1944, Bob Schipf recalls Otillia telling him on several occasions that Phoenix was no more than "twelve mud huts" when her family first moved there. The tale was no doubt allegorical, but certainly not that far from historical fact. By 1880 Phoenix boasted a population of 1708, up from 235 wind-blown, sun-baked residents a decade earlier. The 1880s was also the era of the territory's famed "Apache Wars," though this vicious "Western taming" conflict happily stayed clear of the town's boundaries. In 1889 the bustling "city" of 3000 inhabitants became the new territorial capital. And in 1912 Phoenix truly began to come into its own as a sophisticated Western metropolis when the first 19 blocks of pavement was laid down its two most important streets, Washington and Central Avenues!

Born there on 19 May 1897 was future aviator Frank Luke Jr., the middle child of nine sired by the Lukes of Phoenix. To support this hefty brood, family tradition states that the pioneering Frank Senior successfully introduced cotton farming to the Arizona territory, as well as raised horses. He also took an early and active role in local politics. The family's sizeable spread at 2200 West Monroe Street in Phoenix included a two-story main house, barn and outhouses for the Indian help.

Wilder, however, than the senior Luke's unbroken steeds was his fifth born, Frank Junior. From the day he entered the world, it is said, he seemed to stand out. Whether he cried louder or his small legs flailed harder as an infant or disappeared quicker or got into trouble more often as a youngster, Frank Junior was a decided handful. By the age of four the mysteries and frontiers of the family homestead had long since been explored. The unforgiving world of the Arizona wilderness beyond the gate had become irresistible. Frank Junior, too, had become a collector, be they tarantulas in the family barn or melons and chickens from a neighbor's spread. It was on just such an occasion that he and his teen cronies, among them Bill Elder and Pidge Pinney, were first introduced to the local sheriff.

From a very early age, the feel of a saddle and the grip of a firearm had become second nature to the young Luke boy. His reputation for marksmanship was well earned, as was his prowess as a street fighter and, by the time he was a sophomore at Phoenix High School, a backfield legend on the school's football team.

Frank was an aggressive "line plunger" away from the gridiron as well. Childhood friend Bill Elder's oft-repeated tale of his and Frank's death-defying crossing of the runoff-swollen White River remains a character-defining classic. Such disregard for physical danger was typical of Frank throughout his short life, whether it was a challenge of nature or another man.

LELA LOWENSTEIN

Associate Editor Phoenician '17.
Deutsche Verein '16, '17.
Jeffersonian Contest '17.

*"With a soul as strong as a
mountain stream."*

IDA MAE GOLZE

Girls' Booster Club '17.
Girls' "Y" Club '15. Senior Play '16.
Senior Play '17 Senior President '17.
German Club '16, '17.

*"Her vivacity, charm and grace,
won in all hearts a place."*

GLENN METCALF

Business Manager Phoenician '17.
Spanish Club '15.

*"Poor Wisdom's chance against
a glance, is now as
weak as ever."*

FRANK LUKE

Baseball '14, '15, '16. Track '14, 16.
Tennis '14. Football '14, '15, '16, '17.
Agricultural Club '15, '16.
Junior Play '15. Twelfth Night '17.

*"Too happy-go-lucky to realize
his own talents."*

MAUDE STEWART

Society Editor Phoenician '17.
Pennant '17. Bo'sn's Bride '17.

*"Her enthusiasm knows no
bounds."*

ANITA MARRO

"I can't make my eyes behave."

*The editor's parting observation in the 1917 edition (Volume VIII) of Phoenix
High's* Phoenician *yearbook reads for graduating senior Frank Luke: "Too
happy-go-lucky to realize his own talents."*

Frank Luke Jr. entered the impressive new two-story structure that was Phoenix Union High School in August 1913. His record there ran the gambit from spectacular to mediocre. Academically, Luke's grades, respectable if unexceptional, averaged in the high 70s, or a C+, though the curriculum was most certainly more challenging than the more generally water-downed fare offered by most public schools today. Luke's subjects ranged from Algebra (Luke's final grade: 75) and Ancient History (77) in his freshman year to Physics (75) and American History/Civics (83) in his 1916-1917 senior year.[8] So, too, was the course of study made more relevant for both the era and locale by the inclusion of agriculture courses in both his sophomore and junior years. By the early 1890s more than 80,000 acres within a stone's throw of the city limits were under cultivation.

And though his classroom scores never broke into the A range, this was not true on the field where he excelled in football, performing heroic feats in his senior year as quarterback for the Phoenix Coyotes. Frank Luke Jr. was also a standout in baseball, track, and in general mischief-making. The latter category included the hazing of incoming freshmen, breaking training, discharging firearms on the campus and a spectacularly disruptive, widely witnessed tour of the high school's second story roof!

By the summer after his sophomore year in high school, at the tender age of 16, Frank felt he was ready for the physical demands of working in a man's world at the New Cornelia copper mines at Ajo. At first amused by the young teen's efforts, the veteran miners soon became disgruntled as the muscle-hardened youngster began to out-produce the veteran miners on his shift. Things soon came to a head when a veteran Irish miner named Breen, out of sight of the shift foreman, attempted to cut the young Luke down a notch or two. To the miner's great surprise, Luke's fists flew with unerring aim and swiftness. By the time the foreman arrived the fight was all but over. Luke's man-sized reputation had been established, so much so a summer later he was nominated to take on a touring professional boxer from San Francisco, "The Battling Haney." Having acquired the entrepreneurial instincts of his father,

Frank and Phoenix friend Floyd Carver had opened a dance hall in Ajo where Frank offered dance lessons after working hours. Haney and his manager began counting their winnings when they learned the mining camp was backing a fair-skinned dandy of a dance instructor.

Frank took out the oversized pro-boxer in the first round!

During his junior year at Phoenix High, Frank took in a rough and tumble school tradition called the "Junior-Senior Class Pennant Rush." The winning class of this upper classman brawl had the honor of hoisting the class pennant to the top of the school flagpole. The seniors won. At dusk that same day in 1916, the peace was torn in Phoenix by the rapid report of six Colt .45 rounds. Local law enforcement, rushing to the sound, arrived upon the empty school grounds to find a splintered flag staff and violently abused brass ball at its top. The senior pennant, however, remained, undisturbed flapping in the evening breeze. With no bleeding bodies in sight, the deputies returned to their original duties.

Disappointed by the results offered by his Colt, Frank had soon returned with his 20-gauge shotgun. A pair of explosions ruptured the evening quiet for a second time. Hurrying back to the school, deputies found a clearly satisfied Frank Luke Jr., smoking shotgun in hand, examining the now thoroughly shredded remains of the senior pennant.

In his senior year, Frank and a number of his "gang" were expelled for the hazing of school freshmen. The expulsion was short lived, however, after news of Phoenix High's foremost backfield runner reached the ears of some of Phoenix' most influential citizens. Among them were Dean Scarlett of the Phoenix Trinity Episcopal Cathedral and Dwight B. Heard, one of the young state's wealthiest men and publisher of the *Arizona Republican.*

Frank seemed to justify their faith during the first quarter of Phoenix Coyote's next game with Flagstaff. Despite a broken collarbone, Frank refused to be pulled from the game and went on to make a touchdown.

Later in the season, however, Frank would be suspended from the team for breaking training.

It was a foretaste of what lay in store for the U.S. Air Service and one innocent, by-the-book West Point grad by the name of Captain Alfred Grant.

No one is quite sure why Frank Luke Jr. elected to volunteer to fly with the USAS when the United States entered the Great War in April 1917. Certainly there is no evidence of a rush to duty. Perhaps when the moment finally came, it was yet another challenge he could not resist. Perhaps flying offered a new sense of freedom akin to the freedom he'd come to love in his native Arizona. Almost certainly the prospect of military order and discipline delayed an immediate decision, for it was not until 25 September 1917 that Frank enlisted in Tucson.

From that day, Frank Luke had little more than a year of life remaining to him, but by that time he had found his place in history.

Being granted immediate assignment to the USAS, he was ordered to Austin, Texas, and the School of Military Aeronautics where a ground school class was already in session. Though not known for his academic achievements at Phoenix High, Frank had soon caught up and graduated with his class on 23 November 1917. Upon graduation from ground school, he received orders to report to Rockwell Field in San Diego, California, for primary flight training. On 23 January 1918 Frank was commissioned a second lieutenant in the Aviation Section of the Signal Officers Reserve Corps. That April, Luke had begun his advanced course of flying at Issoudun in Central France. By the end of the month he was flying out of Issoudun's satellite Field Number Five. Frank Luke was ordered on 30 May to the gunnery school at Cazeau in Southern France. He arrived at Cazeau some three months after another "Blue-Collar Cadet," one Edward Rickenbacker, had passed through the same school en route to the Front.

Upon completing the gunnery course, Luke joined the pilot pool to await his combat assignment. While his impatience continued to build, he continued to amass valuable airtime over the next weeks flying a wide variety of aircraft types up to frontline units.

And while Luke anxiously bided his time at Cazeau awaiting

his turn, at the front, "Death," as de Tocqueville had observed nearly a century earlier, was "constantly thinning the ranks, making
vacancies, closing and opening the career of arms...[allowing]
extraordinary men to rise above the common man."[9]

 And, to be sure, the "thinning of the ranks" was very much the
order of the day with America's pioneering First Pursuit Group during July 1918!

*Flight School graduate
Frank Luke in typical
flying gear of the period.*

Chapter Two
Insert No. 1

THE GERMAN IMMIGRATION ISSUE

World War One was an uneasy time for Americans of German ancestry. Anti-German sentiments ran high during the years 1917-1918. The flames of impassioned hatred were fanned to new heights in large measure by the unrestrained wartime propaganda of the day that portrayed the German breed itself in both word and picture as nothing short of bestial.

High profile German ethnicity soon was socially unacceptable, if not dangerous. Once proud Germanic names such as Mueller were anglicized to become Miller; German Shepherd dogs became Alsatians; and Kraut dogs became "Liberty Sausage."

Yet the German element for far too long had been an important member and now too numerous a portion of the American social fabric to be exiled or even interned, as were the Japanese during World War Two.

By the 1910 U.S. census, the last before World War One, citizens of German heritage made up fully 26.4 percent of the United States white population. The German immigration rate, to that year, had been exceeded only by the English. By 1910, a staggering 21,600,000 German-Americans were numbered among a white U.S. population which then was officially 81,731,957.[10]

In the decade immediately preceding the U.S. Civil War, between 1851 and 1860, German immigration had surged past that of the Irish to become and remain the single largest source of new foreigners until the last decade of the Nineteenth Century.

It is estimated some 225,000 Germans had already made their way to the colonies before the Revolutionary War. For the most part, they settled on the frontier, next to their Scotch-Irish neighbors from the Mohawk Valley of New York south into Georgia. Between 1790 and 1820, however, immigration was relatively small with 968 Germans accounted for as arriving at eastern ports in the latter year.

German immigration numbers were a function of both attractive conditions in the young United States as well as dissatisfaction at home.

Immigration had been difficult during the Revolutionary War with England. But a great upsurge in German immigration to the United States began between 1831 and 1840, growing from 10,000 a year at the start of the decade to over 29,000 nine years later. The decade total would reach 152,000 new German arrivals. The Napoleonic wars, over-population, over-crowding of the finite farming regions, heavy taxation and the decline of the cottage artisan trades in the face of the emerging factory system all contributed to unrest at home. So too did the heavy-handed reaction and over-reaction by petty German rulers opposed to the popular freedoms espoused by the German student societies and then enjoyed under the brand of Jacksonian Democracy then emerging in the United States.

So too did idealistic reports of new promise, written by earlier German pioneers in America, begin to make their way back to the fatherland. "America," wrote German-American historian Albert Faust, "offered refuge from economic, social and political evils of these lands."

German immigration increased yet again between 1841 and 1860, reaching 215,009 for 1854 alone! It will be recalled that it was during this period that Lorenz Lueck, with his family – including son Frank Senior, took his leave of the Fatherland to venture forth to the promise of the United States.

The figures climbed once again after the Civil War, when, from 1866 to 1873, German emigrants poured into the country at a sustained rate of 130,000 a year. Many Germans and their families were escaping the mandatory military duty of the great wars of Prussia. In particular, the economic and social stress brought on by the overthrow of the aforementioned petty German states then being merged into the one Germany through the onslaught of the Franco-Prussian War of 1870 triggered a massive exodus. So too did the appeal of homesteads freely offered by the United States government prove an attractive inducement to land-conscious

Germans. The immigration rate was driven to new heights by Europe's financial panic and depression of 1873.

By 1882 some quarter million Germans were arriving in the United States annually. However, German immigration began a steady decline from 1892 as the newly united nation of Germany began to come into its own as an industrial powerhouse.

The German immigrants of the Nineteenth Century collectively called themselves "Volkerwanderung." The first wave was generally made up of poorly educated laborers and peasants who readily took to the hard labors of agriculture on the frontier. The second wave, generally arriving between 1830 to 1860, were often better educated and more skilled. This latter group more often gravitated to the cities where they became merchants, manufacturers and often journalists. There was considerable friction between the older "Graune" or "Gray" German immigrants and the more recent "Gruenen" or "Green" arrivals. Regardless of their different approaches to making a living, when it came to the Civil War, virtually all the German-American population were of one political mind as Jeffersonian Democrats, and as, such strongly opposed slavery. The ranks of Grant's Northern forces were filled with a disproportionately high number of German surnames.

The third wave of Germans, which arrived after the Civil War, were generally a far better schooled lot and often were dissatisfied with the available opportunities in the United States as they were not inclined to the manual positions welcomed by earlier waves of Germans. The later 19th Century arrivals, nonetheless, according to German-American historian Friedrich Munch, would "as a rule prosper well." Many of this latter group turned to commerce, manufacturing, many becoming "prominent in the technical and professional branches."[11]

Chapter Two
Insert No. 2

SETTING THE STAGE
(from an uncredited internet page)

A Hundred Years Ago:
The average life expectancy in the United States was 47.

Only 14 percent of the homes in the United States had a bathtub.

Only 8 percent of the homes had a telephone. A three-minute call from Denver to New York cost $11.00.

There were only 8,000 cars in the U.S. and only 144 miles of paved roads.

The tallest structure in the world was the Eiffel Tower.

The average wage in the U.S. was 22 cents an hour. The average U.S. worker made between $200 and $400 per year.

A dentist averaged $2500 per year; a mechanical engineer made about $5000 per year.

More than 95 percent of all births in the U.S. took place at home.

Sugar cost four cents a pound; eggs were 14 cents a dozen and coffee cost 15 cents a pound.

The five leading causes of death in the U.S. were: pneumonia and influenza, tuberculosis, diarrhea, heart disease, and stroke.

The American flag had 45 stars. Arizona, Oklahoma, New Mexico, Hawaii and Alaska hadn't been admitted to the Union yet. Arizona was admitted in 1912.

Drive-by-shootings in which teenage boys galloped down the street on horses and started randomly shooting at houses, carriages, or anything else that caught their fancy were an ongoing problem in Denver and other cities in the West.

The population of Las Vegas, Nevada was 30, composed of local ranchers and their families.

Plutonium, insulin, and antibiotics had yet to be discovered.

Scotch tape, crossword puzzles, canned beer and iced tea hadn't been invented.

One in ten U.S. adults couldn't read or write.

Only six percent of all Americans had graduated from high school.

Marijuana, heroin and morphine were all available over the counter at corner drugstores. Coca-Cola contained cocaine instead of caffeine.

Punch card data processing had recently been developed, and early predecessors of the modern computer were used for the first time by the government to help compile the 1900 census.

Eighteen percent of households in the U.S. (including the Luke family - author), had at least one full-time servant or domestic.

There were about 230 reported murders in the U.S. annually.

Anonymous

Chapter Three

BIRTH OF AMERICA'S FIRST PURSUIT GROUP

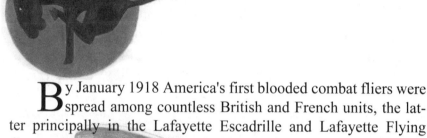

B y January 1918 America's first blooded combat fliers were spread among countless British and French units, the latter principally in the Lafayette Escadrille and Lafayette Flying Corps, along the Western Front. The grim, though priceless experiences of these rapidly-aging young veterans would prove vital to the successful formation of this nation's first American-trained and commanded flying squadrons.

The famed American-manned Lafayette Escadrille was transferred out of the French Air Service on 5 January 1918, though it would not officially become the American 103rd Aero (later Pursuit) Squadron until 18 February. Veteran Escadrille flier Bill Thaw, recently commissioned major, U.S. Air Service, became the unit's first commander. On 10 August 1918, Thaw, soon to be promoted to Lt. Colonel, would take command of the 3rd Pursuit Group. But for those first formative months of the year, the 103rd would continue to fly, fight, and mature while still attached to the French Army, as would the neophyte American squadrons following it. The American 1st Pursuit Group would serve out its first formative operational months with the French Sixth Army.

Another Lafayette Escadrille veteran, Raoul Lufbery, an ace and the former French unit's top scoring pilot with 16 confirmed victories, would also receive a major's commission. Though his

career in the USAS would prove to be tragically brief and personally frustrating, it was nonetheless indispensable for the recently
arrived, wet-eared Americans.

Upon receiving their new commissions, both Thaw and
Lufbery headed for the USAS' new 3rd Aviation Instruction Center
located some six miles outside of the railhead at Issoudun. General
Pershing would call the site, and not without ample justification,
"the worst mudhole in France."[1] In fact, during that wet winter of
1917-1918, this most important U.S. training center was still being
built by Air Service enlisted and disgruntled cadet officer personnel pressed into service as laborers and builders. At Issoudun the
two former Escadrille fliers found the school short of everything
from prepared roads to tools and all manner of building materials.
They were short of everything except that old-fashioned Yankee
pioneering spirit and mud - and more mud.

Rickenbacker, fresh from 25 hours flight training at Tours, had
arrived in late September of 1917 as the field's engineering officer
to supervise the building of repair shops, and the acquisition of
everything from spare aircraft parts to building materials. As was
typical of everything associated with First World War aviation,
there were no rule books and manual guides for such enterprises -
the USAS organization continued to create itself, improvising on
the run to war.

The first French training planes arrived in October 1917 as
construction continued. Field conditions made flying almost
impossible. The mud thrown up from the planes' wheels broke
propellers "almost as fast as they could be put on."[2] Because of the
scarcity of materials, Rickenbacker had yet to build the requisite
machine shops and secure the power source or vital machine tools.
Initially, all mechanical work was limited to two overworked
machine-shop trucks brought over from the United States.

While Issoudun had witnessed considerable progress by the
arrival of Thaw in January and he was able to acquire the American
aircraft mechanics needed for his new squadron, Lufbery would
find only frustration. Presuming to shortly take command of the
new American 95th Aero (later Pursuit) Squadron, Lufbery was

"invited" to a desk while the last elements of the new American training program and the facilities at Issoudun itself were slowly brought together. The assignment was an anathema to every fiber of Lufbery's eternally restless being. Soon, disgust turned to anger as the former Escadrille ace "chafed at his enforced lack of activity"[3] for the next three months. Nor was the freshly-minted major hesitant to let his new superiors in Paris know at some length of his discontent.

There is little doubt why, when the men of the pioneering 95th Aero Squadron became the first American-trained flying unit assigned to the Western Front that February, American authorities had not placed Major Lufbery at their head. A superior's perception of the line between the reasoned demands of a loyal subordinate and a troublemaker can often be thin in time of war.

February saw the 95th assigned to the interim 1st Pursuit Organization and Training Center. As such, its first stop on 18 February was some 20 miles behind the lines at the French aerodrome at Villenueve-les-Vertus, home to Group Menard. Here, it was planned, the veteran French fliers would provide the green Americans with a first hands-on look at the specifics of aerial combat over the lines.

The frustrations first found at Issoudun, however, were only exacerbated at Villenueve. For there the Americans would wait for the next three weeks without a plane to call their own. Finally, around 6 March, the first French-made and unarmed Nieuport 28C-1s began to arrive. On 9 March 1918 the 95th's new commander, Captain James E. Miller, anxious to get on with the war, borrowed three Spads from Group Menard to explore the lines with two of his equally inexperienced men. The small American formation was promptly pounced upon by a veteran German flight, and Miller himself shot down and killed.

It was not an auspicious beginning for the 95th or the U.S. Air Service.

Stunned by the early demise of the 95th's commander, Colonel Billy Mitchell was appalled to discover that this first batch of combat-bound fliers had not even been through the elementary aerial gunnery course at Cazeau. Immediately Mitchell ordered the pilots to gunnery school. They would remain there for much of the next month.

THE HAT IS TOSSED

On 5 March, four days before Miller's untimely death, the men of the 94th Aero Squadron joined the 95th at Villenueve. They had just completed the gunnery course at Cazeau. Among the new 94th fliers was a tall, former auto mechanic and racecar driver from Ohio. Lieutenant Eddie Rickenbacker, after much persistence and to the consternation of his Issoudun commander, Major Carl A. Spaatz, had managed to be reassigned to the 94th on 4 March 1918.

The new unit acquired seven of the 95th little Nieuport pursuits for their own. For Raoul Lufbery, now assigned as a senior advisor to the nearly as ill-prepared 94th, his finest hours and, perhaps, biggest battles lay just ahead. During these last two months of his life, Lufbery fought many of his most important contests. They would, however, be with his Paris superiors. And for even this squarely-built bantam ace there was a concern for the quickening of time.

The shortness of time was also on Ludendorff's mind on the 21st of March when his 43 German divisions began their spring offensive by slamming into the 12 divisions of the British Fifth Army on the Somme. The German general knew that if the war was to be won, or at the very least a favorable settlement made, it would have to be made soon before the flood of fresh American divisions doomed the enterprise. And success did appear to be his as his armies gained 14 miles by the 24th, the greatest territorial advance since 1914. The British Fifth Army and elements of their Third Army to the north were in full retreat.

Reacting to the fluid situation, the unprepared 94th was moved further back from the front to Epiez on 1 April and again on the 7th to Toul. Lufbery renewed his fearless and repeated attacks on AEF headquarters for the equipment the unit still needed to get into the fray. Nonetheless, by the end of the first week in April, the 94th still had no guns for its slowly building inventory of airplanes. In the end, so the story goes, the fiery former Escadrille ace bullied his way straight to the top and into the office of general of all American Expeditionary Forces, General John "Black Jack" Pershing.

The 94th soon had their guns. And by the end of the second week of April the unit had also come up with its endearing and enduring squadron insignia, the famed Hat-in-the-Ring. It was the squadron's commander, Major John S. Huffer, another veteran of the French escadrilles, who'd first suggested the stars and striped top hat of Uncle Sam. And it was the squadron flight surgeon, Lieutenant Gary Walters, who recalled the old American custom of tossing a hat in the ring as an invitation to battle. Another pilot, Lieutenant Johnny Wentworth, who'd been an architect in civilian life, was asked to draw up the now famous insignia. Rickenbacker tells us the insignia was painted on his Nieuport by 14 April. But, as air historian Robert F. Dorr so correctly observed, the 94th "was not nearly as ready to fight as this impudent symbol suggested."[4]

'LUFBERY'S GIFT'

With armed aircraft, the veteran ace could dive into the role for which he'd unknowingly been preparing for the last three years. Shepherding the green Americans over the lines, Lufbery began to share all he had learned of aerial combat and fighting tactics. The first and most important skill was to develop the "flier's eyes," which Captain Miller tragically lacked on that fateful 9 March flight.

Upon return from these early and fortunately uneventful sorties, Luf had asked his fliers what they'd observed - he'd then tell them what they'd missed. On more than one occasion the list included distant enemy formations!

Lufbery's approach to combat was much the same as that of the great British ace Mick Mannock. Aerial dogfighting was a science for Lufbery, and a game to be played by the numbers. A fighter pilot, he insisted, must always weigh the odds before engaging. Advantage and the chance to fight another day were requisites.

Today a fighter pilot would call it "situational awareness." There is no substitute for the successful combat pilot. It was a lesson taken to heart by the supremely pragmatic and seasoned Rickenbacker.

Panic, insisted Lufbery, could be the pilot's worst enemy. And should the worst case scenario occur, an in-flight fire, there remained a chance for the cool-headed pilot who could side-slip his aircraft to keep the flames away from the cockpit long enough to get the plane on the ground.

The chain-smoking Lufbery worked tirelessly with his pilots, making himself available day or night for the endless line of searching questions thrown his way. And his advice was revered, as he was himself, by the pilots. And 8 April saw the arrival of three more experienced fliers from the old Lafayette Escadrille, now the U.S. 103rd Aero Squadron, to help spread the veteran's burden. They were James Norman Hall, Kenneth Marr, and David McKelvey Peterson.

THE FOG OF WAR

Finally, on 14 April 1918 Lufbery and his AEF superiors deemed the 94th ready for the U.S. Air Service first official combat patrol by American-trained fliers.[5] The honor of participating in this first history-making sortie went to Lieutenants Reed Chambers and Eddie Rickenbacker, who were led on the flight by the recently arrived Escadrille veteran Captain David McKelvey Peterson. The two-hour patrol, which began at 0600, extended from Pont-a-Mousson to Saint Mihiel.

"About the time we attained the frigid altitude (of) sixteen thousand feet," Rickenbacker later recalled, "I noticed the captain's machine gliding back to the field."[6]

Thinking Peterson had experienced engine trouble, Rickenbacker took command and completed the patrol as planned. In fact, Peterson had returned because of the dense blanket of fog covering their patrol route. Upon the return leg Rickenbacker and Chambers realized they had to penetrate the solid undercast should they have any hope of getting down in one piece. Luck or

94th Lieutenants (left to right) Oscar Gude, Eddie Rickenbacker, and Alan Winslow with the 1st Pursuit Group's beloved ace/mentor Raoul Lufbery at Toul in late April 1918. Within some three weeks of this photograph, Sunday, 19 May, Lufbery would meet his death at the controls of Nieuport 28, s/n 6178, while intercepting a two-place Albatros reconnaissance plane Gude was unwilling or unable to close on before he exhausted his ammunition. Though Gude had joined the 94th more than a month and a half earlier this was reportedly his first combat. Gude was transferred to the newer 93rd P.S. during mid-July. On 22 October he was at the controls of 93rd P.S. commander Major John Huffer's personal Spad when he inexplicably landed the French-made pursuit at the German aerodrome at Metz and spent the last weeks of the war as a prisoner.

Providence, as was so often the case with the future Ace of Aces, remained close by his side as he entered the blinding white-out, not knowing when or if he would come up against the region's high hills or tall trees. Gingerly finding the ground, Rickenbacker chanced upon a known landmark - a railroad tunnel - and scurried safely back to Toul at a deck-hugging 100-foot altitude. Chambers was nowhere in sight when Peterson angrily greeted Rick as "a bloody fool."[7]

America's opening day of front line operations was beginning to look like a major foul-up. A decidedly depressed Rickenbacker, now out of his flying clothes, had just begun filling out his flight report at headquarters when the phone offered an ominous ring.

Rick 'knew' it would be news of the discovery of the fatal remains of his flying companion's plane. Instead, an excited operations officer called for the stand-by alert pilots, Harvard-educated Douglas Campbell and Alan Winslow, to man their planes. A pair of German Pfalz D.IIIs from Jasta 64 had been spotted near the field. Rickenbacker rushed outside in time to see the flames of the first enemy plane brought down by Winslow within three minutes of his takeoff. Campbell forced down the second Pfalz for the second successful victory of the opening day within as many minutes!

Both German pilots survived to tell their American captors they'd become lost in the fog chasing a pair of Nieuports (Rickenbacker's and Chamber's) patrolling the area! To Rickenbacker's eternal relief, Chambers returned to the field in one piece and to wildly welcoming arms that evening, having made an emergency morning landing not far from the field.

Foul weather kept the 94th grounded for the next few days. It was time enough to reflect on the fortuitous turn of that first day of operations and for Campbell and Winslow to absorb with feigned casualness the deluge of congratulatory cablegrams from superiors and fans throughout the United States.

The celebrity-like adulation was something that Rickenbacker had known all his adult racing life. It was something he thoroughly understood, and would seek out, to the disdain of many, the rest of his days. Over the next days and weeks the tall Ohio son became more determined than ever to make his first score. And while ego has never been in short supply among successful military fliers, Rickenbacker's was seasoned with a native pragmatism brought to maturity by his years of success on the race circuits of the United States and England.

Frustration had dogged his heels until the afternoon of 24 April. Pulling smartly into the rear quarter of an unsuspecting enemy plane below him, the novice combat flier was at once pleased with himself and yet continued to entertain a vague feeling that it had all been too easy. And within those seconds Lufbery's warnings of the clever ways with which the Germans set aerial traps for just such green would-be warriors as he came flooding back into his frozen consciousness.

Rickenbacker shot a look over his shoulder and the red, white and blue striped rudder of his Nieuport in time to see a deathly handsome black Albatros exploding out of the broken overcast behind him. With the powerful and lightning reflexes for which he was so famous, the former racecar driver whipped the agile French pursuit into a stunning climbing turn and within seconds was closing on the second German's tail. With his fingers closing on the trigger, he prudently checked his rear quarter one last time, spotting two more pursuits rapidly closing the distance. Losing all interest in the glory of victory for the afternoon, Rickenbacker safely used the nearby cloud cover to make good his escape to home. There he was to learn that Campbell had been leading the latter flight that he had taken to be the enemy.

Another element of Rickenbacker's complex makeup had come to the fore earlier during his frustrating drive to make his first aerial mark. On 18 April his Nieuport coasted to a stop amid the congratulatory utterings of his squadron mates who'd just received reports of an enemy plane seen going down in the sector Rick had

Despite the camera-ready smile, Eddie Rickenbacker considered it just short of a criminal act for the 1st Pursuit Group to have initially been equipped with the Nieuport 28, a type earlier rejected for front line service by both the French and British air arms.

just returned from patrolling. No doubt the temptation flitted through the synapses of his ambitious brain an instant or two, but in the end Rickenbacker responded that if a plane had gone down it was not by his guns. Remarkably, Rickenbacker later reflected, no one ever came forward to claim the mystery plane.

Rickenbacker's frustrating two-week quest, however, was about to pay off. Flying had been a hit and miss affair due to the typically damp and overcast spring weather. Finally, around noon on the 29th the sun reclaimed its presence. Captain James Norman "Jimmy" Hall and Rickenbacker were on standby alert at five that afternoon when a call came reporting an enemy two-seater entering their sector. The veteran Hall led Rickenbacker into the sun to await the German Pfalz scout spotted approaching north of Pont-a-Mousson. While Hall dove to the attack, Rickenbacker retained his altitude, maneuvering to cut off the enemy's escape route back to his lines. Finally, spotting Hall's Nieuport, the Pfalz D.III snapped over on his wing, hightailing it for his lines - as Rickenbacker had anticipated. The one-time auto mechanic didn't hesitate.

"At 150 yards," recalled Rickenbacker, "I pressed my triggers. The tracer bullets cut a streak of living fire into the rear of the Pfalz tail. Raising the nose of my airplane slightly the fiery streak lifted itself like the stream of water pouring from a garden hose. Gradually it settled into the pilot's seat."[8]

Though the Pfalz crashed at the foot of a woods a mile behind the lines, the confirmation for Rickenbacker's first widely observed aerial victory had already arrived by the time the pair had returned to their field and a cheering crowd. Rickenbacker would go on to write at length in his first autobiography, "*Fighting the Flying Circus*," that there was no substitute in life for such personal adulation. Both Hall and Rickenbacker were to be awarded the Croix de Guerre with Palm by the French government for their action, but U.S. policy at the time forbade the awarding of decorations by foreign governments. This, however, did not stop the flood of news correspondents or Rick's growing volume of fan mail from continuing to pour in from the United States.

Fog slowed the pace of operations over the following week,

though James A. "Jimmy" Meissner's first kill, a Hannover CL shared with Doug Campbell, on 2 May, brought the squadron total victories to four. The following day Lafayette Escadrille veteran David McKelvey Peterson returned with the squadron's fifth victory and first squadron loss. Charles W. Chapman, an LFC veteran, was seen falling, his Nieuport a raging torch from the firewall aft.

And on 5 May, passing almost without notice was the squadron's assignment to what officially had become the 1st Pursuit Group. Adding substance to the new unit had been the arrival, fresh from Cazeau, of the pilots of the 95th "Kicking Mule" Squadron on the fourth.

As if to show off his stuff to the newly arrived squadron, Rickenbacker made his second aerial kill of the war on 7 May. The consequences, however, were only to demonstrate the frustration and price of this new kind of war.

Around eight that morning Rickenbacker, Hall and M. Edwin "Eddie" Green had scrambled into the air on word of four enemy planes flying south over Pont-a-Mousson on the Moselle. The three American Nieuports had dived on the four-plane flight of German Pfalz D.IIIs. Both Green and Rickenbacker each downed one of their prey, but the elation was short lived when Rick realized Hall was missing. Returning to Toul, Green related how he'd seen the entire upper wing of Hall's fragile Nieuport give way in their dive on the Germans. It was a fatal structural weakness that another 94th pilot, Jimmy Meissner, and the squadron had first discovered in a similar dive five days earlier - and lived to talk about.

Not only was Hall gone, but neither enemy kill could be confirmed from the ground, as then required, since the engagement had occurred some three to four miles behind the Allied lines.

So enraged was Lufbery on that 7 May 1918 day by the news of the loss of his old N.124 Lafayette Escadrille flying mate, that he threw on his flight suit and headed deep into German territory in search of revenge. And he found it, though the kill was never to be confirmed. Both plane and pilot returned overdue and spent - the Nieuport flying on fumes.

Happily, some weeks later the squadron received a personal

letter from Hall in a German hospital where he was recovering from injuries sustained in the crash of his Nieuport. Hall, who'd already written two big-selling books of his war adventures, *"Kitchener's Mob"* and *"High Adventure,"* would survive the war to co-write, with Charles Nordhoff, the classic two-volume history of the Lafayette Flying Corps which was published in 1920, and *"Falcons of France,"* a fictional account of the LFC. But the pair's most famous work, *"Mutiny on the Bounty,"* published in 1934, would be penned in their new-found Pacific paradise of French Tahiti.

"Luf's" Final Flight

As for Rickenbacker's second kill, it would not be confirmed until 1960! The Indianapolis racer's second confirmed wartime victory, and third kill, was made ten days later on Friday, 17 May. His victim was identified as an Albatros D.V. That Sunday, the 19th of May, however, Rickenbacker's world, as well as that of his squadron's, came crashing down around their knees.

About ten o'clock that morning a high altitude German two-seater Albatros photo plane was reported over Saint Mihiel and headed toward their field. Lieutenant Oscar J. Gude, the only 94th flier then presumably on standby alert, scrambled to the attack. A crowd gathered before the squadron hangar as the German plane came into view, emerging from the white puffs of Allied "Archie" exploding about him. Suddenly, as the wheels of Gude's Nieuport cleared the ground, the antiaircraft fire stopped and the observation plane, apparently having received a fatal blow, was seen to fall into a quickening spin. But then the Rumpler expertly recovered at a hair-splitting two hundred feet and began heading back for its own lines. Gude went in to the attack but emptied his guns on the obviously skilled German crew to no affect.[9]

As the farce continued to play itself out, Major Lufbery, who'd been watching the events from the field barracks with a group of his fellow fliers, leaped aboard a motorcycle and sped to the flightline. There he found the Nieuport 28, s/n 6178, of former Lafayette Flying Corps flier Phillip W. Davis serviced and ready to go. The former Escadrille ace charged after the prey. Though Lufbery had downed two enemy aircraft, both unconfirmed, since joining the 94th, he continued to look for his first USAS confirmation. No doubt, the target appeared as though it had been served up on a silver platter, appearing as it had on the Allied side of the line, indeed virtually over his home field and in full view of hundreds of potentially confirming pairs of eyes.

As he attacked, the German rear gunner fired. Luf's Nieuport was seen to sharply jerk, or pull away. Was this because his guns jammed, or had a round chanced to enter the cockpit, severing the thumb of his right hand as it held the control column? In either case, the determined veteran ace soon banked in for another attack on the German's rear quarter. The enemy gunner was waiting for him. A well-placed incendiary shell tore through the firewall of the little French fighter. There, it penetrated either the plane's shoulder-mounted oil tank or one of its two knee-level fuel tanks affixed just behind the rotary engine and immediately in front of the cockpit's instrument board.

Instantly, the wind-blasted open cockpit turned into a raging inferno. There was no chance of side-slipping away from the flesh-searing holocaust which now began to consume Lufbery and his plane. The pilot's flying suit had ignited by the time he hauled himself out of the oven of a cockpit and onto the wing. A small stream some 2,000 feet below must have offered some small glimmer of hope for survival. He threw his flaming torso into the brutal slipstream. His forward trajectory, however, carried him some hundred yards beyond the beckoning waters, his badly charred body impaling itself on the garden fence stake of a poor home in the village of Maron, to the north of Nancy.

Rickenbacker reported that seeing the American ace go down, the leading ace of a nearby French escadrille took off in hot pursuit, but he too was downed by another well placed shot "through the heart." Eventually, however, the Rumpler was brought down by the French. Both the Rumpler crewmen from Reihenbildzug No. 3 safely lived out the conflict as prisoners of war.

On 20 May Major Gervais Raoul Lufbery was laid to rest with

full military honors in the field's local Airman's Cemetery. In addition to hundreds of officers in attendance from all the services, there was General Gerard, commander of the French Sixth Army, to which the 1st Pursuit Group was attached; Major General Clarence R. Edwards of the American 26th Division and Colonel William "Billy" Mitchell, commander, Western Front American air forces. At two o'clock Rickenbacker led his Number One flight of Nieuports over the crowded site as the flower-decked casket was being lowered into the ground. A small cloud of freshly cut flowers fluttered down from the passing pursuits.

Today, Lufbery's remains reside at the Lafayette Memorial du Paru de Gorches just outside of Paris. The American ace's score closed with 16 official victories and 13 probables.

Two days later Rickenbacker downed his fourth German plane of the war, an Albatros D.V near Flirey.

A NEW GERMAN OFFENSIVE

General Ludendorff, having failed twice since March to knock the tenacious British out of the war, elected to next make a diversionary attack against the French in an effort to draw off Marshall Foch's reserves to the south. This accomplished, the Germans would once more return to the north and the British for the final "knock-out" blow[10] to end the war before American strength at the front overwhelmed his nearly spent, under-strength armies.

With 41 German divisions poised opposite the Chemin des Dames, the softening up bombardment promptly began on the morning of 27 May. The sector, defended with only four French and three battle-weary British divisions, quickly caved to the advancing Germans. Rapidly advancing to Aisne, the enemy found the bridges over the river had not been blown. By the second day of the offensive, the Germans had advanced 15 miles and by 3 June they had reached Chateau Thierry, less than 57 miles from Paris.

There they would be stopped by French reserves fortified with "the cry not heard since 1914… 'Paris in danger.'"[11] Here, too, the

German armies got their first taste of combat against freshly arrived American infantrymen of the U.S. Army's 3rd Division, and the U.S. Marine 2nd Division at what soon became the legendary Belleau Wood.

On 28 May, the second day of the German Push, Rickenbacker downed his fifth enemy plane, an Albatros C, over Bois de Rate. It would be his fourth official victory of the war. Confirmation of his second kill would not come for another 42 years.

Two days later, on Thursday 30 May 1918, the former Ohio auto mechanic downed his sixth German airplane, another Albatros C over Jaulny. It was another lone wolf volunteer patrol that got off the ground around 7:30 that morning. Rickenbacker had smelled opportunity when the RAF asked the 1st Pursuit Group to provide egress cover for their bombers that morning as they came off their target, the German railhead at Conflaus, and headed back to their own lines.

Rickenbacker elected to follow at a comfortable distance as the dozen 94th and 95th Nieuports headed toward Conflaus and their assigned protection duties. Anticipating the likely German response to an Allied air attack on such an important target, he fairly glowed with the expectation of a target-rich "hornet's nest" of scoring opportunities. His instincts would be right on the money!

Over the lines at 15,000 feet, the picture began to fall into perfect focus. The large RAF formation had dropped its load and was already turned and heading back. Angry black antiaircraft bursts marked their course as the American machines, crossing over Thioucourt, were nearing their British companions' altitude. Further east, Rickenbacker spotted the massed avenging specks of the German Air Service rapidly closing the bombing formation's rear.

Looking again at the American formation, Rickenbacker was surprised to see his group mates being engaged by a second, previously unseen enemy formation of pursuits that were attacking out of the west. Taking note of a lone diving Nieuport with two Albatrosses in hot pursuit, Rick dove to the attack. He hoped his sporadic fire would distract the enemy pair long enough for him to close the range. To his surprise and relief one of his adversaries began "falling to earth, quite beyond control."[12] The second Albatros was soon looking for a healthier environment.

The unidentified pilot, his fighting spirit still intact, followed Rickenbacker as he headed for yet another local contest some five kilometers distant, involving as many as five American pursuits and a like number of Albatros fighters. It was now Rickenbacker's turn to follow as the unknown American dove to the attack. Again Rickenbacker watched as the willful Nieuport heedlessly climbed up the tail of one of the German fighters as a second enemy in turn latched onto his tail. And soon the first veteran Albatros pilot had smartly looped over and behind the overly anxious Nieuport pilot, joining his Teutonic comrade in lethal pursuit of their prey. Rickenbacker was closing the trio as fast as his little fighter would permit, again squeezing off short, hopefully distracting bursts every few seconds. Finally, the tall Ohio son steadied his aim on the closest Albatros and let go a long burst which brutally connected with the doomed German. The gangly American watched as the Albatros, the pilot most likely already dead at the controls, continued listlessly on its course until it crashed into a stand of trees on the east bank of the Moselle.

Both kills, his sixth and seventh, took place behind enemy lines.

As the surviving German fighters elected to head home, Rickenbacker was finally able to close on the lone Nieuport, which had in the meantime managed to shed much of the linen off its top-right wing. Pulling in close to the cockpit of the struggling pilot, Rick was greeted with the toothy grin of Jimmy Meissner. This was the second time Meissner had stripped his Nieuport wing, happily managing a relatively safe return to their field to share the tale. Meissner had gotten his second German that day and would end the war in command of the 147th Pursuit Squadron, having amassed a remarkable eight victories along the way.

Though Rickenbacker had scored twice again on his 30 May flight, his fifth confirmation would not arrive until well into June.

In the meantime, the honor of history's first official American-

Harvard-educated Douglas Campbell was credited, with Alan Winslow, with the 94th Squadron's first two official aerial victories on 14 April 1918. By virtue of an earlier confirmation, Campbell would also beat out Eddie Rickenbacker to become the unit's first official ace. Campbell would end the war with six official victories and would later serve 24 years with Pan American Airways, becoming its general manager in 1948.

trained ace had already gone to the clean-cut youth from Harvard, Lieutenant Douglas Campbell. Campbell had gone out on the morning of Friday, 31 May on a voluntary patrol the day after the Rickenbacker/Meissner fight and officially downed his fifth enemy plane. The victim was another snooper, a high-flying Rumpler C from FA(A) 242 downed over Lironville. As the plane crashed well within Allied lines, the confirmation was made official within hours of his safe return to Toul.

Six days later, on 5 June, Campbell earned his sixth and last victory while stopping a bullet in the back. He would read of the balance of the war's progress while recovering from his wounds in the United States.

Rickenbacker's own continuing operational status was little more secure than that of Campbell's. The senior flier woke up Saturday morning on 1 June feeling generally lousy. His head pounded and he was sure he was running a fever. Steering clear of the flight surgeon's tent, Rick quietly flew the day's assigned mission and headed for his cot.

Sunday, the second, proved a rewarding day on several counts. Poor flying weather permitted Rick to catch up a bit on his always sizeable pile of stateside mail. This was later interrupted with the welcome arrival of the new men of the 27th Aero Squadron, commanded by Major Harold Hartney and that of the 147th, commanded by Major Geoffrey Bonnell - both senior officers late of the RFC.

At long last the 1st Pursuit Group was made whole!

The following day Rick found only frustration when he climbed up the tail of a new Fokker with jammed guns. Tuesday, 4 June, should have been a joyous day for the ill-feeling Rickenbacker when he was appointed deputy commander of the 94th. Perhaps, most importantly, for the highly competitive former racing champion, he no longer needed to seek approval for his favored voluntary patrols.

Rick's frustrations, compounded by his throbbing head and aching bones, reached the breaking point when he again found the enemy on his next combat patrol. Not only did his guns again jam, but his Nieuport's cranky rotary engine gave up the ghost entirely. With a curse on his lips for the frail beast, Rick managed to glide safely back to his field at Toul. There he promptly reported to the medical tent where a 48-hour leave in Paris was prescribed.

It was a slow beginning in a strangely slow month for both Rickenbacker and the group. The end of June would find the group with only six confirmations for the period and Rickenbacker back in a Paris hospital with a misdiagnosed "three-day-fever."

Rickenbacker's one bright spot for the month of June would be the confirmation of his fifth victory on the 9th. The 94th had its second ace.

Though the month remained generally quiet, July anxiously waited in the wings. And with it would come a new offensive, a new plane - and new competition for one Edward V. Rickenbacker.

Chapter Three
Insert No. 1

CONFIRMATION OF AERIAL VICTORIES

Not surprisingly, the U.S. Air Service system of officially confirming an aerial kill in World War One was adopted in total from
that used by the French. The majority of Americans volunteered to
fly and fight for the French before direct U.S. involvement, and
later the USAS operated within the French Sixth Army during its
first formative months of combat operations. Essentially, a kill had
to be confirmed by independent observers not part of the aircrew
making the claim. This was not always possible deep behind
enemy lines. Or, the wreck of the claimed victim had to be found
at the location of impact as identified by the victorious combatant.
Unlike the British system which assigned victories for enemy aircraft perceived to be 'out-of-control,' an American/French victim
had to be seen to come apart in the air, or to be on fire and impact
the ground. Making a controlled landing within Allied lines with
inevitable capture provided the ultimate evidence for a positive
confirmation.

And while American fighter pilots from World War Two on
were assigned fractions of kills for shared victories, WWI
American/French fliers were awarded a full credit for kills rendered
by upwards of six pursuers. So it is that today many of the WWI
American scores have been significantly reduced as a result of
close reexamination, during the late 1960s, by the Historical
Research Division at Maxwell AFB, Alabama, which employed the
post-WWI accounting policy now in place. Today, Frank Luke's
original score of 18 (some have suggested it should be 21) is officially given by the USAF as 15.33. Rickenbacker's total of 26 is
now officially 24.3 and Wehner's 6 is now officially listed as 3.5,
though the actual kills of all three may, in reality, be in excess of
even their original official scores.

Chapter Four

WHAT PRICE GLORY?

A s the automobile and auto races had captured the imagination of the pre-war American public, so too had aviation in the public's mind come into its own during World War One.
Flying was widely seen as the grand adventure by many young men
of the war years. It was, many perceived, if only subconsciously, a
sure road to personal fame and glory. A certain glow of dashing
romance and derring-do away from the mud and masses surround-
ed flying. More than one writer of the day cavalierly had likened
flying to the grand knighted duels of an earlier time. Yet there was
about this new adventure, bound on the wings of a technology still
in its infancy, the conceited flash and excitement of Twentieth
Century modernity.

To be sure, when intelligent, upper crust college men were
sought out for that exciting new job classification of "flyer" there
was no shortage of willing, indeed anxious, volunteers. Yet, behind
the glamour lay a road of unimagined technological challenges and
untimely failures, a cruelly inhuman working environment and
impersonal death, occasionally of the cruelest kind, continually
thinning the ranks - as de Tocqueville suggested - bidding, always
bidding the next adventure-seeking youth to join for the ride of a
lifetime.

Housing

No doubt, the promise of white sheets and a warm, dry bed and a hot meal at day's end contributed to the allure. And, to be sure, the average American flier had it all over his mud-soaked, trench-bound comrade. The contrast, however, did begin to pale for First Pursuit airmen as they journeyed closer to the front.

For many of the original members of the 94th and 95th Squadrons, "reality" hit the road in France with stunning immediacy in the mud of Issoudun. There, at the half-built training facility, the would-be airmen were handed a shovel or hammer and quickly turned into laborers to help construct their simple, slab-sided wooden shelters!

Neither Rickenbacker nor Hartney offered much insight into living conditions at Villeneuve, some eight miles behind the front, though reference is made to the "mud" of Epiez. The 94th moved north to the field outside Toul on 7 April and were joined there by the 27th on 1 June. Hartney recalls inheriting the little stone house that had been Lufbery's billet. He would call the long established aerodrome "the finest we encountered in our entire stay in France...Officers and men were assigned to comfortable stone barracks. We found the hangars of steel and very roomy...What a relief to promenade on concrete walks after the ankle-deep mud of Epiez and Issoudun!"[1]

If Hartney admired Toul, he fairly waxed poetic over the group's next all too brief stay in residential housing around Touquin, beginning 28 June through 9 July. The squadron commander would call their accommodations there in the 900-year-old Mirabeau Castle little short of "Paradise."

"Each officer," recalled Hartney, "had a room about an acre square and one of them actually had white sheets. We hated to leave..."[2]

Saints, the staging point for much of the group's early combat, on the other hand, was anything but commodious. Initially, the officers quartered themselves in the nearby Hotel de Marie. But the structure, which had earlier been used as an Arabian hospital, was, as Hartney would term it, "infested with cooties."[3] Whatever man-ner of infestation this covered, be it lice, bedbugs, roaches, it was sufficiently extensive to drive the officers into field tents, "an invention of the devil," Hartney would call them. There they took up residence little removed from the inclement elements to live among the rats and flies, atop the bare earth, or mud, when the shel-ters leaked - as they often did.

Not all of the 1st PG squadrons based at the Saint Field, though, appear to have had it so bad. A replacement pilot for the 95th, Norman Archibald related in his 1935 autobiography, *Heaven High, Hell Deep*, that his squadron was billeted in the village of Saints, a half mile from the field itself. The 27th, he tells us, resided another eighth of a mile further down the road, many of the officers of the latter squadron also taking up residence in local pri-vate homes.

Archibald was assigned one of two adjoining second-floor rooms of an old house with fellow newcomer Grandville Woodard. Archibald wrote the stairs were: "creaking, misshapen....Doors were askew; the roof sagged; cement and plaster had fallen in numerous places. In one room was a marble top dresser and a feather bed piled high with softest quilts. The other room, except for a low rocking chair, was void of furniture. Who would occupy the luscious bed? We tossed a coin. Luck again! But as Woodard began to set up his folding cot, I assured him of the feathered nest every other night.

"On the lower floor lived the owner, a dear old lady of eighty. An accident two years before had left her badly crippled, with one arm not properly set, bent in an awkward position. Unable to go about she had not crossed her threshold since the mishap. Kindly neighbors brought warm food, gossiped and cared for her tenderly during the declining years of tedious old age. Happy and coura-geous, but with trembling lips, she told in vivid terms of 1914, Germans had occupied this village and Prussian officers, living in this very house, had forced her to prepare their meals and obey their commands. Her eyes sparkled as she thanks the 'Bon Dieu' for the young Americans who now shared her home."[4]

Over the course of three days, beginning on 1 September, the 1st PG's four squadrons began moving back to the Verdun sector. There they settled onto a remarkably small field, which two years earlier had been used by the Germans. It was called Rembercourt. The front lines resided 12 miles to the east. There the group would remain flying and fighting through the last months of the war. Group headquarters was located in a rundown shed, while officers again made themselves at home in their ubiquitous and despised field tents.

Nor was the food anything to write home about. Tasteless hardtack, a saltless hard biscuit or bread, canned army beef and coffee served as the core of the airman's diet - and too little of that, especially for the group's enlisted personnel.

FLYING FIELD CONDITIONS

Typically and ideally, a group aerodrome, accommodating the 80 to 90 airplanes of its four squadrons, was laid out in a rough square. At each corner of the square would be located one or two inward-facing hangars and related support facilities of a different squadron.

More specifically, Archibald described the 1st PG airfield at Saints as: "…approximately square. Two sides were flanked by majestic poplars. A road bounded the third side and on the fourth an open field, studded with barbed wire entanglement, was a reminder of earlier war days."[5]

For a flying unit on the move, as were most combat units responding to the ebb and flow of the war's fluid fronts, the famed Bessonneau Hangar, most typically of the 20 x 24 meter size, was the maintenance shelter of choice. The canvas-covered structures were supported by a light timber frame that could rapidly be dismantled and moved forward or back as the demands of war dictated. So popular was the structure that German air units, such as JG.1, were quick to adopt its use when fortunate enough to capture one intact! But perhaps the mobile structure's greatest enemies

For a flying unit on the move, as were most combat units responding to the ebb and flow of the war's fluid fronts, the famed Bessonneau Hangar, most typically of the 20 x 24 meter size like these at Orly Field, was the maintenance shelter of choice.

were natural: high winds and accumulating roof snow.[6]

An aerodrome's mess and sleeping quarters, be they local requisitioned housing, hurriedly constructed wood structures or tents, for the 31 officers and 181 enlisted men of each squadron, were located not far from their respective hangars - if possible, under the concealment of a nearby stand of trees. When the members of the headquarters staff, a searchlight company, telephone squad, the men of the lighting plant manning the truck-borne portable electric generators, field-defending antiaircraft gun crews, and Red Cross and YMCA staff are added, a group aerodrome became home to over 1,000 individuals. This sizeable aggregate was amassed to support the tip of the spear, its 80 combat fliers and their aircraft.

The pilots needed every measure of support they could muster for this new kind of war. For their challenges were, by today's standards, truly all but insurmountable!

For beginners, there was the quality of the field's flying surface itself. The fliers of the 94th and 95th Squadrons had gotten an early taste of the, often, virtually impossible field conditions in the mud at Issoudun's flying training fields. And while some fields were certainly better than others, the airmen had their work cut out for them at Epiez. There they were located on the side of a hill. Upon landing, pilots had to use extreme caution, for if the flier lost control of his light plane in an unforeseen wind gust these early pursuits, built without benefit of brakes, simply continued rolling down to the bottom of the hill!

And then there was the extremely rough, 30-acre postage stamp of a field at Rembercourt, which demanded an extra measure of skill from its pilots on approach and simple luck upon touchdown to avoid a rut-upending flip onto one's nose or back.

War on High

But the flier's greatest challenges awaited him once he became airborne. World War Two Eighth Air Force B-17 crews, in their electrically-heated flying suits, routinely went on oxygen at 10,000 feet en route to targets over Nazi-occupied Europe. World War One fliers routinely flew to a mind-numbing 18-to-20,000 feet without oxygen while sitting in sub-zero open cockpits.

Literally facing hundred-mile-per-hour arctic blasts of air as frigid as a minus 30 to 60 degrees Fahrenheit for most of their two hour patrols, a warming facial shave before a high altitude flight was not recommended. The razor's destruction of the face's outer skin layer could lead to a serious case of frostbite. Many wartime fliers smeared a protective layer of whale-oil on their faces immediately before a flight and, aside from the standard leather flying helmet and goggles, covered that part of their face below their eyes with a protective covering. Nuchwang dogskin from China was particularly valued by British fliers.

Eating was another consideration before an early morning high altitude sortie. Flying on an empty stomach or reckless overeating, for that matter, led to an extreme form of nausea at altitude with painful cramps, "...projectile vomiting and lengthy spasms of retching with clammy skin and racing pulse..." generated by intestinal gases expanding to more than double their sea-level volumes.[7] Nor did the castor oil, a powerful vegetable oil laxative widely used to lubricate aircraft engines of the day and regularly thrown back

Lafayette Escadrille and U.S. 1st Pursuit Group ace Raoul Lufbery is transformed by the heavy, multi-layered clothing required to function in the frigid, subzero higher altitudes that became the World War One flier's arena of battle.

into the pilot's face during flight, help settle matters. As for the genuinely disgusting odor generated by burnt castor oil, it was a smell not soon forgotten by aviators of the Great War!

Correct clothing was vital to a flier's survival at altitude. To avoid overheating prior to flight, flight clothing was carefully layered on as close to flight time as possible. While, it had been found by 1918, any dry trapped air was a reasonable insulator, excessive moisture generated by preflight sweat would freeze at altitude, defeating the protective intent of the clothing.

World War One air historian Denis Winter outlined what the well-dressed British flier of the day included in his extensive wardrobe.

"Dressing would... be a strict sequence. Silk underwear. Close-woven woolen underwear duplicating the silk and worn loose. Cellular two-inch-square vest. Silk inner shirt. Army khaki shirt. Two pullovers. Tight-woven gabardine Sidcot suit lined with lamb's wool. Muskrat-lined gauntlets with silk inners.

"The final adjustment (prior to pulling on the leather helmet and goggles was)...a silk scarf...wound carefully round the throat to prevent air entering the vulnerable neck area and getting inside the flying suit as well as preventing skin chafing from constantly turning round in flight to check for an enemy behind the tailplane.

"Thus dressed, the pilot could withstand temperatures of minus fifty degrees centigrade."[8]

To have an altitude advantage on your enemy was as important in aerial combat over WWI France as it was over Korea's MiG Alley 35 years later. But that precious element of height came with its price for early fliers. Extended, oxygen-starved flights at altitudes of 18 to 20,000 feet could easily take the edge off a sharp mind, lead to disorientation and more often than not a raging headache, not to mention a bursting bladder by the time the thoroughly chilled aviator returned from his typical two-hour patrol.

THOSE CANTANKEROUS "KITES"

The four initial squadrons of the 1st Pursuit Group operated, in turn, two principal types of French designed and built chasse or pursuit-type aircraft, the Nieuport 28C-1 and Spad XIIIC-1. The appraisal of these two distinct "machines" or "kites," as the pilots of the day were wont on occasion to call their airplanes, clearly depended upon who one listened to. What was clear, opposing views were firmly divided between the fliers of the 94th and 95th Squadrons and those of the 27th and 147th. Indeed, the positions were so strident at times, one wonders if they were talking about the same aircraft.

"None of us in France," Rickenbacker once commented while referring to the Nieuport 28, "could understand what prevented our great country from furnishing aircraft equal to the best in the world... American pilots did the best they could with the second best (airplanes)."[9]

And yet, when the little fighter gave way to the new Spad, 27th commander Harold Hartney was outraged.

"And now another catastrophe befell the squadron - they took away our beloved little Nieuports and gave us ... (that) 'bloody brick'..."[10]

So opposed and vocally adamant was 147th commander Bonnell with the planned transition in type that he was promptly fired on 22 July 1918, and replaced by a commander more willing to accept the inevitable.

Yet, at this time Rickenbacker recalls the 94th holding a diametrically opposed response to the same re-equipping program. "Our whole squadron was fitted out with the machines (Spads) which we had so long coveted. The delight of the pilots can be imagined."[11]

Was the Spad XIII a "bloody brick" or the "staunch and strong" airplane of Rickenbacker's estimation? The simple answer is yes, on both counts! In fact, both the Nieuport and Spad had their strong points and infuriating down sides, though on balance, the Nieuport 28's negatives seemed to have outnumbered those of the Spad by a large margin.

THE NIEUPORT 28C-1

Even as the U.S. Air Service set about ordering 297 Nieuport 28C-1s for its first pursuit squadrons, Colonel "Billy" Mitchell had viewed the type as an interim stop-gap aircraft to be employed only until the arrival of the Spad XIII. And though the batch sold to the USAS had been earlier rejected by both the French and British air arms, the type did have its admirers.

The Nieuport 28 has been called "the most elegant aeroplane of the First World War."[12] The look was imparted, in no small part, by its relatively long, slim, gracefully tapered aft fuselage. Unique to the N28 and because of its narrow fuselage, its two Vickers machine guns were set collectively off center forward of the cockpit. The first gun was located on the top of the fuselage to the left of center and the second weapon was located still further down the left side of the fuselage resting on a shelf just below the wing center section left strut.[13]

Though the Nieuport 28 was remarkably maneuverable and had a good rate of climb, it remained unpopular with most, though not all, American fliers. To find those reasons, there is no better starting place than the heart of the Nieuport 28: its demanding rotary engine.

Though the rotary engine was an American invention, first used in the Farwell automobile, it is most widely remembered as an

James Norman Hall's Nieuport when it crashed 7 May 1918 behind enemy lines. Note separated upper wing fabric at left. Hall had "pancaked" the Nieuport with such force he tore off his under carriage and dislodged his engine - the impact throwing his head into his dashboard panel.

A wounded and captured James Norman Hall photographed some two hours after his 7 May 1918 crash by the D.V Albatross pilot who claimed the victory. Hall would credit the downing primarily to antiaircraft fire. 94th flier Edwin "Eddie" Green would tell Rickenbacker after the combat he saw Hall's upper wing fabric separate.

early aircraft powerplant. This innovative honor, should it be called that, went to the French in 1908. And, to be sure, there were significant advantages to be found over the troublesome complexity and weight of the early water-cooled engines and the low-speed heating problems encountered with the fixed radials of the day. The rotary was a relatively light, simply constructed air-cooled engine boasting an outstanding power-to-weight ratio. The latter consideration has been a prime concern for aircraft designers since the origin of the job classification.

That said, however, it was mostly downhill from there!

The engine's most remarkable feature was that the entire powerplant spun around a fixed crankshaft, its propeller bolted to the crankcase! The corresponding gyroscopic effects on the airplane itself, especially on highly-maneuverable, small-winged pursuits, could be truly frightening for novice fliers. Put simply, as the engine rotates at high RPM to, say, the right, the airframe wants to compensate by rotating around its directional axis to the left. Bank the little rotary-powered pursuit to the right and the nose tends to pitch down, bank left and the nose wants to pitch up. The application of corrective power on landing approaches, in particular, could have immediate, and often fatal consequences for the uninitiated.

Further, the engine had no carburetor. It was up to the pilot, therefore, to regulate the flow of both the air and gasoline from a two-function "throttle," called a "manette," in the cockpit. In reality, however, the engine had a limited speed range, most typically being run either full bore or momentarily cut out by a button on the top of the Nieuport's control column. The mastery of formation flying took on an entirely new dimension for rotary pilots!

Here too, since the rotary engine received its oil and gasoline through the same port, traditional mineral oil, which contaminated the fuel and in turn was diluted by the gasoline, could not be used. The solution, "simple, over the counter (medicinal) castor oil," would prove a boon for busily employed wartime farmers.[14]

Further adding to the physical hazards was the use of improper annealing of the plane's copper fuel line and lack of a flexible coupling joint at the engine. Among the complexities of engine operation, without going into the details of that operation, Nieuport pilots had the option under varying conditions of firing one, three, six or all nine cylinders of their 160 hp Gnome Monosoupape Type N rotary engines. The constant vibration and start-stop jerks of the engine on the rigid fuel line led to more than a few in-flight fires in the days before the regular use of parachutes.

Fires, too, as Hartney experienced first hand, could just as easily result from inattention to proper engine operating procedures. On 22 October Hartney took up a Monosoupape (rotary) - powered Camel from the group's new dedicated night-fighting 185th Squadron. Once at altitude, the American night fliers, taking advantage of their mounts' extraordinary glide-ratios, would shut down their engines for as long as ten minutes at a time. The search light crews on the ground could then listen for the approaching rumble of the giant Gotha bombers on their way to bomb Paris. Once the distinctive sound had been picked up, the lights would arc into the sky to illuminate their prey for the waiting pursuit.

On one occasion that night Hartney had inadvertently switched off his engine without also switching off his gas jet feed. Fuel began to flood his crankcase. When next he flicked on the engine, a blinding flash of flames erupted around the cowling. Hartney would later say he was "badly frightened" by the experience. The fire continued to blaze for the better part of a minute as Hartney labored to keep the flames away from the cockpit until they burned themselves out - the engine no worse for the experience.

So, too, the linen covering over the leading edge of the upper wing had a nasty habit of pulling itself free during unusually high dive angles of attack. The resulting loss of lift led, at times, to the further failure of the nose rib section of the upper wing frame itself.

There is little wonder that American pilots of the 94th and 95th Squadrons resented their "cast off" Nieuports. All the greater was the outrage, as no forewarning of the French chasse's shortcomings came with the ($18,500 per plane) bill of sale. The fliers had to find out to their peril in the heat of combat. Twice during the first weeks of operation had the 94th's Jimmy Meissner stripped his wings, and twice had he returned by the narrowest of margins. The

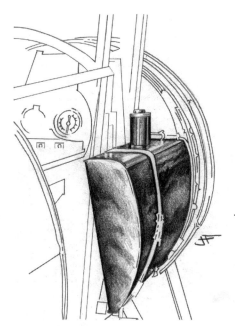

Seen here at the right is the Nieuport 28's reserve tank, located adjacent to the cockpit and similar to the one which had burst into flame on 19 May 1918 forcing an already badly burnt Raoul Lufbery to jump to his death from his doomed Nieuport.

failing had caused pilot/author James Norman Hall an early end to his flying career and an extended stay as a prisoner of war. And so, too, had Rickenbacker discovered, on 17 May 1918, that the ample application of power gave him the slimmest of avenues back to a safe landing at his home field.

It was a failing British-trained RFC veterans Hartney and Bonnell knew all too well before taking their 27th and 147th commands to France. So forewarned, neither squadron experienced the structural failures endured by those of the 94th and 95th. So insistent, in fact, had Hartney been on the point of excessive dive speeds, that he was forced to send one heedless pilot packing for fear he'd kill himself.

As if to add insult to injury, Hartney and his squadron amazed both French factory representatives and 94th and 95th commanders by getting an amazing 30 hours of life from their rotary engines between overhauls. The 27th's Sergeant Albaugh had discovered that drilling holes in the engine cylinders improved the circulation of the raw gasoline/castor oil mix, thereby improving overall engine cooling and extending the engine's operational life.

On 2 May 1918, the 94th's "Jimmy" Meissner had first discovered the weakness of the Nieuport 28's upper wing fabric and would endure the same affront a second time on 30 May. The pilot had the distinction of being the only 94th pilot to successfully nurse his plane back to Allied lines on both occasions. Meissner is pictured here on 2 May 1918 beside the tattered upper wing of his "Dark 14."

THOSE DAMN VICKERS!

Once the fliers had learned to regulate their food intake, to dress properly and at the proper time, mastered the endless in-flight demands of their troublesome Gnome engines, learned the discipline of task-focusing in their frigid, oxygen-starved environment and, finally, found the enemy's rear quarter - there remained no guarantee their guns would even fire!

Much of the trouble centered round the American ammunition which was 3mm larger than that demanded by the Vickers machine guns. Consequently all ammunition boxes and machine gun breeches were modified. Still, as many as one in five shells could be expected to jam the breeches! Nor did the thick flange, which activated the extraction function moving the round from the belt to the breech, properly set into the groove of the gun mechanism.

"Both malfunctions, the enlarged ammunition and the thick flange, left the pilot unarmed since repairs could not be made to either problem in the air."[15]

Another common machine gun malfunction due to an improperly depressed cocking lever, however, could be solved in flight with a good old-fashioned whack from a small hammer or mallet atop the offending armature. Rickenbacker carried such a hammer strapped to his wrist for just such occasions!

Though the ammunition problem had not been solved by war's end, the careful examination of individual belted shells by each flight of four planes' three gunnery specialists had gone a long way toward alleviating, if not eliminating the problem. In the end, as the learning curve continued to climb toward the fall of 1918 jams were occurring less and less often and only after "prolonged" periods of firing.

If it were possible to find an aircraft machine gun more despised by American fliers, it was the U.S.-made 30-caliber Marlin. The design was based on the Colt-Browning Model 1895 and adapted for wartime use by the Marlin-Rockwell Corporation. So bad were the jams with the type that Americans soon returned to the Vickers. The type's notorious wartime reputation led directly to postwar American authorities ordering the type being destroyed en mass!

Another armament issue centered upon the controversial Buckingham incendiary bullet used to good effect by Luke in flaming enemy kite balloons. Around the time of the Arizonan's arrival at the front, the French issued a bulletin telling of a captured German aviator fearing he would be shot for carrying incendiary bullets in his machine gun without a special order on his person restricting his mission to that of balloon attacks. Similarly captured English and French aviators found with Buckingham shells in their guns and no corresponding special orders were, reported the Germans, being shot.

Allied squadron commanders were consequently issued Operations Order No. 39 requiring that a copy of Operations Order No. 38 be carried by all pilots flying over the lines armed with incendiary ammunition, along with a daily order specifically limiting the pilots' missions to attacks on balloons.

Operations Order No. 38 read:

1. Incendiary ammunition must not be used except for attack-

ing captive or dirigible balloons.

2. Its employment is forbidden in aerial combat between aeroplanes.

Norman Archibald of the 95th Pursuit Squadron no doubt spoke for most of his fellow fliers, thinking the orders "absurd" since ground combatants were using every weapon available to man and science to kill their enemy.[16]

THE SPAD XIII

Rickenbacker had flatly called them, "the best ships I ever flew." And, to be sure, when the Spad VII first began replacing the Nieuport 17 in the French escadrilles during September 1916, a revolution in aerial performance had arrived for the Allies. The 110 hp Le Rhone rotary-powered Nieuports had found their match in the Central Powers' new 160 hp Mercedes-powered Albatros D.I and D.IIs. Though both the Nieuport and Albatros had service ceilings within a few hundred feet of each other at some 17,000 feet, the German pursuit boasted a 6 mph margin in speed at 109 mph. And, perhaps even more important, the Albatros was equipped with two 7.92 mm Spandau/Maxim machine guns to the French pursuit's lone 303 Vickers.

The 180 hp V-8 Hispano-Suiza powered Spad VII arrived in French units with a top speed of 129 mph (20 mph faster than the Albatros) and a service ceiling of 21,490 feet - more than 4,000 feet above that of its German opponent. And to a pursuit pilot, superior altitude offered advantages difficult to overcome.

But there was more to the early Spads than performance; the M. Bechereau-design weighed in empty at nearly 300 pounds heavier than the earlier Nieuport 17. Air historian Michael Jerram has called the Spad, "structurally one of the most advanced aircraft of the conflict."[17]   Indeed, there was much about the Spad that American fighter pilots of the Second World War would use as the standard for rating their own later mounts: superior speed and altitude capabilities, rugged construction and superior diving speeds.

Eddie Rickenbacker had finally arrived when he found the mount of his desires in the sturdy, nonetheless problematic Spad XIII C.1.

Simply put, the heavier Spad's structural density and redundancy in everything from heavy trussing and the doubling of bracing wires to some three times as many wing ribs as the earlier Nieuport 17 spoke of a ruggedness ready to handle the most demanding maneuvers. The beefed-up structure also permitted the Spad to endure the kind of enemy punishment that would have destroyed the lighter-built Nieuports. It was the kind of structure that made heroes of fliers the likes of Frank Luke, Jr.

By the late summer of 1917 a marginally larger rendition of the Spad VII, the Spad XIII, had begun to enter frontline units. The airframe had been further beefed up to accept the larger 220 hp Hisso engines which brought the pursuit's top speed to over 130 mph - a speed superior to virtually all its opponents for the balance of the war. But the S XIII's most important improvement was the doubling of its offensive firepower from one to two 303 Vickers machine guns.

The Spad's heavier construction certainly had performance consequences for American pilots used to the lighter Nieuports. Its added weight and absence of a rotary engine made for a more stable gun platform. And though the Spad XIII was less maneuverable, it could be aggressively horsed around the sky and dived without fear of compromising the structure. And too, its new structural density gave it a superior dive rate.

Closer to the ground, however, that increased dive rate translated into a noticeable 'sink' rate which required the "Brick," as it was derisively referred to by the uninitiated, to be powered, not glided, in for a landing. And once on the ground, the French pursuit had a wicked reputation for ground-looping on rollout.

The Spad's lack of dihedral also made the pursuit marginally unstable, or "sensitive" in the roll. Actually, this was a desirable quality for a pursuit. On the other hand, the Spad was not a "hands off" machine, but rather a demanding and fatiguing pursuit requiring constant hands-on attention in the air over the course of a typical two-hour patrol. Still, the wings' relatively thin cross-section gave the pursuit an admirable climb rate, while its pushrod-activated ailerons helped to keep stick forces light for the pilot.

Any piece of man-made hardware is only as good as its weakest links. On the minus side, the header tank for the Spad's water-cooled V-8 engine was positioned in the upper wing's center section and was known to spring a leak from time to time, invariably spraying scalding water back into the pilot's exposed face.

And while the American Spad XIII's were powered by the powerful 220 hp version of the water-cooled V-8 Hispano-Suiza engine (the "220 Hisso""), with an honest-to-goodness throttle, there remained aspects of this relatively new powerplant found wanting. In fact, Bechereau had designed his remarkably compact and stout airframe around the new, rugged and light-weight aluminum-block V-8, created by the great Swiss engineer Marc Birkigt, because it promised such a revolution in power-to-weight ratio over the established and problematic rotary designs of the day.

Rickenbacker's exasperation with the many weaknesses of the Nieuport 28 often had him ranting "It should be shot!" Had it been a living thing, he surely would have willingly performed the execution. On a good day he simply called the machine "flimsy;" on bad days when the upper wing linen was shed or the engine seized, he'd take to accusing the Nieuport of no less than treason for "betraying" him and his men. But he referred to the Spad as "the machine which we (of the 94th and 95th) had so long coveted...a staunch and strong (pursuit plane)."

It has been said that "love is blind," and this surely was true of Rickenbacker's unrestrained, and unamended endorsement of the Spad XIII! Nor was it the "catastrophe" that Hartney had called it - though the type was directly responsible for nearly causing the latter's untimely end. Reliability, unfortunately, would not be a by-word for the American Spad XIII's early 220 Hisso engines!

The occasion was a protection mission on 16 August 1918.[18] Hartney had led twelve 27th and three 94th Squadron Spad XIIIs assigned to protect an American 88th Observation Squadron Salmson on a photographic sortie over the lines. In the end the Salmson was not found.

During these first weeks of operations with the new Spad, Hartney reported the men of the 27th and 147th had "no confidence" in the new machines. And with good cause. On the Fere-en-Tardenois to Fismes leg of the flight, while climbing to 18,000 feet, Hartney watched one Spad after another drop out and head for home, aborting the mission with engine trouble. By the time he reached altitude there was only one plane left flying his wing - manned by a new replacement pilot, Frank Luke, Jr.

"It was one of those grim, heat-hazy days," Hartney later recalled, "when it was particularly difficult to spot enemy ships. The first intimation of their presence would be the streaks of tracer bullets and that nasty click-click as hostile missiles snapped menacingly past our ears."[19]

Both Hartney and Luke, alone and badly outnumbered fought for their lives that day and lived to fly another by margins too thin to recall with any fondness.

The Spad's Achilles' heel and source of the mass aborts was its engine's poorly designed reduction gear housing. Hartney relates that the slightest propeller imbalance, even a small nick incurred by a thrown field rock, could throw the reduction gear out of alignment. The resulting engine vibration would begin to loosen the water-cooled engine's plumbing, leading to overheating and even seizure.

So serious was the problem that the 90 percent operational rate for Hartney's Nieuports dropped sharply to 50 percent and less when tending the new Spads. Hartney relates that where four hours was all that was required to overhaul the relatively simple air-cooled rotary engine, four days were needed to thoroughly overhaul the new water-cooled Hisso powerplants! Nor was the problem limited to Hartney's 27th, but rather was found throughout the American pursuit community. During its first weeks of operation the 3rd Pursuit Group's 93rd Squadron reported as few as "3 to 5" of its 22 Spad XIIIs operational at any one time.[20]

Frustrated 93rd ground crews discovered "their sensitive Hispano-Suiza engines...required constant tune-up, gapping of spark plugs and carburetor adjustment. Poor propellers were on the first lot of Spads, and had to be replaced. Also there were broken exhaust pipes and fuel and oil lines."[21]

If American wartime fliers royally cursed the French aircraft industry for their unreliable steeds, the French fliers of the famed Storks Group operating the same Spad types down the road from Hartney's group were themselves no less frustrated by the same maintenance issues. So bad was the Hisso engine problem at one point, that Colonel Mitchell asked Hartney to send his maintenance chief to the French unit to let them have the wisdom of the American ground crews experience in dealing with many of the same issues.

Clearly, "quality control" had yet to become a heralded byword of France's pioneering and overtaxed wartime aircraft industry.

Equally clear was the fact that the seemingly endless and often ruthless challenges of a 1918 combat flier began long before he met the enemy over the line. The sheer frightfulness of conditions and the flier's sense of vulnerability, had one consciously dwelled on them, came to be accepted as the price of being a member of this elite group. And at times the sense of vulnerability invaded their psyche regardless of their steel-nerved, fatal outlook. As one Vietnam-era "Wild Weasel" pilot shared with this writer, it was not the decidedly hazardous daytime missions which bothered him so much as his unwelcome nighttime dreams of a fiery end. Conversely, it was this shared trial and responsibility which engendered a comforting kind of comradeship, a bond which crossed barriers of rank and background - most readily within American, Canadian and Australian units.

And while the qualities of superior general intelligence, physical well being and a certain focused intellectual discipline, as then demonstrated by collegiate accomplishments, went a long way toward providing the base material for a successful peacetime military officer, this would, of itself, prove insufficient for the demands of wartime flying. The peacetime importance placed on an unwavering regard for regulations, good discipline, attention to paperwork, a fanatic attention to personal appearance and that brand of apple-polishing politics which all too often won peacetime promotions, were not, of themselves, the qualities which won wars.

The wartime qualities requisite of a successful aviator were certainly less clear. To be sure, a feeling of almost supernatural skill, call it "ego," went a long way toward meeting the extraordinary challenges of the combat flier. Invaluable too were those qualities of aggression, determination, imperturbability in the heat of battle, and the ability to quickly process and evaluate a fluid situation. To make correct snap judgements and act without hesitation, and, yes, even to be something of a non-conformist, proved essential to martial the wherewithal to cut through the fog of conformity to find the new answers for their ever-changing situational demands.

It was this latter irreverence for the status quo, the innovative can-do spirit found in rich abundance within the democratic American culture, which would ultimately prove so valuable in the months ahead.

Chapter Four
Insert No. 1

CIVIL NIEUPORTS

While the U.S. Air Service purchased some 893 Spad XIII
C.1s and only 298 Nieuport 28 C.1s, it is the graceful lines of the
latter type which became most immediately recognizable to the
post-WWI American public. This was due principally to the universal appeal of the motion picture and film stunt flier Garland
Lincoln.

French-built Nieuport 28s first passed into civilian hands in
this country from stateside surplus U.S. Army/Navy lots around
1927-1929. The Navy had acquired 12 of the type (A5794 through
A5805) in August 1919 from the U.S. Army to be experimentally
flown as the "eyes of the fleet" from platforms mounted atop the
forward turrets of American battleships.

By the end of the 1920s Lincoln had amassed 11 of the rotary-
powered French pursuits. His Nieuports were featured in a long
string of Hollywood feature productions, including both the 1930
and 1938 versions of the classic WWI epic *Dawn Patrol*,
Heartbreak (1931), *The Lost Squadron* (1932), *Ace of Aces* (1933),
Hell in the Heavens (1934), *Suzy* (1936), *Men with Wings* (1938).
Stunt Pilot (1939), and *Captain Eddie* (1945).

By 1931 or 1932, however, Garland Lincoln's fleet of fragile,
tired Nieuports was down to four airplanes. Their airworthiness
was marginal at best and most certainly not up to the rugged
demands of a modern screen "dogfight." So it was that Lincoln,
with the financial support of the RKO Studio producer of 1933's
Ace of Aces, set about building a lone, new, rotary-powered
Nieuport 28. While the reproduction externally resembled the original French pursuit, its top wing was built without dihedral, and
both wings were some 40 inches shorter in span. So too was the
graceful fuselage, now made of sturdier stuff. Steel tubing assembled in the manner of the famed Fokker D.VII with crossed bracing
wires spanned the interior bays.

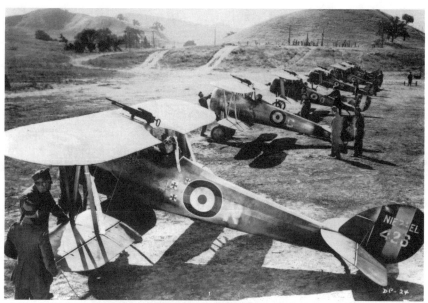

Stars of the classic 1938 remake of the Warner Bros. - first national feature film, Dawn Patrol, *Errol Flynn and David Niven, occupy the cockpits of the first two of the four Nieuport 28s supplied by Garland Lincoln for the Hollywood production. By this late date the fragile World War One veterans were no longer deemed airworthy, the aerial sequences fleshed out with disguised and newer civilian types.* Author's collection

The clean, elegant lines of the classic French Nieuport 28 belied its demanding, fragile nature. Here a line of 95th Pursuit Squadron Nieuport 28s prepare for takeoff sometime in 1918.

And while Lincoln's authentic Nieuports were relegated to background static props as vintage "set dressing" on the *Ace of Aces* airfield location, Lincoln's new, up-graded Nieuport reproduction put on a stellar aerial performance for the RKO cameras.

The shrill, raspy sound of the 160 hp rotary Gnome added further to the authenticity of the film's sound-track, though the 15-year-old powerplant was about at the end of its life. Modern pilots were too ill-equipped to deal with its unforgiving, irascible nature.

So Lincoln set about once again building a newer Nieuport reproduction based on the up-graded version of the original Lincoln design, powered by a new, more reliable and heavier 200 hp Wright J-4 radial engine. The new film 'pursuits,' known as Garland Lincoln LF-1s, took on a huskier appearance, belying the Nieuport's original elegant, even delicate demeanor. Nonetheless, Lincoln's new LF-1s were remarkably rugged and remarkable performers, one reportedly exceeding 250 mph in a dive!

Nine LF-1s were said to have been made by Lincoln, though there is no cinematic evidence of such numbers. Only three LF-1s have been specifically identified by U.S. Civil Registration number, these being NR-75W, NC-1405 (or NX-10415?) and NX-12237. The latter Lincoln reproduction, the last known to still exist, was widely flown through the 1950s and 60s with master film stunt pilot/owner Frank Tallman at the controls. His N-12237 was featured in the 1958 Warner Bros. film *Lafayette Escadrille* and later in single episodes of the 1960s television series *Get Smart* and *The Twilight Zone*.

By the year 2001 only one Nieuport 28 replica, a Jim Appleby-built, and Central California-based craft, is known to be still flying.

Chapter Four
Insert No. 2

CIVIL SPADS

By the end of 1922 the Spad XIII had disappeared from the stateside inventory of the U.S. 1st Pursuit Group, though the type soldiered on into 1929 as a trainer with the 43rd School Squadron at Kelly Field, Texas. The 43rd supplied a number of Spads in 1928-1929 for the *Wings* silent film production shot on location in Texas. Unlike its fragile predecessor, the Nieuport 28, the Spad's time on the Hollywood screen was strictly limited and consequently its type's preservation in civilian hands was equally limited.

While Hollywood stunt flier Paul Mantz during the 1930s had found a Spad VII in the basement of an abandoned California hotel and resurrected it, at least to static condition, it was not to see any airborne screen time during the remainder of its stateside tenure. Mantz's Spad was displayed hanging from wires for a series of publicity stills for the 1938 Paramount feature *Men with Wings*. Seven years later it appeared for less than a minute as a static process and background prop in 1945's *Captain Eddie* and for a final brief moment 22 years after that in the 1976 Mel Brooks comedy *Silent Movie*. All told, its screen career was anything but spectacular!

Whether it's because of the innate complexity of the Spad's wing and other structural components, or the fact that the original plans were destroyed in 1940 France in the face of the Nazi invasion, aircraft homebuilders have generally avoided the type with a passion. When the World War One aviation era began to be revisited in earnest after the 1966 motion picture release based on Jack Hunter's classic novel, *The Blue Max*, German Dr. I triplanes, the relatively simple early Nieuport types, and the boxy SE-5s seemed to be the aircraft homebuilder's types of choice. The definitive American-manned WWI pursuit type, the Spad - the mount of Rickenbacker, Luke, and so many other American WWI aces, was nowhere to be found outside of a museum.

Then in 1978 Carl Swanson completed the first of three replica and airworthy Spads. Added to this in the 1980s was a fourth airworthy replica built by Dick Day for the Champlin Museum. Further sweetening the mix, as of this writing, are several more Spad replicas under active construction. The Spad's future has never looked brighter since its service retirement during the early 1920s.

Chapter Four
Insert No. 3

FLYABLE SPAD REPLICAS, ca 2001

1. The Dick Day-built Spad XIII for the Champlin Museum of Mesa, Arizona. Now part of the Boeing Museum collection in Seattle, Washington. (Comment: among the most authentic replicas now on exhibit. In the markings of Frank Luke. Planned for static display only.)

2. The Carl Swanson-built Spad VII/N-9104A completed in 1978. Now part of the EAA Museum display in Oshkosh, Wisconsin. (Comment: flyable, recently limited to static display.)

3. The Carl Swanson-built Spad VII/N-8096L shown here. Now part of the Old Rhinebeck collection in New York state. (Comments: steel tube fuselage, 150hp Lycoming engine, tailwheel and brakes. In markings of the French Storks. Flown regularly.)

Photo courtesy Dan Taylor

4. The Carl Swanson-built Spad XIII/N-14574. Now part of the Owl's Head Transportation Museum in Maine. (Comment: flown regularly.)

Chapter Five

HARTNEY'S GANG

It was Alexis de Tocqueville who first observed and put to word the remarkable duel nature of a democratic nation whose people, or at least the major segment of that people, enjoy equal opportunity. All things being equal, he noted, there is no other form of government or people who value peace more, for such times best permit its citizens to pursue that which they value most: the improvement of their personal lot in life. This is usually achieved through some form of commerce or industry.

Conversely, in time of war, these same democratic principles render possible and fuel the desires of even the lowest, upwardly mobile soldier to acquire that same success through military honors won on the battlefield. In either case, in time of peace or war, de Tocqueville pointed out, the principle of equal opportunity, regardless of position, fuels within a free man the same ambition for accomplishment - only the methods vary.

Most Americans readily take the above observations for granted - a given. To be sure, the U.S. Army, through the years, has had its share of celebrated, highly visible enlisted soldiers who, on the strength of their performance on the battlefield, have moved up through the ranks. Many of these just as easily received battlefield commissions as officers, based on their proven military abilities. Certainly, Audie Murphy, the most highly decorated American soldier of WWII, comes most quickly to the American public's mind. Murphy, true to de Tocqueville's observations, was able to convert his early success on the battlefield into a successful postwar film career as a boyish American leading man, principally in low-budget Western features. His most famous role, however, will remain that as his wartime self in the 1955 feature "To Hell and Back" based on his autobiography.

So also did highly decorated WWII army combat veterans George Kennedy and Neville Brand translate battlefield honors into successful postwar Hollywood careers as in-demand character actors.

The U.S. Air Force, too, has its measure of success stories. Today, the archives of the Air Force Enlisted Heritage Research Institute, Gunter Annex, Maxwell AFB, Alabama is filled with tales of enlisted airmen who pursued their unfettered dreams to become officers. "Mustangs," they're called. Forty-eight, as of this writing, have risen on their abilities to become general officers. Among them was a poor West Virginia farm boy whose father's Old World German name had been Jager. Prophetically, it means hunter. Ultimately, the young Mustang, with the eyes of an eagle, found his way into the U.S. Army Air Corps where he moved up from enlisted aircraft mechanic to a WWII ace and, in October of 1947, became the first man to officially fly faster than the speed of sound. Over the years the Old World name had been phonetically changed to Yeager.

Had his father resided in the Old Country in Luke and Rickenbacker's time there is little doubt that the gifted Jager son would not, could not have risen above his class in the enlisted ranks to become Brigadier General Charles "Chuck" Yeager.

Few today appreciate how truly revolutionary was this so-called classless "American phenomenon." It was most certainly a remarkable social condition when viewed by our Old World Allies and enemies shortly after the beginning of the Twentieth Century.

It was no accident that Germany's "Red Baron" was Manfred von Richthofen - the "von" signifying his family's aristocratic origins. Indeed, there was no shortage of "vons" among the long list of German aces. These included Manfred's own brother Lothar, von Beaulieu-Marconnay, von Barnekow, von Althaus, von der Osten, and von Hantelmann, whom we'll meet again in following chapters. War's impersonal attrition, however, soon thinned their limited numbers. Initially at least, personnel filling the officer ranks of Old World aristocratic nations were most often determined by birth and social position rather than native ability.

De Tocqueville wrote, during his 1830-1831 visit to the United States, that in many Old World aristocratic nations "birth is the only source of rank...the same inequality exists in the army as in the nation; the officer is noble, the soldier is a serf.

"In aristocratic armies, the private soldier's ambition is there-fore circumscribed within very narrow limits. Nor has the ambition of the officer an unlimited range. An aristocratic body not only forms a part of the scale of rank...but it contains a part of the scale of ranks within itself: the members of (a given social rank)...are placed one above another...(accordingly in their corresponding military ranks), in a particular and unvarying manner. Thus one man is born to the command of a regiment, another to that of a com-pany; where once they have reached the utmost object of their hope (as prescribed by their social rank), they stop of their own accord.

"A nobleman who embraces the profession of arms follows it less from motives of ambition than from a sense of duties imposed on him by his birth."[1]

De Tocqueville, himself a French aristocrat, spoke in idealistic terms of the extraordinary, socially charged nature of a democratic people liberated to pursue their ambitions for personal success and recognition in time of war.

But, what of a democratic system, such as that of Great Britain, which has been fused to an Old World aristocratic order? Clearly, old ways die hard.

Originally, the British, as had their German counterpart, acquired their first officer-class pilots, some 200, from the ranks of their cavalry officers - all "gentlemen of class" - upper class, that is. By 1916, however, the Royal Flying Corps' original "gentle-man-pilots" were beginning to observe, with no little disdain "what

Lacking the "social preconceptions" and " preconditions" of their English and other Old World Brothers, the Canadians - as the Americans - were viewed by most in the established Royal Flying Corps as "a strong, rough crowd ... wild and keen of spirit." And to be sure, that "rough crowd" of Canadians brought with them that unique New World pioneer fighting spirit which was to claim the lion's share of the RFC's WWI aerial victories. No more sterling example of that 'spirit' could be found in the Canadians - or the RFC - than in 72-victory Allied ace, William "Billy" Bishop.

a mixed crowd" the RFC was becoming.[2] The warring Old World nations had little choice but to eventually fill their officer ranks with "plebeians." By the Armistice, the Royal Flying Corps would have 26,000 airmen in uniform.

Such sudden and unexpected social mobility proved troubling for this carefully stratified society. The British, however, soon found crudely dehumanizing means to keep those of 'lowly' birth in their place. First, a large pool of NCOs - non-commissioned officer-pilots - was created. Secondly, adding insult to injury, only officer-pilots officially received personal credit for aerial victories within RFC squadrons. Those kills scored by NCOs went to the credit of the British squadrons as a whole and not to the individual.

And then there was the not uncommon indignity recorded by an RFC NCO pilot named Butcher. While on leave in London, the combat veteran was bodily kicked out of a Haymarket theater upon entering through the main lobby by officer cadets and told to use the side door as was expected of '*his kind*'.[3]

When placed within the context of the times and locale of the First World War, the "American phenomenon" presented quite a challenge for Old World traditions. But this "lack of social preconceptions" was, in reality, a larger phenomenon, generally encompassing all the pioneering nations of the English-speaking New World. These included those World War One fliers from Canada, Australia and New Zealand. One high-ranking English RFC officer viewed such men as generally " 'a strange, rough crowd' but approved their 'wild, keen spirit.' Bigger, richer, more self-assured, North Americans remained distinct to the end."[4]

Perhaps more disturbing to European sensibilities was that by war's end those same free-spirited, rough-hewn Canadian pilots serving with the gentleman's club that was the RFC/RAF had shipped home with the majority of that Old World service's aerial victories!

Clearly then, there was a new social dynamic at work in New World squadrons and Europe's First World War presented the comparative laboratory to try the relative merits of both the old and new social systems. American fliers arrived in Europe short on experience, but fairly bursting with a spirited homespun aggressiveness and ambition to succeed. Their backgrounds may have been unusually top-heavy with economic position and higher education levels than the average doughboy, but their preconceptions were few. If judgments were to be made of their fellow fliers, as they most certainly would be, they would be based on the here and now. Social pretense was shunned, or, more precisely, simply viewed as not relevant. So long as everyone could begin on a level playing field and agreed to play honorably by the rules, sharing mutually accepted sacrifices, friendships of a kind not found in peacetime flourished with a previously unimagined intensity which only death could extinguish.

Yet unseen, within this happily innocent international polyglot group of freeborn patriots remained issues of national loyalty and trust that would first be put to the test, and could only be tested over the foreign fields of war-torn France.

ENTER THE 27TH AERO SQUADRON

The 27th, the U.S. Air Service's first pursuit squadron, could trace its founding roots back to Company K of the 3rd Aero Squadron, so designated on 8 May 1917. A month later, on 15 June at Camp Kelly (soon Kelly Field), Texas the unit was redesignated the 21st Aero Squadron. This soon proved something of an embarrassing clerical error as another 21st Squadron had been authorized on the same date in San Diego, California. More than a week passed before the Camp Kelly unit was allotted, on 23 June 1917, its permanent designator: 27th Aero Squadron.

The new outfit's first weeks were involved in infantry drill and poorly-received labor duties clearing the raw desert landscape of scrub brush and cactus - duties not unlike those their future brethren had endured at Issoudun. The Texas site would soon be called Kelly Auxiliary Field Number Two. On 16 August the squadron, under the temporary command of a Lieutenant Fred Harvey, boarded a train bound for Toronto, Ontario Canada and their first taste of good British military order. After the group had been divided up for various trade school classes at stations around the province, the squadron rejoined and headed south across the border back to Texas, this time with a new commander.

The new squadron commander, Major Harold E. Hartney, was a recent Canadian import, a former British Royal Flying Corps ace with emergency residency papers only days old. Hartney had joined the squadron in Canada during the last week of October, four days before their 26 October departure for Texas.

Hartney would call "those American boys" of his new command "one of the finest groups of men ever gathered together anywhere...earnest, brave, intelligent."[5]

Earlier, de Tocqueville had spoken of how once war attracts positive public attention and it is seen to offer the chance of "a greatness of vivid and sudden lustre (sic)... to create high reputations" it will begin to draw to it the "choicest spirits" from all the country. Such citizen combatants "soon make good soldiers, when

Canadian son, Major Hartney, the new commander of the 27th Aero Squadron, would call his men, with typical Hartney enthusiasm, "those American boys... one of the finest groups of men ever gathered together anywhere... earnest, brave, intelligent."

they are aroused from their business and their enjoyments... the desire of advancement is universal, it is ardent, tenacious, perpetual... (allowing)... extraordinary men to rise above the common level... bent on advancement at all hazard."[6]

De Tocqueville went on to say that free men, for the most part, "worship chance" and that war accommodates such risk-takers. "Death is constantly thinning the ranks, making vacancies."[7]

True to de Tocqueville's vision, Hartney had been greeted that late October day in 1917 with a remarkable assemblage of those "choicest spirits." Among those 60 pilots joining the 27th by war's end, six had been graduate engineers before the war, another three lawyers, four salesmen, two journalists, a cotton planter, a theater owner, a banker and a stock broker, and a concert pianist. Many others had left their college campuses without their degrees to answer the call. And still others in this democratic society with less distinguished backgrounds were nonetheless welcomed for the chance at a measure of military luster - risking nothing more than their lives.

Of these 60 fliers, 13 would pay the ultimate price by war's end and another seven would cheat death by becoming prisoners of

war. Twenty-one, mostly late arrivals, would survive to the
Armistice and another 13 were transferred out, an unspecified number failing both their own high personal expectations as well as
those of their squadron. For many, such revelations are nearly as
close to a life-altering state as is death itself, since the psychological consequences linger for a lifetime.

Back in Texas, by 29 October 1917, flight training in the ubiquitous OX-powered Jenny trainer had begun in earnest at Hicks
(later Taliaferro) Field - when not helping build the 'frontier' camp
itself. There, too, Hartney introduced the traditional British six-
plane flight unit, three flights per squadron, to the 27th. Though
Hartney was initially criticized for the innovation, it was eventually adopted by the whole of the U.S. Air Service as the organizational standard. The Canadian war veteran also revolutionized the
standard training within the squadron and was again roundly criticized for his efforts, but the results spoke for themselves. While
daring to actually teach rudimentary and "showy" aerobatics and
such "unthinkably dangerous" though life-saving techniques as
power-off landings to his pilots, the squadron remarkably finished
their flight training period with but one flying fatality.

The unit arrived in Garden City, New York on 26 January
1918, for embarkation across the Atlantic, finally arriving at
Issoudun in France on 29 March. There, Hartney took great delight
in introducing his airmen to the agile Nieuport.

The 27th Pursuit Squadron finally arrived, with the 147th, joining the 1st Pursuit Group at Toul on the first of June 1918. Though
the weather was marginal the next day, 95th veterans began leading
small groups of 27th fliers on "Cook's Tours" patrols to familiarize
the green airmen with the local terrain and landmarks. Other 27th
fliers began standing alert, though, fortunately little action was in
the offing.

During the course of the first week, the 27th logged 19 patrols.
From the beginning, it was evident there was something special
about the new squadron. For, while June was a dry month as a
whole, four of the six confirmed aerial victories recorded by the
group for the period were scored by the green, though decidedly

aggressive, quick-study fliers of the 27th.

Such credit inevitably flowed up to the squadron's deceptively petite, almost effeminate looking commander with the pencil-thin mustache, Major Harold E. Hartney. And, indeed, first impressions can be, at times, deceiving. Hartney had spent much of his youth growing up on the vast, untamed Western prairies of Canada, to which he returned as a young man and freshly-minted lawyer to practice in Saskatoon. A master shot with a rifle, Hartney had joined the 105th Saskatoon Fusiliers of the Canadian Militia (national guard) to pursue his pastime at government expense. Mobilized in October 1914, Hartney would be one of the unit's small handful of survivors when he transferred to Britain's Royal Flying Corps in late 1915 to take up flying. By mid-February of 1917 the Canadian had become an ace, flying FE-2b and 2d two-seat pushers with No. 20 Squadron.

Earlier in his British flying career Captain Hartney had agreed to offer his services to instruct American fliers, should the occasion arise. He was, however, completely unprepared for the 21 September 1917 cable from headquarters ordering him back to Toronto, Canada, for immediate transfer to the U.S. Air Service with the rank of major. In Canada, he was to train and take command of the newly formed 27th Aero Squadron. Hartney, by his own account, was delighted. He and his young family were granted U.S. residency. Permanent citizenship would follow during the first years of the next decade.

From the beginning, it was clear Hartney had a winning command style. For though he could chew on a subordinate for obvious stupidity or other misconduct with the best of them, he was firmly opposed to what he called "bulldozing," command by intimidation. Rather, he strove for a level of enthusiastic cooperation among his men, generated by a spirited example and affirmation seldom seen in other squadrons. Nor did the wisely perceptive, gutsy barrister from the wilds of Saskatoon fail to risk either controversy or his position braving latitudes or even ignoring time-honored traditions of military seniority for the sake of his command. Early on, Hartney instinctively understood the uniquely individualistic nature of the First World War flier and was quick to recognize potential in the most unsuspecting places.

To be sure, there was no more enthusiastic booster of the 27th than Harold E. Hartney, who never shied from the boast to fellow commanders or superiors that he had: "...one of the finest groups of men ever gathered together anywhere."[8]

It had only been 11 days since the 27th first joined the group that Lt. John K. "Mac" MacArthur, a Buffalo, New York electrical engineer before the war, scored the squadron's first victory. MacArthur, with his patrol, attacked eight Albatros pursuits attacking two Allied reconnaissance planes. His patrol brought down three of the Germans and dispersed the others. The new squadron also sustained its first combat casualty this 13 June when Lt. William H. Plyler was shot down, to survive the conflict as a prisoner of war.

On 17 July, MacArthur would become the 27th's first ace.

As if to celebrate another important date in the 27th's brief career, Rickenbacker, the group's master party giver, threw a gathering on the field the evening of 22 June on the eve of the 27th's first anniversary. Aside from the resident group of officers and invited neighboring British and French personnel, Rick had spent most of the previous day on the phone locating all the available nurses and Red Cross girls within traveling distance of Toul.

The party proved a roaring, alcohol-laden success - so much so that little flying occurred the next day.

Being temporarily hung over was one thing, and Rickenbacker could hold his own with the best. But, in fact, the game Columbus, Ohio native had not been feeling well all June. As early as 1 June, the day the 27th and 147th joined the group, Rick's diary reflects his "feeling seedy...his head ached...and (he) suspected he had a temperature."[9] The tall former-auto racer nonetheless stayed clear of the medical tent to fly the day's assigned patrol. Bad weather and gun jams foiled his efforts the next two days.

On 4 June, Rickenbacker was appointed deputy commander of the 94th. Most importantly, he no longer needed permission for his favored and most productive lone-wolf voluntary patrols. On his

Mechanics prepare to pull the chocks on a flight-bound 95th PS Nieuport. Under-carriage brakes had yet to become standard aircraft equipment.

next such patrol, however, his frustration reached the breaking point when he again found the enemy as, unfortunately, his guns jammed once again. The engine added to his woes as it seized, forcing a stretched and nerve-trying glide back to the field.

This time, a thoroughly depressed and under-the-weather Rickenbacker headed straight for the medical tent complaining of "aching bones." He was prescribed a 48-hour leave in Paris.

Rick arrived in the French capital Saturday, 8 June. The ace found his greatest restorative powers at the American aircraft depot in nearby Orly where he had his first close look at the Spad XIII. As a man first spotting a woman he knows he must have for his own, so such a bond, as instinctive and intangible, perhaps even irrational, as it may be, sparked between the flier and the new machine. A rejuvenating glow surged through the worn fiber of his being as he looked and pulled at the control surfaces of this compact, low-slung rock of an airplane. Here, he was sure, rested the success yet awaiting him in the air.

Before returning to the field, Rick renewed himself on his last night in Paris by indulging in a luxuriant dinner with an attractive acquaintance.

Bad weather, which always seemed to greet Rick's return, persisted at Toul.

On 20 June, Rick's plans to down his first balloon were again put on hold by inclement weather. Continuing bad weather the following day gave Rick time to make arrangements for a party on the 22nd.

Despite the generally hung-over nature of the group's fliers on the 23rd, Hartney's squadron was not to be denied a blowout party of their own the following night to properly celebrate the unit's one-year anniversary with a big dinner with ample stocks of beer and wine. Interestingly, according to 27th chief motor mechanic Walter S. Williams, a German spy brazenly landed on the field for the occasion in a captured French plane, perhaps on the basis of an intercepted wireless invitation, wearing a French uniform and speaking English with a convincing French accent. He just as brazenly congratulated the men of the 27th on their recent arrival. This was reportedly confirmed after the war by a returning prisoner of war who'd seen the photo of the 27th fliers he'd taken that evening![10]

What Hartney was to later call "the luckiest break I ever had in my life" occurred two days later on the 25th. It was an unsettling period as the group began to pack for the move to their new field at Touquin. On nothing more than a "strong hunch," Hartney joined MacArthur and Robert E. "Bob" Hill on the evening alert. Hartney's hunch proved right on the money, as the trio was soon off the ground after a pair of German planes was spotted over the lines.

Hartney, boasting to have the best eyes in the outfit, soon spotted over Lorry a Rumpler C two-place scout with an escorting Albatros D.V trailing above his altitude. The sun was still up at the time, 6:40 in the evening. Hartney dove and took out the Rumpler's rear gunner before pulling off to let MacArthur finish the kill and receive official credit. Unfortunately, in the meantime the Albatros was diving to his companion's defense, downing Hill in the process. Hartney, in turn, latched onto the German pursuit's tail and promptly dispatched him.

Hartney's sixth official victory this early in the game at the front gave him a heightened credibility and respect among his green pilots he couldn't have purchased for a million dollars. From then on, Hartney later observed, "not one word that I uttered nor any wish that I expressed was doubted or debated by my men, officers or enlisted. So far as discipline or confidence were concerned, it was the luckiest break I ever had in my life."[11]

The 26th proved an even happier day for Hartney when a cable arrived announcing that his wife of three years, Irene, had given birth to their second daughter in Saskatoon.

Being ahead of the game, Hartney assured his officers a little good news of their own when he got word of the group's imminent move to Touquin. Hartney had sent forward Russel Pruden, his resourceful supply officer, to make some most rewarding arrangements. The first units of the 27th began making the move on 25 June; the move had been completed by the 29th. But when his officers finally did arrive at Touquin, they found themselves quartered in the magnificently appointed 900-year old Mirabeau Castle. Hartney called the stay "Paradise."

At the other end of the spectrum, at the 94th, accommodations were not nearly as grand, nor was the hospitalized Rickenbacker's vague condition improving. Doctors told him he had something called a "three-day-fever."[12] By 2 July Rickenbacker was feeling somewhat better and was transferred to a nearby chateau for convalescing officers.

For the 27th Pursuit Squadron that second of July offered the unit its biggest aerial contest to date. The new squadron had arrived in the big leagues, thrown, as it was, up against Richthofen's old Flying Circus, personally led this day by its current commander, Ernest Udet. And though Hartney was not leading this particular nine-plane patrol, his veteran's hand was very much in evidence. Udet was suckered in by the oldest ploy in the book over Etrepilly-Verdilly when his nine-plane formation dove on Don Hudson's flight. With an apparent two-to-one advantage over the American Nieuports, Udet believed it was easy meat on the table. The misconception, however, was soon erased when Fred Norton led the second, higher half of the 27th formation down on the tails of the unsuspecting Germans in a classic, perfectly executed and sprung

trap. The ensuing battle raged with these seasoned German veterans for an epic 35 minutes. When the dust cleared, the novice
Americans had downed four of Udet's oft-celebrated fliers, two of
which were later confirmed, for the loss of Ed Elliott, the
squadron's first combat fatality and Walt Wanamaker. Wanamaker
would survive his captivity to become Judge Wanamaker of Akron,
Ohio.

The 27th had only been at the front four weeks, but the spirited aggressiveness of its inspired pilots, its ability to find the enemy
and make things happen when other more experienced 1st Pursuit
Group units couldn't, was beginning to draw attention to itself and
its commander in high places.

This July day, however, it was no surprise to Hartney when his
men had found the enemy in number. He witnessed for himself
from the air hours later the massed buildup of German ground
forces taking place around the Chateau-Thierry Salient. It was no
secret on the streets of Paris that the Germans were feverishly
preparing for their all or nothing offensive to win the war before
American strength and numbers finally and irrevocably pushed the
scales in favor of the Allies. And where offensive German divisions were present, Hartney knew, its supporting tactical air arm
was sure to follow.

Two days later, on Thursday, the Fourth of July, Rickenbacker,
in the company of fellow convalescing officers, drove into Paris.
And though he was regaining his strength and was delighted to be
able to lift a glass or two in honor of his nation's birth, he remained
depressed. His squadron was continuing to make a poor showing
with but one confirmed kill for all of the month of June. Much of
the continuing malaise he attributed to the "bum" Nieuports his
men were forced to fight with. Rick again sought to buoy his spirits by driving out to the Orly depot. That Saturday, impulse got the
better of him and he talked the field superintendent into letting him,
without orders, pick and fly out a new Spad to his home field.

Although Rick had been released by his doctors and had
returned to operational duties, his health remained marginal. His
return to the field would not be a long one. Almost immediately his

fever and general overall seedy feeling localized in his right ear where the pain, at times, became nearly unbearable. An old wives remedy consisting of a bag of hot salts on the offending ear at nights offered only a brief respite. Nor could sleep easily come to the healthiest of field personnel given the nearly nightly shelling of the aerodrome. Add to the mix yet another disruptive move three miles up the road to Saints on 9 July.

Finally, one morning around 10 July, Rickenbacker was found lying on his army cot in a semiconscious state. Paul H. Walter, the squadron doctor, immediately packed the Ohio native off to Paris for the first of two mastoid operations.

On reflection, the nearly two month absence from the fighting may well have saved the future Ace of Ace's life. For in this new game of aerial warfare there was no system in place for rotating veteran fliers home after a given number of combat sorties or time spent over the lines. As the Germans and Japanese continued to practice in World War Two until their defeat, combat fliers simply fought until war's end, capture, or their death.

The average life expectancy of a WWI flier at the front was said to have been three weeks. As it was, Rickenbacker would far exceed his "welcome," due, many would say, to his oft-credited "luck." When asked about "luck," Rickenbacker would not hesitate to suggest Divine oversight. Most, however, would agree the Ohio native's maturely pragmatic, intelligently calculating approach to the "risk factor" went a long way toward his remarkable ultimate success over his foe - and his final survival.

There is, no doubt, no stronger material evidence of his mental approach to this challenge than his practice of having his aircraft mechanics paint a small white circle with a black Maltese cross at its center over each patched bullet hole on the canvas-covered airframe of his Spad. For Rickenbacker each diminutive German symbol represented a lesson learned, a notice of an aerial mistake not to be made again. Each was a lesson taught by the ultimate instructor - his opponent, the veteran German flier.

At their new field of Saints, group personnel were again relegated to living in tents. Hartney would call them the "invention of the devil."

On 13 July the group was inspected by Colonel Mitchell and French General Henri Giraud. Tension was building on the field as the beginning of the German offensive was obviously close at hand.

The following day, on the occasion of the French national holiday of Bastille Day, the 95th's Quentin Roosevelt, the favored youngest son of the former president, asked Hartney to bring his compact cornet for a celebration at the Hotel de Ville in Coulommiers that evening. It had been many a night that demanding squadron paperwork had kept Hartney up long hours past those of his junior fliers. And in the quiet of those late hours, Hartney's cornet could often be heard, almost hauntingly, echoing an old hymn across the silent field. As a calming requiem, the notes offered a wistful ending to another uncertain day survived, and a blissful few minutes of solitude for its player to collect himself and help order the unrelenting deluge of demands and problems which inevitably flow across the desk of a squadron commander.

Quentin Roosevelt, who'd scored his first confirmed kill three days earlier, would never make his party that evening. Earlier that day, he was posted missing in action. An intercepted German wireless message spoke of the president's son, "after conspicuous bravery...without regard to danger" being shot down and killed by a "more experienced opponent" over Chamery.[13]

Leutnant Hans Christian Donhauser, an accomplished ace from Jasta 17 who ended the war with 19 official victories, took credit for the downing.

Those who had known the good natured flier and his daredevil bent at Issoudun had felt, "it's been suggested, that once Quent's combat career had been launched, it would be poignantly brief."[14]

Roosevelt's example was but a foretaste of events to come.[15]

Sounds of another venue made their presence felt during the early morning hours of 15 July when the shattering resonance of German artillery from Soissons to Reims announced beginning of the long awaited German offensive. Fifty-two enemy divisions moved with grim determination through ill-prepared French and Italian positions toward the Marne. British troops, hastily thrown

Quentin Roosevelt, the favored youngest son of the former president.

into the Italian line, held the advance, but above Reims, German troops reached and began to pour across the Marne. There, in the Chateau-Thierry Salient above Reims the freshly arrived American 3rd Division offered a spirited defense that finally ground the rapidly expanding enemy bridgehead to a halt.

That first morning, even Rickenbacker, from the "safety" of his Paris hospital bed, soon learned first hand the offensive had begun. The American ace had been "lying half asleep" when a loud, window-jarring explosion from a long range German railroad gun erupted in the French capital itself. Startled, Rick could only imagine what his fellow 1st Group fliers were up against.

Hartney's pilots averaged five hours in the air that first day. All the pilots were assigned strafing patrols. Their targets: the endless sea of soldiers, trucks, horses and guns which swarmed the roads. As soon as the American airmen had emptied their overheated guns, they'd scurry back to Saints to rearm and refuel on the run.

Meanwhile, field crews prepared for the worst. Men were assigned to the hangars with lighted torches ready to destroy any equipment that could not be flown or driven out on short notice. Trucks had already been loaded with baggage and spare equipment. Rifles were ready to be issued to field personnel should the enemy advance not be stopped.

A lieutenant and sergeant roared onto the field that evening with word the lines were holding. Nevertheless, Hartney pursued his contingencies and ordered a truck convoy of spares, supplies and men back to Melun, 30 miles to the rear.

For all the low altitude strafing that first day, Hartney had not lost a man. The strafing patrols continued on the 16th. For the next week, Hartney wrote, "pilots and mechanics were on the job for 18 to 21 hours a day."[16] Three days after the start of the push, weary German lines began to collapse as the Allies launched their counterattack.

But these tide-turning sorties did not come without a price for the group or for the men of the 27th. Lieutenant Malcolm Gunn was shot down and killed on the 16th; Robert "Bugs" Raymond, the squadron's able violinist, was also downed and lost to the unit, surviving the war as a POW. On the 19th Ralph Schmitt was wounded on an afternoon patrol and sent home for the duration. But it was on 20 July that Hartney called "one of the most disastrous (days) in the history of the 27th Squadron."[17]

Five pilots took off at 0700 that morning on a voluntary patrol. The prevailing west to east winds were unusually strong that morning and blew the frail, underpowered American craft deep into German territory. The group was set upon by seven Albatros pursuits. In the end, only freshmen fliers Ivan Roberts and Leo Dawson, both in their fourth day with the 27th, returned. Killed was John MacArthur, who'd become the squadron's first ace three days earlier, and Fred Norton, the former All-American football star. Zenos "Red" Miller, who already had three victories to his credit would survive captivity to become a postwar Princeton doctor.

The most poignant loss was that of Fred Norton who was found by advancing Allied soldiers critically wounded in a hurriedly abandoned German hospital. Norton died two days after being downed, in the bed of an Allied troop truck headed back to Allied lines. A deeply moved Hartney was given the note the dying airman had scribbled moments before his passing.

"27th, more power to you."[18]

Between 16 and 22 July the squadron had lost six fliers in combat, eight since the second, more than a third of its flying offi-

cers within the last two and a half weeks of protracted, bone-numb-
ing engagements.[19]

Between 23 and 25 July, twenty-five replacement pilots
arrived at Saints, the largest number of these green pilots, ten,
assigned to the beleaguered 27th Squadron. The first two replacements arrived at Hartney's command on the 23rd, the day after
Norton's death.[20]

Among the five replacements assigned to the Kicking Mules of
the 95th Squadron were Grandville Woodard and Norman
Archibald.[21] Archibald lent a human touch to the otherwise statis-
tical accounting of the arrival of group replacements on 25 July in
his 1935 autobiography. He and Oliver T. Beauchamp boarded
their train in Paris headed for Coulommiers. With many of the train
car's seats unoccupied, the two found two other 1st PG replacement
pilots also headed for Saints: Grandville Woodard and Frank Luke.

"The train stopped frequently. Every five minutes of waiting
was unbearably long. About four-thirty in the afternoon we jerked
into Coulommiers....A truck from the Group met us. Twenty minutes later we drew up before the headquarters tent and reported for
duty.

"An officer, seated behind a desk in the corner, looked up and,
smiling, greeted us. We handed him our orders and received a
questionnaire. We must fill in the blanks: our parents'
names...home address and whom to notify in case of death...

"Fully a dozen times had I answered these same questions, filling in these same blank spaces and it always seemed a useless, red-
taped procedure. But now - WHO SHALL BE NOTIFIED IN
CASE OF DEATH stood out. It was, after all, necessary and
important. For the first time the question seemed sane and logical."[22]

Beauchamp was assigned to the 27th and would be killed in
action on 1 August. Archibald and Woodard were assigned to the
95th and both would be prisoners of war by 29 September.

Among the eight 27th Squadron replacements arriving on the
25th, Edwin Kingsland and Harry Harkins would be transferred out
of the unit within weeks of their arrival. Though the reasons

remain unspecified, a measure of the demands placed upon a new 27th airman may be gauged by Hartney's introductory welcome, a hard-edged classic not soon forgotten:

"If when you get up there over the lines," Hartney tells the replacements at one point, "you find you want to come back that means you're yellow. I do not ask you to be brave enough to go over, I only ask you to have enough guts to come back and tell me so and get the hell out of this outfit...you are in the 27th in name only. When you have shown your buddies out there that you have guts and can play the game honestly and courageously, they'll probably let you stay. You'll know without my telling you when you are actually members of this gang."[23]

Among the remaining six replacements arriving on the 25th, only Donald Donaldson and Ernest Hewitt would remain to fly with the squadron until the Armistice. Arthur Whiton would become a POW in little more than a week. Ruliff Nevius would not survive August, nor would Joseph Fritz Wehner and Frank Luke, Jr. survive September.

The latter two, however, would take to their graves more than 40 percent of the squadron's total First War aerial victories and the first Medal of Honor to be awarded to an aviator!

Chapter Six

A COWBOY DESPISED

Though Hartney viewed the new group as certainly anxious enough to show what they could do, they remained, to his practiced eye, sorely ill-prepared for frontline operations.

The demands of the last week of July proved unrelenting. Hartney made the time to fly mock combat engagements with each of the new men, each of whom he bested with painful ease. And though the enemy continued to be pushed back, the temporary aerial lull was a wary day-to-day trial. And amidst the daily ration of scheduled patrols, protection missions, training flights and "Cook's Tours" for the new men, the squadron had to contend with the arrival of what Hartney had occasion to call, if not too loudly, "those damn Spads."

While 27th aircraft maintenance had become the envy of the group when it came to the operational availability of the cantankerous Nieuport 28, the Spad's poorly designed engine reduction-gear housing initially dropped the squadron's, and indeed the group's, aircraft-available figures to an all-time low. Unprepared pilots, unreliable aircraft and a critical shortage of spare parts only added to the burden of an overtaxed squadron CO whose men had been stretched to the limits of emotional and physical endurance for the last two weeks. Yet for all the challenges shared with the group, by the end of July Hartney's fliers had repeatedly found and engaged the enemy. They had, as had the neighboring 95th, racked up nine victories during the month for the costly sum of eight casualties. All the 94th had to show for its four losses was a single aerial kill. The month's winner, by a nose, however, was the 147th which brought in ten scalps for the loss of three of their own.

Given the scope and shear mass of information and action-demanding problems cascading over his desk, Hartney, though caught unawares, had little patience for army intelligence warnings of one of his new men's German immigrant heritage. America, after all, was a nation of immigrants. This was, however, the United States first major contest on the international stage. Many of its young countrymen were now fighting over the grounds of their parents, many opposing with arms their Old World kin. Echoes of a Civil War little more than half a century old resonated just beyond the veil. Truly, here resided a test of loyalties, a test of young bonds yet untried beyond the Atlantic, bonds that cleave a free people as one, as something new, the ultimate strength of that young union so far from home an unsure, untried thing.

The confidential information certainly warranted a second look at the handsome, well built, immaculately appointed six-footer with the erudite Bostonian lilt. Now that Hartney thought about it, Joe Fritz Wehner was something of a loner, certainly he didn't volunteer any more than was necessary in conversation. His carefully crafted bearing and neat presentation, however, spoke volumes, suggesting, perhaps intentionally, a persona and collegiate standing which was not entirely his.

The son of a Boston German immigrant shoe cobbler who'd brought his craft with him from the Old Country, Joe had excelled on the playing fields at Everett High School and the Exeter Academy. A trusted team player, he'd captained both schools' football teams. On graduation, Joe volunteered to work with the YMCA in German prison camps before diplomatic relations cooled between Germany and the United States. Returning to his homeland, Wehner volunteered again, this time for the Air Service, only to discover that now his heritage and recent time in Germany made him suspect. He'd already been arrested and briefly detained as a

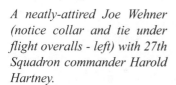

A neatly-attired Joe Wehner (notice collar and tie under flight overalls - left) with 27th Squadron commander Harold Hartney.

possible enemy agent in Texas and would be detained again on Long Island by suspicious authorities before shipping to Europe.

As far as Wehner knew, as did Rickenbacker before him, there could very well be one or more undercover agents in camp now watching and reporting his every move. It was certainly enough to make the Bostonian a guarded, closed-mouth, bitter young man.

As for Hartney, the proof of the pudding would be found in the air, not in the unfounded paranoia of a so-called intelligence report. Judgement, as with all his pilots, would be restricted to the arena of combat, the ultimate test of a flier's resolve and convictions.

The first day of August 1918 would be variously remembered as "That Awful Day" or "Jonah Day." Eighteen 27th pursuits left Saints at 0705 that morning on a protection patrol, escorting a pair of French Salmsons on a photographic reconnaissance mission in the Fere-en-Tardenois region. Led by Texan Alfred "Ack" Grant, a hard-nosed, by-the-book West Pointer, the formation was initially attacked at 10,000 feet at 0810 by eight Flying Circus Fokkers. Soon the melee was joined by crack German pursuits from Richthofen's Jastas 4, 6 and 10, as well as Jasta 17 - all first string units. Six of the 18 American fliers would not return. The veteran

In character, a pug-faced, ill-tempered Alfred Grant, recently promoted to command of the 27th Squadron, stands by the cowling of a 1st Pursuit Group Spad XIII.

Jason Hunt and recent replacement fliers Arthur Whiton and Chuck Sands were killed in action. Squadron veterans Dick Martin and Cliff McElvain survived the war as POWs. Oliver Beauchamp, with the squadron little more than a week, managed to nurse his shattered Spad back to Saints, only to lose control over the field and spin to a fiery death before hundreds of waiting ground personnel.

But the veteran Germans also paid a price. Donaldson, in his first combat, scored three witnessed, though ultimately uncon-firmed victories. Hudson amassed another three kills, later con-firmed, while Ivan Roberts acquired a single victory, and Jerry Vasconcells and Ruliff Nevius shared another confirmation. Also among the German casualties this day was Jasta 17's six-plane ace and commander Gunther Schuster.

Though costly, the 27th had again returned with a winning score. Interestingly, both Luke and Wehner were also on this patrol. But, in the case of Luke, no combat time is credited. Had he, as some biographers suggest, already begun his wayward lone-wolfing ways and broken away from the formation before contact had been made with the enemy? More than likely.

Rickenbacker would characterize Luke as "an excitable, high-strung boy...his impetuous courage was always getting him into trouble."[1] Hartney further rounds out the picture of the Arizonan, telling of his unfortunate propensity for brash boastfulness, of mak-ing claims for great accomplishments yet to be demonstrated.

From the beginning, it seems Luke's abrasive behavior, perhaps motivated by his own insecurities, put distance between himself and many of the squadron's other fliers. And all his fellow airmen could see, all the actions upon which to judge the new man, was his continual flaunting of orders, of refusing to stay the course, of breaking formation. No one believed his excuses, "engine trouble" most often. Many, however, began to wonder if all they had on their hands was a loud-mouthed coward. A lying "four-flusher" (sic) some had called him, though, doubtless, not to his face.[2]

Norman Archibald, the 95th flier, recalled, "Luke was being talked about.

"His own squadron almost ignored him. So, he would come over to see us, Woody (Woodard) and me, for he had known Woody in the States and I was an amused listener.

"The tales he told.

"He insisted he always left the formation.

"One evening in front of the operations tent, Luke again was narrating about his prowess. Said he left the formation, saw a German plane about a mile over the lines, had a terrible fight and his opponent went down in flames.

"Another flyer was standing near by. 'Those kinds of victories are easy,' he said with dry sarcasm. 'You better go back and get confirmation.'

"Luke looked a bit hurt. But launching afresh into another yarn, he novelized a hair-raising air battle in which, as always, he was the hero.

No one believed him. No one ever saw his conquests. Luke still came over. His stories, more self-trumpeting as time went on would have paled the 'Penny-Dreadfuls.' (pulp fiction)"[3]

The large engagement had been actively witnessed by two cheering divisions of American troops and their accompanying correspondents. A number of the newspapermen arrived at Saints the following day to recount their view of the "magnificent flight." They also told of the wrecked aircraft, both German and American, with their dead crews left unattended on the field of battle.

Hartney was shocked at the news and within minutes had taken

The 1st PG's new Spad XIIIs with their poorly designed engine reduction gear housings initially dropped the unit's aircraft available figures, what the U.S. Air Force by the year 2000 would call: "mission capable rate," to new lows - as low as 15% in some squadrons. By point of reference, in the year 2000 the USAF mission capable rate standard for their new C-17 jet transport was 87.5%. Here a mechanic pulls through the prop on a new, and as yet, unassigned Spad XIII at the 1st Air Depot. Squadron insignia and individual aircraft fuselage numbers would be applied upon delivery to the squadrons in the fields.

to the air skimming the region's wheat fields and stands of trees, in now famous Belleau Wood, then headed north to Cantigery and Villers-Cotterets and the vast expanse of battlefield beyond. What he saw sickened even this veteran soldier. A broken ball race (bearing housing) on his Packard prevented an early drive to the front to inspect first hand the remains. Hartney's touring car repaired, he planned another drive up to the front on or shortly after 4 August. It was on this trip that the small major from Canada first took special note of the misfit from Arizona. Hartney had agreed to take the young flier up with him, though not without reservations.

With a driver, the pair headed to the front in Hartney's Twin-Six Packard. The shy, boastful Luke began to talk of his formative years in the Southwest. His Indian encounters, his days as a semi-pro boxer, his horsemanship and experience with a gun all came to the fore. His words, once released, fairly exploded forth in that strange, high-strung staccato manner of his which contrasted so markedly with his long, socially insecure periods of off-putting, sullen silence. When he talked, Luke's deep blue Germanic eyes blazed with passionate resolve, his rugged blond, muscular good looks and powerful body language spoke of an energy, a coiled resolve lacking only focus.

As a lawyer appraising his client, Hartney sensed this was a young man who would not respond to the traditional modes of military discipline. Yet when Luke spoke of his determination to make good, his squadron commander gleaned a glimmer of an extraordinary, if unrefined, potential. Such men were no strangers to Hartney. He'd seen scores of just such strong willed, individualistic youth on the Western prairies of Canada. Hartney recognized the drives, the coarse, irreverent bent that, if properly channeled, could well serve the squadron. And then, perhaps, Hartney recalled his Bible and the Exodus admonition "...not to oppress the stranger, since you understand the soul of the stranger." Both men, in their own ways, were strangers out of their element. Hartney was the foreigner from Canada leading this rugged band of spirited Americans, among them Frank Luke who'd been thrust into a world and social setting as foreign to his being as if he'd landed on another planet.

"Hundreds of times," Hartney would later recall, "I have seen professional officers shocked by the apparent informality of flying men and attempt to 'put the fear of God into them,' meaning to give them the rigid military discipline so necessary in the infantry (or) some of the other mass-thinking branches... Rob an aviator of the rugged individualism which led him into the flying service and you have zero."[4] Hartney had soon made his own silent commitment to this rough-hewn Westerner. With his mind's eye on the larger picture, he would risk, by careful measure, the perception of good military order. He'd play out the reins a bit on this one, and give him his head. It was a gamble, to be sure, but the rewards seemed justifiably promising.

And the first test lay just ahead. Two of Don Hudson's 1 August claims had come at the expense of two German two-place Rumpler Cs which had collided and fell to their doom trying to

evade the American's guns. Hartney and Luke found the inter-
locked remains of both planes and their dead crews still in their
cockpits, faces blackened from their rapid decomposition in the hot
summer sun. The wrecks were resting in an otherwise undisturbed
wheat field.

As Luke looked on, Hartney walked the few hundred yards to
the crest of a nearby hill. Silently, grimly he looked beyond.
Moments later, Luke had joined him. Below the crest, played out
a hundred cruel acres of silent death. The trampled and charred
ground lay wounded, littered with hundreds, perhaps thousands of
corpses, both German and American, resting where they had died
whole or torn by the angry spray of heavy caliber machine gun fire,
individual rifle rounds and fixed bayonets. Much as Picket's
Charge had less than 60 years earlier, hundreds of American dough-
boys marked the exposed path they had followed into the teeth of
withering enemy fire and bayonets, their number made staggering
by the modern, more efficient machine gun and the rearguard
German crews sacrificed to buy time for an exhausted army in
retreat. The silence was deafening, the stillness disturbed but incidentally by the lone army chaplain collecting identity papers.

Hartney and Luke drove up the line finding more German and
British planes, but no American wrecks. Nearing Fere-en-
Tardenois, Hartney reports he and Luke witnessed the successful
attack by a German Albatros on an American observation balloon.

Little was said on the long drive back to the field. That Luke
was giving personal reflection to the events of the day Hartney
could have little doubt. But had he let the young flier see too much
and too closely the vast impersonal savagery that is modern war?
For many pilots keeping the killing at arm's length, destroying
planes and not necessarily men was an important psychological distinction. Death at close quarters would certainly have a devastat-
ing effect on another American Ace of Aces, World War Two's
Dick Bong.[5] For Hartney, only time would tell with Luke. The
time, however, would not be long in coming.

The first half of August was a period of relative quiet in the air
for the 1st PG. It was a time of getting the squadron's green pilots

up to speed and contending with the trouble-prone new Spad pursuits.

The latter on-going problem was no more apparent than on the morning of 16 August when 11 planes took off from the advanced field at Coincy on a protection patrol to cover the flight of an American 88th Observation Squadron Salmson.[6] Luke was also scheduled for the mission but got off an hour late due to mechanical problems. In the meantime, one by one, Hartney's Spads dropped out of formation, aborting the flight and returning to their field with reduction gear problems.

Finally, as Hartney tells the story, he is left with a lone Spad, that of the recently arrived Frank Luke. It was at this opportune moment that the pair was jumped by a sizable flock of the enemy. Only the inspired defensive flying of the two Americans and luck prevented their destruction.

Hartney, in his 1940 autobiography "*Up and at 'Em*," certainly reconstructs a vivid picture of this important moment in the evolution of Luke's social dynamic within the squadron. It provides, what a dramatist would enthuse, is the motivation for the central character's all-important drive for vindication. Escaping the Germans by the narrowest of margins, Hartney flew back to the mission's field. There he cursed up a blue streak among the waiting 10 fliers who'd earlier aborted with engine problems. At the height of his animated diatribe, all eyes began turning to the sound of a last Spad approaching for a landing.

"Here comes your boy friend now," mused one of Hartney's chaffing fliers. "He said he was going to get his first Boche today or never come back. Let's see what the blowhard's got to say for himself. Bet he claims one.[7]

A group of the fliers trotted over to Luke's ship. Soon they returned to tell Hartney, "What did I tell you? He says he shot one off your tail."[8]

Hartney took Luke aside and was soon convinced the Arizonan was telling the truth. Few others in the group, save Wehner, believed the boastful cowboy. Nor was Luke's claim ever confirmed.

From that moment, wrote Hartney, "Frank Luke was a lonesome and despised man..."[9]

Luke's unmitigated flair for frontier-style individualism, while perhaps a sideshow amusement for some, represented something of a threat to many of his fellow fliers with their fashionable walking sticks and thinly applied veneers of pseudo-sophistication and conforming Twentieth Century modernity. Luke, perhaps unstable, nonetheless possessed and gave life anew to their shunned, raw, untamed roots, that "rude vigor of thought" de Tocqueville had so eloquently spoken of. Luke, perhaps reminded his fellow airmen that they had paid a price for their conformity.

To be sure, their intellectual association with the group had given the fliers a stake in their micro-society, "a sense of responsibility and self-importance that (kept) them from being 'lost in the crowd.'"[10] But, the price of that association had been personal liberties grudgingly given up. It is a subtle thing, but a highly valued American commodity. Should there not, therefore, be a degree of jealousy among a squadron's members when an individual was permitted to remain in their midst who steadfastly refused to give up the same measure of his personal sovereignty? It was, many perceived, an injustice and a grating reminder of what they had already lost.

Luke's fate, it appeared, remained his own, his destiny that of his own making. Yet, it was the judgmental tyranny of the majority, which ultimately triggered the deep-welled pride and challenged Luke's own loudly proclaimed, nonetheless fragile self-concepts of daring, courage and skill. The personal validation and social exculpation became everything - the cost incidental.

Regardless of Luke's ultimate, and amply demonstrated successes, many resented to the end his refusal to "play the game" by the established rules.

As the bulk of the 27th fliers turned their backs on Luke, so did Luke, deeply hurt by the unit's distrust, turn within himself, breaking the silence only to taunt his fellow fliers with physical challenges and cutting sarcasm. On the ground, he spent his time in the orderly's tent pecking out, with two fingers, confirmation forms and

Twenty-Seventh Squadron commander Hartney found Frank Luke, Jr. as ill-prepared for combat as the rest of his recently arrived replacement aircrews.

at the machine gun range perfecting his already considerable skills as a marksman. As Wehner before him, Luke was now an angry man determined to prove himself - damn the price. What tolerance he had for the arbitrary ways of the military was ebbing away. More and more the Westerner finds it impossible to hold his position within formations unable to find the enemy.

To be sure, Hartney felt he had his hands full managing Luke and the 27th, but demands were about to quadruple. On the afternoon of 21 August upon landing after another mock combat with a new pilot, Hartney's orderly, Dudley, told him he'd just been promoted to group commander. Initially, Hartney thought the Southerner daft. Nor had the "petite major" from Canada given the group post a second thought.

Hartney's superiors, however, had an eye on him from the start, and they liked what they had seen. From the beginning, Hartney's inexperienced squadron had out-shown the group's established squadrons across the board from aircraft availability and squadron scores, to sheer energy and enthusiastic command by example. By the end of August and since their arrival on 1 June, the 27th, under Hartney, had amassed 18 confirmed aerial victories, compared to the veteran 94th's three, the 95th's 12 and the 147th's

11. And, unlike the 147th's Bonnell, Hartney knew when to keep his mouth shut and follow orders.

And while Hartney moved up to the unrelenting round-the-clock demands of a group commander, Lieutenant Alfred "Ack" Grant moved into the vacated squadron command post. While Grant was neither particularly impressive in the air or, so it would prove, on the ground, he did have the seniority and a West Point ring. Grant was a solidly built bull of a man. He was a commander possessing neither the handling skills nor the subtle insights into the human character of a Harold Hartney. Rather, he believed, perhaps simplistically so, that an outfit and its men should be run by the book. Privately, he no doubt harbored a strongly disapproving eye for the dangerously permissive manner in which the Canadian commander had dealt with "that headstrong boy from Arizona." What Grant understood most thoroughly was his position of authority and the Army Manual of Arms. The men were his to command and mold in his image.

A couple of lines from the wartime diary of 27th aircraft mechanic Walter S. Williams is insightful. The date of the entry: 10 September 1918:

"Capt. (sic) Grant decides the squadron needs more military efficiency. We have regular reveille calls, roll call formations, morning exercises, spit and polish inspections, inspections of quarters, night roll calls, etc."[11]

For the free-spirited Frank Luke, who never had a strong affinity for military life to begin with, the situation on the ground was becoming more intolerable by the day. Continually frustrated in the air by the lack of engagements, the Westerner found no respite from, nor chance to disprove the condemning stares and attitudes of his fellow fliers smothering his waking hours. And now Grant. Luke had lost his senior mentor, his emotional backstop and shelter amid a sea of predators. Joe Wehner, "the spy," and Frank Luke, "the liar" - the squadron's odd men out. Though different from each other in so many ways, they found they had few others to rely on besides themselves. The pairing of the polished, quiet-spoken gentleman from Boston and the loudmouth Arizona ruffian, that had, at first sight, seemed unthinkable, proved ultimately inevitable.

On the evening of Hartney's appointment to group command he quietly left the field to attend a staff meeting with Colonel Mitchell. Clearly, Hartney had entered the big leagues of the U.S. Air Staff at the front. But no less exciting than the news a few hours earlier of his own promotion was Mitchell's announcement that as of that evening U.S. air units had been detached from the 6th French Army and assigned to the newly formed U.S. 1st Army. Hartney jubilantly called the reassignment "a powerful stimulant."[12]

Mitchell outlined the coming American offensive at Saint-Mihiel. That evening, America had 24 operational air squadrons on the line: 12 pursuit, 11 observation and, so far, only one bombardment outfit, the pioneering "Red Devils" of the 96th Bombardment Squadron.

New squadrons and groups were feverishly being readied for action. Four American and one French observation group, comprising 19 squadrons and equipped variously with French-made Salmsons, Spad XVIs and even a handful of the aging Breguets (9th Night Ob. Sq.) and recently arrived American-made/British-designed DH-4s, would be available to the American command by 12 September. Since the operational debut of the 94th and 95th Pursuit Squadrons earlier in March 1918 and the subsequent formation of the 1st Pursuit Group, two new American and Spad XIII-equipped pursuit groups had been formed. Both the 2nd and 3rd Pursuit Groups, the latter formed around the expertise of the U.S. 103rd Pursuit Squadron (the former Lafayette Escadrille), would play a major role in the forthcoming offensive. So, too, would the three squadrons of the newly formed 1st Day Bombardment Group be ready with its compliment of American-made DH-4s and French Breguets.[13]

The American air arm was growing up fast. Further adding to the offensive might of the pending advance of the new U.S. 1st Army would be seven French Chasse (Pursuit) and five French and two British bombardment groups. Add to this a 30-plane Italian contingent and 15 American observation balloon companies.

All told, Mitchell would have nearly 1,400 Allied aircraft under his command.

With the 150,000 ground-troops of the U.S. 1st Army poised to strike, Hartney could not help but to be fairly overwhelmed by the magnitude of the pending operation. Turning to the 1st PG commander, Mitchell's finger stabbed at a minuscule point on the room's massive wall map. He identified a 30-acre postage stamp of real estate near Rembercourt. Hartney was to prepare the forward field and his group for a secret move up to the front area. All efforts - repeat - all efforts must be made in secret and under cover so as not to alert the enemy.

Hartney offered his enthusiastic trademark 'Can-Do' response. Fortunately for the Canadian commander, the lion's share of the next two weeks offered a combat lull, a chance to acclimate to the all but overpowering demands of his command and prepare for the move to Rembercourt.[14]

It appears Grant was quick to take advantage of pending events. He promptly grounded Frank Luke, Jr., who, in his eyes, was his new command's single greatest affront to good military order. Grant, by all accounts, was prominent among the large number of 27th fliers who did not believe the Arizonan's claim of 16 August and had least appreciated his formation-breaking lone wolf ways. In a simple-minded effort to 'straighten out' the wayward airman, Grant grounded Luke, making him the squadron's new engineering officer. He was given the task of supervising the construction of the new facilities at Rembercourt.[15] True to his Arizona bad boy's character, Luke fairly railed at his time in purgatory. Here Grandville Woodard would take delight in sharing with this writer the perhaps fanciful tale of how Luke soon took to the motorcycle. How he delighted his construction crews with his remarkable marksmanship skills rendered with a pair of .45 automatic revolvers while standing on the seat of his roaring bike.

Whatever the specifics of Luke's defiant exuberance, Grant's frustration with both Luke and his blatantly ineffectual approach to command, at least as far as Luke was concerned, could only have grown as the days passed without respite. However unmilitary was Luke's approach to the task at hand, Rembercourt was ready when the Word came down.

On the afternoon of Sunday, 1 September, the group began the move up to the new field. The planes, those that were airworthy, began to leave in small, less conspicuous groups. Convoys of trucks loaded with ground personnel and equipment began the drive forward on roads choked with troops and covered by concealing canvas and burlap camouflage stretched between bordering trees and poles. Squadron Rear Parties remained behind laboring on those 'hangar queens' still not flyable. The last of the serviceable planes and Rear Party personnel would not arrive at Rembercourt until the evening of 7 September.

Field personnel were told to stay under the field camouflage; the group pilots, in formations no larger than five planes, were to stay well away from the lines and observant enemy field glasses.

Joe Wehner was part of the first patrol sent aloft from Rembercourt.

As tensions built, looking forward to the pending assault, an ill-advised, overly aggressive pilot from the 95th, Luke-mentor Norman Archibald, had sneaked over the line on the eighth and was promptly shot down and captured. Fortunately, and to the great relief of an outraged high command, the new pilot had sufficient wits about him to keep his own counsel and word of the new operational field to himself.

The final cast member for the concluding third act contest arrived on Monday, 9 September.[16] Eddie Rickenbacker, his health now restored, was delighted to have returned to his squadron at Rembercourt. Successfully recovering from a second mastoid operation on his right ear, the Columbus native had finally been declared "ambulatory" on 1 September, the day the group began its move to the new field. The 4th had been Rick's last day in the hospital. A few days earlier, Rick had been approached in his hospital room by a publisher's agent asking how he felt about authoring a book about his wartime experiences. Rickenbacker, no doubt, brought up his seventh grade education and his limited writing skills. He was assured a ghostwriter could be assigned to the project. Rickenbacker agreed to give the proposition some thought. The more the senior flier thought about the proposition, the better it sounded. The one-time auto mechanic began to keep a daily diary.

Rickenbacker had received word of the approaching offensive and was anxious to get back in the cockpit. And the fliers of the 94th were anxious to have him back. The Hat-In-the-Ring Squadron had fallen on miserable times in his absence, with only three confirmed kills to show in as many months. The 94th had, by a long margin, the poorest three-month record in the group. Many of the men blamed the poor showing on Major Ken Marr, the squadron's C.O., and his lack of aggressive leadership. Many, if not most of the college-schooled fliers felt the self-made former auto racer from Ohio was just the kind of leader the unit needed to get back on top. Squadron rivalry among the group units had always been intense, the relative standings the source of continual ribbing and, on occasion, less-than subtle verbal volleys. To remain in the basement over so long a period with so poor a showing was hard to take.

The socially astute Rickenbacker was flattered, but, for the moment, he wisely offered little more on the subject.

THE SAINT-MIHIEL OFFENSIVE

On Tuesday, 10 September, the Allies' massive 72-hour artillery bombardment got off to a thunderous, nerve shattering start. At 0500 Thursday morning, 12 September, the U.S. 1st Army attacked.

The weather was miserable, with ceilings as low as 100 feet above the ground, with pouring rain and occasional strong wind gusts. By noon the gray ceiling had marginally retreated above the 500-foot mark, but no one at Rembercourt had yet ventured aloft. While the rest of the fliers headed for lunch, Rickenbacker proposed to Reed Chambers that they sneak up for a look around. Chambers agreed.

The pair opened their throttles and successfully drove their Spads through the lifting rain and clinging mud, climbing to the cloud base at about 600 feet. The two had set out on what is today called a weather-evading "Scud Running" flight, as deadly for a non-instrument rated private pilot in this age as was fighting the Flying Circus in its day.

Rick and Chambers headed east for Saint-Mihiel, crossed the Meuse and turned north up the river valley toward Verdun. Dirty columns of charcoal-gray smoke cluttered the gray sky, marking enemy supply points set afire by the retreating German Army. South of Vigneulles the pair found the main northbound highway heading towards Metz alive with retreating troops, and hundreds of motor and horse-drawn vehicles. They found irresistible a report-ed half-mile long column of horse-drawn three-inch artillery flee-ing harm's way. The two Americans made pass after pass on the column. Chaos reigned as panicked horses, still in harness, and men broke on the run, many falling in their tracks amid the angry explosions of mud marking the rapid impact of the Americans' air-borne rounds.

The pair returned to a waiting crowd at Rembercourt with word of the widespread German withdrawal and improving weath-er.

Hartney ordered his squadrons into the air. Luke, as a regular member of Lt. Kenneth S. Clapp's C Flight, soon was airborne with an eight-plane patrol hugging the base of the local 600-foot over-cast. Mist and high-velocity rain stung the fliers' faces as they searched out the retreating enemy in the gloom. At an early point Luke grew weary of the chase and ventured out on his own. Near Lavigneulle the Arizonan chanced upon one of the few groups of enemy aircraft found in the air that day. His long-term frustration, however, only grew as he lost the trio of German aircraft in heavy clouds.

What transpired next depends on who's telling the story. As there apparently were only three Allied parties witness to the action the rendition of the events leading up to Luke's first confirmed kill fall into essentially two camps. Luke's principal biographers, Hall,

Whitehouse and Hartney, have relied upon the accounting or embellished upon Luke's own subsequent combat report.[17] Put simply, Luke stumbled upon the German balloon in the air, downed it and landed at an American balloon site across the line to personally insure confirmation. Soon after he took off, his plane's engine began to miss and he returned to the balloon site for a deadstick landing and later returned to his field by motorcycle sidecar.

The second accounting does not seriously contradict the above rendering. It does, however, shed considerable new light on the event - should its veracity ever be confirmed. The second set of witnesses that 12 September day were Lieutenants Maurice R. Smith, commander of the nearby American 5th Balloon Company, and his observer, Joseph M. Fox. Both were up observing on the hour in question. Smith's rendition of the events came to public light some 40 years after the war. The testimony arrived via a rather circuitous route in the form of an undated letter from the 1960s written by WWI 2nd Balloon Company veteran Craig S. Herbert to then Air Force Museum curator and long-time American Aviation Historical Society member Royal Frey.

What follows then is based on Smith's first person accounting of Luke's first official kill.

Approaching Marieville, Luke spotted an observation balloon and promptly banked into an attack run. He charged his guns as the bag grew in the gray overcast before him. Now aligned on the balloon's beam, the Arizonan spotted the roundel of an Allied balloon company. Thoroughly frustrated, the 27th flier landed near the American balloon site and called up to the observer on the phone line at the end of the tether. At the time, Lt. Smith was observing and Lt. Fox was handling telephone duties in the basket as it hugged the base of the overcast. Smith took the call. He told Luke that "if he wanted to shoot down a balloon, to shoot down a Boche one, and (Smith) would confirm it."

The balloon commander told the Arizonan he could see one across the line near, as Smith recalled many years after the war, at Hatton Chatel. Luke agreed and headed back to his nearby Spad, its engine still slowly ticking over, and headed for the German

drachen. American balloonists, at that stage of the war, generally
had a rather low opinion of their heavier-than-air brethren. "In
fact," Herbert wrote Frey, we were downright ashamed of their
actions - turning tail and running without firing a shot."[18]

But, as intimidating as were the veteran fliers of the German
Air Service, the vast majority of Allied fliers much preferred to
face an enemy Fokker rather than take on the massed arms of a
drachen nest.

Because of their concentrated, extraordinarily lethal defenses,
balloons had long been a voluntary assignment among most bel-
ligerents' fliers. Though a large target incapable of evasion, the balloon's ring of defending machine guns and artillery positions radi-
ating out from its winch truck on the ground - not to mention as
often as not a waiting air patrol above - made the target one of the
deadliest and most costly at the front. Only their premium value to
the enemy as a vital 'high-ground' observation post could demand
the toll Allied air command paid in fliers and equipment for their
destruction.

Once the balloon commander spotted Luke's approaching
Spad, the race was on. Could the Germans winch down the bag
before the American could flame it? With each passing second the
balloon descended, beckoning, as a spider to its unsuspecting prey,
to come closer to its nest of waiting guns, closer to sure destruction.

Mist permeated the air, the surface of the German sausage glis-
tened with dampness as it bobbed and jerked ever closer to its
winch truck and grounded "nest." Surely the American would end
his craziness, break off any moment now. Luke's determination,
however, knew no bounds. He dove at the balloon, his carefully
placed rounds puncturing the stubborn bag again and again without
result. The Westerner, intent on his target, refused to be dissuaded
by the heavy concentration of ground fire directed his way, or the
occasional ominous thud of a round tearing through the frail airframe's canvas and wood. Nor was any thought given to the illu-
sion of protection suggested by his linen-covered fuselage and own
wicker seat.

One trip through the deadly gauntlet would have been enough

for most pilots. Smith and Fox could only look on in amazement as Luke made a second pass and a third, each time more rounds finding their mark. Luke pulled away to work on both his guns that by now had jammed. Fixing the left machine gun, the hard headed airman turned to begin a fourth run when his eye caught sight of a flame and then a great burst of light and heat as the bag, now close to its nest, first shuttered and then began to collapse in on itself. Flaming gas and canvas ripped through the winch crew as they vainly sought to outrun the holocaust.

Jubilant, Luke turned back toward the American balloon site. According to Smith, the flier circled the 5th Balloon Company post waving down a victorious 'thanks' before heading back to Rembercourt. Before the Arizonan flew out of sight his Hisso engine began to miss and before long cut out entirely. The heavily damaged Spad turned back toward the friendly balloon site and Luke was able to glide the sturdy pursuit in for a successful dead-stick landing.

According to Smith, "(Luke) stayed with us 2 (sic) days and then I sent him back to his outfit in a motorcycle side car. But during the two days I gave him the plan for shooting down balloons, which he used with great success. I told him that balloons were most vulnerable in the early morning before they had gotten to their forward observation post, where the most anti-aircraft fire was in position or, in the evening, when they left the forward post, where it had maximum fire protection. While the balloon was moving forward or backward it had less than ½ (sic) the fire protection and of course at night when it was bedded down, it was less than that."[19]

While Luke is widely acknowledged for introducing the dawn/dusk balloon attack technique to the American Air Service, there is little evidence his attacks enjoyed seriously reduced numbers of defending guns. What is clear, when Luke's Spad was finally trucked back to the field it was so badly damaged by ground fire that it was written off and salvaged for useable spares, principally guns, instruments and engine parts. It was the first of at least five Spads so disposed of by Luke during a remarkable, if brief career.

And though Hartney lent immediate recognition to Luke's first

*An extremely rare photograph of an exuberant
Frank Luke, Jr. about to deplane his Nieuport.*

'official' kill, the actual confirmation would not be received from 1st Army headquarters until 26 September. It seems Luke had strayed a bit into Colonel Davenport Johnson's 2nd Pursuit Group sector, "poaching," as Hartney would later term it on Johnson's personal "preserves."[20]

There is little doubt Rickenbacker heard of Luke's success that 12 September. If not, the Columbus, Ohio native's attention was more than focused when the rogue cowboy from Arizona stole his Ace of Aces honors within the remarkably brief span of the next four days!

Chapter Six
Insert No. 1

THE GREAT GERMAN-AMERICAN WITCH HUNT

Preparing to deliver his request for a declaration of war to Congress, President Wilson foretold: "Once lead this people into war, and they'll forget there was ever such a thing as tolerance...the spirit of ruthless brutality will enter into the very fever of our national life, infecting Congress...(even) the man in the street."[21]

By mid-1917 the American public had moved an epoch away from the debates of isolationism and pacifism of but months earlier. The popular 1915 song, I Didn't Raise My Boy to be a Soldier, was but a distant memory.

"To question the nobility of the war effort," wrote one historian, "was tantamount to treason."[22]

And the ongoing public revelations of the U.S. Secret Service only added fuel to the once innocent, internationally naive, now growing American belief, indeed the realization, that German agents had long and covertly been at work in a one-sided war with the American people and their industry. The outrage only grew from July of 1915 as the contents of the captured papers of Germany's top spy, Dr. Heinrich Albert, were revealed. Tales of widespread spying and sabotage, bombings of U.S. munitions plants and England-bound U.S. freighters. Revelations of a German-inspired strike at Bethlehem Steel, and imported German and Central Powers propaganda funneled through a German-owned New York daily newspaper, The Main, helped seal the fate of the German cause in U.S. minds. It all served to fuel the growing distrust of Germans generally and German-Americans specifically.

The spy scare had soon cast doubt on anyone with foreign ties, especially those of German ancestry. German-Americans, once regarded as ideal, even superior citizens before the war, were now seen as treasonous by nature. U.S. psychologist G. Stanley Hall, once an outspoken admirer of the positive influence of the "Teutons" in American society, now declared "there was something fundamentally wrong with the Teutonic soul."[23]

Washington further fueled the hatemongers by ordering employers to investigate their workers nationalities and assure their loyalties to the United States.

The subsequent and unregulated prejudicial abuses at the hands of the populace at large often ranged from overt public humiliation to homicide. A number of German-Americans, on the thinnest of pretexts, were publicly flogged and tarred and feathered, and at least one was lynched in Illinois. Many were fired outright from their jobs. Some, who kept their jobs, but had distinctive accents were forced to their hands and knees and made to crawl across the workshop floor before their fellow employees to kiss the American flag. At some bond rallies Americans of German ancestry were compelled to march as public objects of scorn.

Amidst the anti-German frenzy of the era Americans began calling hamburger "liberty steak," sauerkraut "liberty cabbage," and German measles "liberty measles." In Cincinnati pretzels were outlawed!

The popular arts were no less infected. The works of Beethoven and Mozart disappeared from symphony selections across the country. And Hollywood contributed mightily with a long series of less than subtle hatemongering propaganda films. Among them: *To Hell with the Kaiser*, *The Kaiser*, *The Beast of Berlin*, and the *Wolves of Kultur*. Erich von Stroheim, the famed German-American actor/director and co-star of the 1950 classic American film *Sunset Boulevard*, made a comfortable living during the First World War playing one bestial German soldier after another on the silent screen. Perhaps his most memorable screen moment is that as a lusting German officer, wanting to get at a cornered American nurse, tears a baby out of her arms and throws it out a second story window - all to the outraged screams of American audiences.

Conformity was the order of the day. Congress enacted stiff

laws and penalties for criticizing the government. Historians were even prohibited from disagreeing with official rationale for the start of World War One, which squarely placed Germany at the center of the issue. Further, the Post Office was forbidden to mail any periodicals which "did not completely echo the governments' policies."[24]

Clearly, the years 1917-1918 were not happy times for either advocates of the U.S. First Amendment or German-Americans!

Chapter Seven

THE ENEMY

The Allies' St. Mihiel Offensive began on 12 September 1918. By the 20th, fliers of Hartney's First Pursuit Group were facing deadly red-nosed Fokker D.VIIs flown by the "sharp tools" of Jagdgeschwader (JG) II, and JG I - Richthofen's justly famed and lethal "Flying Circus." They were gifted opponents of the first order. By war's end the eight undersized squadrons of these two elite German "Circuses" numbered among their members, past and present, 147 aces - and nearly 1,400 aerial victories! The Americans had been thrust against arguably the best dogfighters the world had yet seen. Without their knowing it, these freshly enthusiastic, though thoroughly green fliers had been hurled into the "Big Leagues" of classic aerial combat. And so it would remain till the Armistice two months hence.

ORIGINS OF THE GERMAN FIGHTER COMMAND

As was the common military thinking of the day, at the time of opening hostilities on 4 August 1914, the principal and universally-perceived role for military aviation was observation - being the long and short-range "eyes" for their respective land armies and naval arms. Within the German Imperial Army this took the form of 33 Feldflieger Abteilung (FA) - one assigned to each of the eight

Army Headquarters and 25 Army Corps then operational.

Two months into the war these initial preconceptions began to be altered with the downing on 5 October of a German Aviatik from FA 48 by French airmen of an Escadrille V24 Voisin. Their improvised weapon: an infantry rifle. With this unanticipated, first fatal aerial engagement, aviation's role was soon expanded to include the "prevention" of the enemy's aerial mission in order to help assure the success of your own country's airmen. Soon two-seater reconnaissance aircraft of both sides were going aloft with machine guns mounted to the rear cockpit. These early aerial engagements continued to go the Allies' way until 28 April 1915 and the German's first successful aerial victory over a Voisin at the hands of an FA 48 Aviatik.

Ten days earlier the French aviator Roland Garros of Escadrille MS 23 was captured along with his Morane-Saulnier. Examining his monoplane, the Germans discovered Garros had added metal propeller cuffs designed to deflect the occasional bullet from his single, forward firing machine gun. The simplistic 'fix' did, however, endanger both pilot and aircraft, Garros finally bringing himself down behind enemy lines when impacting bullets damaged his prop and consequently his frail engine mount. Though the method proved crude, the ability of the pilot to align his entire aircraft with that of his target assured a truer aim. Garros' own three quickly acquired aerial victories were proof enough of that.

Responding to and making practicable the Frenchman's "through-the-propeller" concept, Dutch designer, Anthony Fokker, had devised within five weeks his revolutionary interrupter gear and mounted it on one of his Eindekker monoplanes. The Fokker synchronization gear permitted the mounting of a forward firing machine gun whose bullets would let fly only when the blades of the plane's propeller were safely out of the line of fire.

The first interrupter-gear equipped Eindekker had reached the front by 23 May 1915. That June, Fokker was demonstrating his revolutionary machine at Douai, home field to FA 62. There, Max Immelmann and Oswald Boelcke, two of the unit's young L.V.G. fliers, were immediately captivated with the new single-seater and

Anthony Fokker at the controls of one of his 1915 monoplanes. Fokker's Eindekker single-seat monoplanes with their synchronized forward-firing machine guns were history's first dedicated fighter aircraft.

its lethal potential. On 1 August, Immelmann received official confirmation for the first Fokker victory, though this may have actually occurred a month earlier at the hands of FA- 6's Kurt Wintgens.

Fokker's single-seat Eindekker, with its light construction and synchronous forward-firing machine gun, had given history its first dedicated fighter aircraft. By the end of 1915 as many as four of the fighters were assigned to the more active front line abteilungen. Already at this early juncture Eindekker fighter pilots were specially picked from their FAs on the basis of their technical competence and "aggressive" inclinations.

So began what the Royal Flying Corps was to call the "Fokker Scourge" of December 1915 to March 1916 - though the Germans never had more than 20 to 30 available Eindekkers. Such was the impact of history's first dedicated fighter aircraft.

The tide turned back again in the spring of 1916 with the arrival of new Allied types such as the Nieuports, DH.2s and FE.2bs in ever-increasing numbers. Should dates be sought for the end of the "Fokker Menace," the 18 June death of Max Immelmann might be one, though the massive 1 July British offensive of the Somme pressured the outnumbered German Air Service as it had not before.

The Fighter Jasta

It was during the summer of 1916 that Immelmann's former FA 62 flying mate, Oswald Boelcke - already with 19 victories to his credit by the end of June, first recommended to the German High Command separate, dedicated fighter units. The first eight were formed that August; these new squadrons, completely separate from the traditional abteilungen, were called "jagdstaffel" or hunting squadron, but were soon referred to by the short-hand term "jasta."

The legendary Boelcke, known today as "The Father of Air Fighting Tactics," first put together the doctrinaire rules of fighter pilot engagement, which remained as valid in jet filled skies over Korea as when they were originally penned in 1916:

The Boelcke Doctrine
  1. Always try to secure an advantageous position before attacking. Climb before and during the approach in order to surprise the enemy from above, and dive on him swiftly from the rear when the moment to attack is at hand.
  2. Try to place yourself between the sun and the enemy.
  3. Do not fire until the enemy is within range and you have him squarely within your sights.
  4. Attack when the enemy least expects it.
  5. Never turn your back and try to run away from an enemy fighter. If you are surprised by an attack on your tail, turn and face the enemy with your guns.
  6. Keep your eye on your enemy and do not let him deceive you with tricks. If your opponent appears damaged, follow him down until he crashes.
  7. Foolish acts of bravery only bring death. The Jasta must fight as a unit with close teamwork between all pilots. The signal of its leader must be obeyed.[1]

Boelcke himself took command of the soon-to-be-famous

The Fokker D.VII was arguably the finest fighter of WWI. Though some 10 MPH slower than Allied contemporaries, such as the Spad XIII, the D.VII was strong, easy to fly and extremely maneuverable at great altitudes. Entering service in May 1918, by that autumn the type equipped the majority of the front line jastas. Especially prized by German fliers was the BMW-powered D.VIIs. So respected was the Fokker D.VII by the Allies that the surrender of the type was made a condition of the Armistice terms!

Jasta 2. The brilliant 25-year-old tactician will be killed in a mid-air collision on 28 October - two days after his 40th and last aerial victory. Now equipped with the new Albatros D.Is and IIs, the Jastas, notably 4 and 6, began to make their presence felt over the Somme. With the arrival of the improved Albatros D.IIIs during the spring of 1917 the Jastas were truly coming into their own - leading to a period the RFC was to call "Bloody April."

The British offensive at Arras had begun on 9 April - Easter Sunday. Though again outnumbered, the German Jastas began downing British machines at a remarkable rate. "On April 6 alone," writes WWI air historian William Barrett, "the day that the United States declared war on Germany, 44 British ships were destroyed. The British lost five planes to every one they brought down during 'Bloody April,' but for all the emphasis upon that month, April was little worse than March or January or February."[2]

Though Boelcke had been killed, his lessons were taken to heart by a gifted cadre of up and coming pupils. Among this rapidly rising roster of stars were Erwin Bohme, Dieter Collin, Max

Muller - the most successful NCO pilot of the period, Hans von Keudell, Wilhelm Frankl, Werner Voss - and Manfred von Richthofen. While von Richthofen is most remembered for his personal skills as a combat flier, his gifts as a combat leader were ultimately to best serve his nation's cause.

Noted for his ability to spot talent, Oswald Boelcke had originally recruited von Richthofen in September 1916 to fly with Jasta 2. By 14 January 1917, von Richthofen had 16 victories to his credit and had been awarded the Pour le Merite - the famed Blue Max. On that day, von Richthofen, the rising star, was given command of Jasta 11, a unit, though its ranks boasted experienced pilots, that had yet to score its first kill since its operational debut the previous October. From 22 January through the end of March under von Richthofen's command, Jasta 11 scored 36 kills - and another 89 in April. These 125 victories, representing about a third of all RFC losses for the period, had been "achieved by a unit averaging," writes WWI air historians Franks, Bailey and Guest, "less than 10 aeroplanes. This feat... made von Richthofen not only the most successful German fighter pilot with 52 victories, surpassing Boelcke's 40, but also confirmed him as Boelcke's successor as best leader and developer of talent."[3]

Though Jasta 11's meteoric ride to fame was exceptional if not typical, the validity of Boelcke's original organizational concepts, combined with the timely arrival of the Albatros series, nonetheless, had returned the German Air Service to an unquestioned position of aerial dominance that fall. Capitalizing on their newfound success, 33 Jastas were in place by the spring of 1917.

So many of the seasoned German veterans the Americans would meet a year and a half later over St. Mihiel, Bayonville and Stenay had cut their combat teeth in the skies over the Arras front.

Despite their aerial successes of March and April 1917, it was becoming increasingly obvious to the German Air Service that their undersized Jastas would remain outnumbered by their Allied counterparts. Their continued control of the air over the front would remain a close thing if something were not done. The concentration and projection of a superior sized force has long been an essen-

The Pfalz D.III appeared in the summer of 1917. Unfortunately, its performance did not coincide with the sleek appearance of its monocoque fuselage. It was not uncommon for jastas of the period to be operating several types; because of the Pfalz's poor rate of climb and maneuverability, the type was often relegated to a unit's beginners or poorer pilots.

tial military principal. In an effort to retain a more commanding authority on the aerial battlefront, jasta commanders such as Jasta 11's von Richthofen and Jasta 4's Kurt von Doring began flying joint patrols in April. By the end of the month, as many as four jastas were massing to fly on joint patrols. That June the first official grouping of four jastas into a jagdgeschwader (JG) occurred when Jastas 4, 6, 10 and 11 were brought together to form JG I. Not surprisingly, the command of this first jagdgeschwader was given to the gifted Manfred von Richthofen. The enlarged unit was to be an elite, highly mobile force able to move, much as a circus, on short notice to a critical region of the front to quickly establish air superiority.

The first test of Jagdgeschwader I came within days of its inception with the British offensive at Flanders. Victories continued to mount, though against growing odds, as JG I was again thrown into the breach at Cambrai that November. It was not long before both sides were referring to JG I as "Richthofen's Flying Circus."

Moving into the fall of 1917, however, German fliers were once again on the defensive as the Allies invested their growing number of squadrons with much improved designs, including the SE.5, Bristol fighters and Sopwith Camel. New German models such as the Albatros D.V, Pfalz D.III and the nimble though frail Fokker Dr.I triplane proved only marginal improvements over earlier equipment. Nonetheless, the skilled and hard-pressed German fliers continued to bring down large Allied numbers. Their score on 17 September alone far exceeded that of "Bloody April."

"THE AMERIKA PROGRAM"

During the winter of 1917-1918, in an effort to counter the anticipated influx of American units into the line, the German Air Service was greatly expanded. The effort was part of what the Imperial High Command officially called "The Amerika Program." While the desperate effort looked good on paper, the doubling of the Jasta strength from 40 to 80 organizations was considerably less than it appeared at first blush. Each of the new jastas were equipped with only eight to nine aircraft, generally obsolescent types such as the Albatros D.V and Pfalz D.III variety. More promising, was the February 1918 organization of two additional jagdgeschwadern. Both 23-plane ace Adolf von Tutschek's JG II and 22-plane ace Bruno Loerzer's JG III enjoyed the arrival of fresh talent culled from the two-seater organizations, as well as those units earlier withdrawn from the Russian front.

It was also during the winter of 1917-1918 that the German High Command began planning a "final" offensive in an "all or nothing" effort to gain a favorable decision on the battlefield before the full weight of the Americans could be brought to bear at the front. The first of what ultimately proved to be a series of "final" German offensives began against British lines on 21 March 1918. And though the three 'Circuses' were in the thick of the intense, often bitter fighting, aerial dominance was never achieved. Further, JG I's esteemed commander, 80-plane ace Manfred von Richthofen was shot down and killed on 21 April on the Somme

Front.

Befitting the respect von Richthofen commanded on both sides of the lines, the Allies buried him with full military honors.

April also saw the arrival of the first of the superlative Fokker D.VII fighters - arguably the finest German fighters to see combat during the war. This was especially true of the highly-prized BMW-powered version of the type. By June their numbers would begin to be reflected in Allied squadrons' growing roster of losses.

Though the elite and consistently productive circuses continued to be supplied with first-line equipment, by July the lesser jastas began to feel the pinch of fuel and production shortages, as well as the decline in pilot training standards.

And though the near-exhausted German army had advanced to within 56 miles of Paris by early June, there they were held. The 15 July German offensive against French and American lines soon failed as well, its lines in turn counterattacked by the French on the 25th. Above the fray, the months of June and July witnessed some of the most intense dogfighting of the war. The growing list of German aces voraciously fed off their French victims.

Thrown into the maw for the first time that June were the inexperienced, French-trained airmen of the American First Pursuit Group. Their introduction into combat in the Soissons sector at Chateau Thierry would soon become the stuff of legends.

DRACHEN

The fighter's reason for being was and is, contrary to its traditional and disproportionate public notoriety, essentially an ancillary one; that is, to secure air superiority. Its mission is to insure the safe operation of its army cooperation, bombing and reconnaissance units - and, conversely, prevent the safe operation of its enemy's respective units. And while bombing - particularly strategic bombing - took on growing importance, especially for the Allies during the latter months of the war, the safe execution of aerial surveillance operations would remain the highest calling for the era's military aviation organizations.

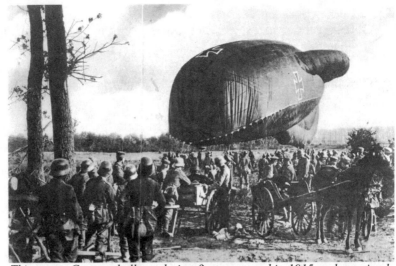

This newer German balloon design first appeared in 1915 and remained in service throughout the remainder of World War One.

Initially, the German High Command had intended long-range reconnaissance to be carried out by their unequalled fleet of airships, while the abteilung aircraft assigned to their respective army corps would perform short-range surveillance duties. But the static nature of the conflict's trench warfare soon changed the nature of air operations. Airships were no longer practicable over the Western Front. Aircraft were given additional ground-support duties, including infantry cooperation and artillery observation.

This latter role had its limitations. The aircraft's airtime over the front was strictly limited, so too was the quality and clarity of the era's wireless radios used to transmit an aerial observer's findings.

Far more practical for long-term surveillance of a given sector of the trench line was the observation balloon, which had first seen combat during the American Civil War in the early 1860s. Major von Parseval of the German Army first conceived the kite balloon in 1885, and it was the Germans who first began to employ the drachen, as they called them, during the Great War.

The drachen were fixed observation posts serving as the eyes of the artillery. Observers also monitored enemy troop and transport movements as far as 20 kilometers away - on a clear day. The drachen represented a serious threat to the Allies and particularly to those Allied aviators whose job it was to bring them down.

The balloon itself was an inflated sausage-shaped container with a rudder to the rear which served to help keep the nose stabilized and pointed into the wind. Incredibly, both sides used explosive hydrogen to float their balloons - even though the United States possessed untold reserves of the thoroughly stable and benign helium gas. Unlike the English and French balloons which were made out of silk, the German drachens were fabricated from more accessible, though doubly heavy rubber-impregnated cotton.

"We tried to get the balloon up to a 1000 meters," recalled Imperial German Balloon Corps observer Karl Kuster, "and on a wind-still day we could make it, but we could always tell that the French and English (balloons) were above us."[4]

The captive kite balloon was attached by a series of 3/8" steel cables to a main cable and phone line that was attached to a winch truck. Suspended below the balloon was a small wicker basket carrying five ballast bags and a parachute canister. The cramped basket itself was equipped with a direct-line phone, a phone battery,

Gunner stands by "Flaming Onion" antiaircraft artillery piece commonly enployed in defense of German balloon positions. Its visual and psychological impact far outweighed its practical lethality.

large map board, altimeter, binoculars - and an artillery lieutenant-
observer.

Though such men were artillery officers, as observers they
were also considered "Air Service" and consequently as the
German Air Service before them, received extra pay. The unique
posting was denoted by a blue pip added to the collars of their
artillery uniforms.

The German observation balloons came into their own in 1915
during the battle for Verdun. It was also in 1915 that a drachen was
first downed from the air. This occurred on 20 January when the
crew of a French Voisin happened to connect with a well-placed 20
pound bomb. But this was the exception rather than the rule.
During the first year of operations airsickness was the observer's
greatest enemy. On calm days their tours aloft lasted four hours.
On windy days two hours was more than enough time! Generally,
dusk and dawn presented the most fruitful and haze-free periods for
observation.

Artillery rarely attacked the balloons which generally sat back
some six to eight kilometers behind the front lines. And "No one
dreamed in those days (1915-16)," adds Kuster, "that planes would
bother with balloons and not one of the observers had his parachute
with him."[5]

For Kuster and his fellow observers that was to change after
the May 1916 rocket attack by a French Nieuport - possibly a
Nieuport 11 of Lafayette Escadrille (N.124) - which cost a kite balloon and the life of its observer. From then on Kuster's balloon
acquired a ring of six nest-based machine guns ready aimed above
the balloon, and what the Allies soon came to call a "flaming
onion" cannon. Once at altitude, the projectile burst with much the
same acoustics as any other antiaircraft shell. But rather than letting loose with a black cloud of shrapnel, the "onion" let fly a ball
of fire which then proceeded to corkscrew erratically about the sky,
taking out anything or anyone in its path. Its effect on most Allied
fliers was quite unnerving.

German balloon companies also had the support of several
local antiaircraft batteries - though they were not under the com-

mand of the balloon captain. Additionally, a lone German plane began to be assigned to watch over Kuster's line of six balloons, each set about a kilometer from its neighbor. As such, Kuster's initial aerial umbrella was decidedly thin. As the war progressed Allied aerial attackers also adjusted their tactics, bringing along a second plane to handle the top cover. Eventually, attackers met with German jasta patrols of increasing numbers. By 1918 the stakes and level of drachen protection had grown markedly. On hazy days the German balloons were often given a pass by Allied commanders. But on clear days "we would be attacked…a balloon was lucky to last through the day."[6]

Under aerial attack the drachen commander would make every effort to reel in the balloon into its grounded "nest" as quickly as possible. In 1914 the chore required an hour. By 1918 the time of the newer three-speed winches was down to four minutes. It was still an eternity for its hard-pressed ground crew and an oft-times lethal lure for the unwary Allied pilot who was brought down into the nest's chattering ring of machine guns and heavier artillery.

The Americans' own AEF balloon company records offer every measure of the hazards involved. Thirty-five balloons were flamed by enemy aircraft while another 39 were so badly holed

Far more lethal for airborne "balloon busters" than the "Flaming Onion" was a concentration of dedicated machine gunners.

they were downed - even though they failed to burn. Another 12 balloons were destroyed by enemy artillery. Keep in mind these numbers are limited to the last five months of the war!

A flaming kite balloon near its nest was a lethal hazard of the first order for its necessarily quick-footed ground crew. It was a scene much as the one pictured here that greeted the German balloon crew of Frank Luke's first official kill on 12 September 1918.

Chapter Eight

THE CONTEST

- 13 September through 29 September, 1918 -

Major Hartney had prided himself in understanding the nature of that new military anomaly - the World War One pursuit pilot. It was an honest, singular liberality of view, he was convinced, not narrowly colored by that of a career officer's self-defeating, traditionalist paradigm. For, while a team player was vital to a combat command, once a dogfight had been entered "individual initiative is at least ninety per cent (of the mix required for a successful engagement)."[1] Hartney understood, as no ground officer of his time could, that once aloft in their cruel realm his pursuit fliers had themselves become their own masters, truly the captains of their own ships and their destinies. It was, and remains, a daunting challenge few are equal to.

Hartney also knew - all too well - that personal war most of his fliers waged within themselves between their natural instincts for survival and their desire to conquer their own fears as well as the enemy. To lose either contest was unthinkable; death was perhaps the easier consequence to bear than a postwar lifetime of acknowledged personal defeat. Fears had to be overcome, shut out, denied their place. There alone, amidst the elements, often beyond the view of either superiors or companions there, Hartney knew, was found the true measure of such men.

The demands of new, imperfect technologies aside, the job was

really a throwback to that old-fashioned, pragmatic brand of pioneering courage and self-reliance found in great abundance within
many of the often misunderstood sons of the recently arrived immigrants. They generally were of superior intellect and certainly stout
heart, daring to leave their Old World, generally middle class lives
behind. Here they braved a foreign shore with nothing save a
dream, and with no one to rely upon but themselves and their own
resources. Such times are a breeding ground for the kind of
dependence-free mental toughness, innovative resourcefulness and
a wiliness which had served our forefathers so well - and which
remained strong within these new ones, these sons of the newly
arrived.

They had arrived with nothing but the freedom of their new
homeland and the challenge, that burning native ambition for the
kind of betterment and recognition de Tocqueville had so often spoken of, and for which they had left their homelands. They had very
little to lose, save themselves. Their potential: unlimited.

One hundred and thirty fliers would pass through and collectively serve with the 94th and 27th Pursuit Squadrons during the
First World War. Combined, these top two American pursuit organizations amassed an unequalled 123 confirmed aerial victories by
war's end. How is it, one may ask, that three under-educated sons
of working class immigrant families, three of 130 such airmen,
were responsible for over forty per cent of their two squadrons' aerial kills?

Clearly, a remarkable confluence of native gifts and technical
acumen had been grafted to uncommon, and perhaps uncommonly
passionate, motivations to fuel a record of achievement extraordinary by any measure. And while the methods and approaches to
these historic benchmarks were as varied as the unique personali-
ties involved, there is no denying their uniformly extraordinary
resourcefulness and desire to succeed.

The events that transpired within Hartney's group over the next
two and a half weeks, from the 13th of September through Sunday,
the 29th, comprise a tale, and a contest, of epic proportions. Its
moralistic underpinnings remain as true today as when the ancient

Greek writer Aesop first penned his classic fable of the steady tortoise and flashy hare.

On Friday the 13th, the day after Luke's first confirmed balloon kill, the weather had improved slightly. Visibility was up to 1200 feet. Hartney had sent up nearly two dozen patrols to pursue the enemy withdrawal. The salient would be gone within three days. Few German planes were spotted, though Rickenbacker, anxious to improve his score, flew three two-hour sorties, two of these lone wolf affairs, on the 13th. All, however, he had to show for his efforts was a single, ominous bullet hole through his fuselage turtle-deck headrest, inches from his head. The famed "Rickenbacker Luck" would hold steadfast that jinxed day.

Over at the 94th early the next morning, Saturday, the 14th, Rick was off early on another lone sortie. Quickly gaining altitude, as was his practice, he finally spotted a flight of four nondescript Fokker D.VIIs that were trailing a returning formation of American DH-4s. Rick dropped out of his favored sun position and pulled - still undetected - to within 50 yards of the last Fokker. Rickenbacker, the city kid who had not fired his first gun before his adult years, made a practice of pulling close enough, if the opportunity presented itself, "to throw a bat" at his opponent. The practice paid off handsomely before and would again. A twin stream of rounds exploded through the aft fuselage and cockpit seat of the rearmost, unsuspecting Fokker. The time was 0815.

The remaining three, previously unidentified D.VIIs erupted into action. In unison, they whipped around on their assailant. These were real pros, Rickenbacker recognized, as he came, almost before he realized it, face to face with the blinking front end radiators of three very angry and skillfully flown Fokkers. Their red cowls announced the arrival over the lines of Germany's finest, the Richthofen Circus. Whatever experience or shortcomings Rick may have lacked as a marksman, he more than made up for in natural agility and reflexes, and he needed all of it this morning. The

Fokkers seemed to anticipate his every turn. Minutes became an eternity until he finally found an opening and dove for home. His successful survival was as close a thing as he'd yet experienced.

Rick's news of the Circus' arrival spread among field personnel like wildfire, but Hartney had other more immediate concerns on his plate that morning. Word had come down from headquarters that two German observation balloons had to be brought down that morning. He'd quickly called his squadron commanders to his office. Flights from their squadrons would fly diversionary patrols while the 27th was given the job of actually taking out the balloons at Buzy and Boinville.

Why had Hartney assigned his old outfit the balloon job? There can be little doubt Luke's wily old mentor had him in mind. He knew pursuit pilots, as a breed, found balloon attacks as distasteful as they were dangerous. He also knew it was now Grant's job to ask his men for volunteers. Hartney could have little doubt as to the outcome. He nonetheless more than likely forced down a smile when minutes later a committee of 27th fliers, headed by Grant, returned to his doorstep with a proposition. The group was rounded out by Lieutenants Leo Dawson, Tommy Lennon and Luke's flight commander, Ken "Gonny" Clapp. Clapp laid out the terms. Grant would put Luke, "your boy friend," they called him, on the job; but if he faltered they wanted his obnoxious loud mouth out of the squadron. They had labeled the Arizonan "a menace to morale."[2]

Hartney quickly agreed, but warned the group that if the 27th didn't get the balloon at Boinville down that morning, he'd give the job to the Kicking Mules of the 95th.

The 27th flight, with Luke in tow, took off at 0930, within an hour of Rickenbacker's return with his sixth official victory. Luke made a mind-numbing six passes at the Boinville balloon and a defending antiaircraft battery. And though it didn't explode, it was so thoroughly holed that it limped to the ground in "a very flabby condition."[3] The time was approximately 1000 hours. Interestingly, credit for this stubborn balloon would also be shared with his former nemeses, Dawson and Lennon, both of whom braved the concentrated fire to dive on the balloon, assuring its descent - as well as Luke's retention in the squadron.

Equally telling, there is no record of Grant himself taking on the balloon.

Hartney and Wehner joined Luke and the rest of the 27th formation for the afternoon sortie against the Buzy balloon. The group left Rembercourt about 1430. This time, the balloon exploded early on; nonetheless, Luke made a final pass, spraying the already flaming target on its earth-bound descent.

For the first time this day much of the squadron fliers had front-row seats to witness Luke's stunning and repeated acts of courage in the face of overwhelming enemy fire. So, too, this day did Joe Wehner's stock rise as he dove headlong into a formation of eight Fokkers headed for Luke. He was joined, in short order, by Clapp and the rest of the flight. Luke, for his part - his guns jammed after the second balloon run - dove for the lines. His Spad was taking hits as Joe closed on and attacked two of the Fokkers. And though Clapp was seen by a number of the airborne fliers to actually down one of the Germans, he would never receive ground-based confirmation.

All the group returned to the field - except Luke. For most, their opinion of the daring Arizonan had made a sea change over the last few hours. Luke's earlier, loudly stated claims were now supported by widely and enthusiastically retold accounts of his bold actions. For some, however, the intemperate aviator would always remain a "four-flusher."

Hartney, in his 1940 autobiography, reconstructed the post-mission events of that late afternoon. Shortly after landing and settling himself into his group headquarters office, he was joined by the "highly excited" trio of Grant, Clapp and Dawson. Hartney recalled Dawson opening the passionate conversation.

"Listen, Major, we want to take that all back. Boy, if anyone thinks that bird is yellow he's crazy. I'll take back every doubt I ever had. The man's not yellow, he's crazy, stark mad. He went by me on that attack like a wild man. I thought he was diving right into the fabric."

Clapp, who hours earlier wanted Luke out of his flight and the squadron, now, according to Hartney, had tears in his eyes for the missing flier. "Gosh Maj,... who spread that dribble around that Luke is a fourflusher? I'd like to kill the man that did... He had to go right down on the ground to get that second balloon and they've got the hottest machine gun nest in the world around it. They couldn't miss him."[4]

At this moment Hartney received a call from 27th maintenance that Luke had finally returned. It appears he once again stopped by a local American balloon outpost to have signed another of his handcrafted confirmation forms. Luke, his fighting blood up, now wanted the mechanics to refuel and rearm his shattered Spad as quickly as they could so he and Joe could down another German balloon at Waroq. The operations officer had told Hartney Luke's Spad was in no shape to fly again.

The headquarters group sprinted the quarter mile to the 27th hangar where they found the mechanics had already foiled Luke's attempts to get back in the air. A good two square yards of linen had been torn off the fuselage aft of the cockpit and a similar amount off a wing surface. The exposed innards revealed shattered wood spars, metal fittings and wire.

Luke innocently didn't give a second thought going over Grant's head appealing directly to his mentor, Hartney, for another Spad and his approval. Grant jumped into the conversation staking out his authority in the matter. Grant felt Luke was turning his military organization into a circus sideshow. Hartney withdrew as Grant heatedly shouted his rash subordinate into submission.

Defeated, Luke slunk away. Hartney caught up with the Arizonan to praise his success and advise patience if he wanted to become an old man. Hartney recalls his comment elicited a strange expression from the Westerner, an expression which suggested he'd never thought about a life beyond the here and now.

Upon return from his initial 12 September balloon victory, Luke had already begun speculating about the advantages of a dusk method of attack on enemy balloons. Hartney, as a wise basketball coach dealing with one of his high-priced and high-strung players,

The 27th Squadron and 1st Pursuit Group's leading ace, Frank Luke, Jr. (third from left) poses with his ground crew at Rembercourt around the middle of September 1918. Of Luke's personal three-man ground crew, only Lou Flanner (extreme left) has been positively identified.

refocused Luke's passions into working out the details of such a revolutionary technique. The approach worked. Luke retired to his quarters.

Hartney returned to the 27th ramp where Joe Wehner was studying a handcrafted three-inch square map routing him to the Waroq balloon. The Bostonian told him of his planned attack. In the end, Wehner arrived in time to witness a French Stork Spad flame the balloon. He, however, downed two Fokkers attempting to stop the Frenchman. He would never receive credit for either kill.

Though Luke's twin victories had culminated that afternoon with a dressing down from Grant, his day was not yet over. Hartney had taken a call from Colonel Billy Mitchell who was overjoyed with word of the downed balloons. The colonel arrived at the field on toward evening to personally congratulate Hartney and the 27th on their success. He also wanted to learn more about the plan to strafe balloons at dusk. Hartney invited the shy, ill-at-ease Arizonan into the colonel's presence to lay out his plan.

Hartney recalled, "Poor Frank was quite flabbergasted as he came before the (colonel) in his untidy uniform and cloth puttees. He was bashful and silent."[5]

Colonel Thomas Milling, Mitchell's deputy, put Luke at ease and soon his plan began to flow forth in his quick-paced, Arizona drawl. He set the trial show for the following day. Gathering steam and bravado as he went, Luke brazenly invited Mitchell back the following day to witness the event.

The impetuous Luke, however, would soon upset his own schedule.

Sunday, 15 September, dawned crisp and clear - perfect flying weather. Rickenbacker was not slow in taking advantage of the early hour. Once again he left the field shortly after sunup on a lone patrol. As fortune would have it, he spotted a formation of six Fokkers as he reached the lines near Bois De Warville. And, as was his practice, he immediately began a climb into the sun. He had not yet been spotted when finally he dove on the enemy, themselves about to pounce on a flight of American Second Pursuit Group Spads. And again Rick climbed up the tail of the last Fokker and let fly a 150-round burst into the unsuspecting enemy pursuit's cockpit. The engagement was over within seconds as the Fokker burst into flames, impacting a mile east of No Man's Land. The balance of the German group scattered east, having little desire to take on either Rickenbacker, outnumbered as he remained, five to one, or the Second Group Spads still strafing enemy ground locations below.

Back at the field, Rick commandeered a car and headed for the front to get ground confirmation for both that day's, as well as the previous day's victory. He acquired both signed affirmations by nightfall. The confirmations would earn him his sixth and seventh official victories and the much sought after newspaper title of American "Ace of Aces."

That same morning, Luke ignored Grant's orders again and joined on his own initiative two 27th patrols. He then dove away to flame both the new Boinville balloons earlier slated by him for destruction at dusk that evening. He'd used the accompanying Spads as his unbriefed top-cover to fend off the defending Fokkers. Two of the Fokkers were downed by Wehner, who also downed another two balloons on his own for an unconfirmed day's score of four. He would only receive one confirmation, a Fokker D.VII, for his day's remarkable pre-dusk efforts.

What celebratory events awaited the new Ace of Aces at day's end were overshadowed by the arrival of colonels Mitchell, Milling, Sherman and Inspector General T.I. Donaldson that evening to watch the show planned by Frank and Joe. Though the Boinville balloons had been downed by Luke earlier in the day, another two remained in the Verdun area near Spincourt and Chaumont respectively. Mitchell doubted a balloon, let alone two, could be planned for destruction five hours in advance and their demise predicted to the minute, let alone in the pre-night gloom then about him. Nonetheless, Mitchell's party with hundreds of other field personnel mounted the crest of a nearby hill. An American artillery barrage had begun to entice the German sausages to remain aloft. Luke's plan was working perfectly.

Though Mitchell had his misgivings, he continued to glance at his wristwatch every few seconds. As the second hand neared the announced time of destruction, 6:58 PM, all eyes began to stare into the gathering blackness toward Spincourt. Within seconds of the designated minute a dazzling light erupted on the horizon.

Seconds passed and a second finger of flame roared into glaring fullness, then sank sickly earthward toward unseen German crews scrambling for their lives.

"By God, there she goes!" Mitchell shouted.[6] The normally composed senior officers reportedly began to dance and shout for joy as the night reclaimed the darkness.

Luke and the 27th fliers had also come up with a technique for recovering their aircraft in the darkness. Over the last few days a control tower, perhaps the world's first, had been erected over the group headquarters building. Upon the sound of approaching aircraft engines, a colored Very pistol flare was fired from the tower. Moments later, an answering alternate colored flare blossomed in the distant sky. As Mitchell looked on in amazement, a kerosene-fueled runway flare path was lit by runners. Moments later, Luke and Wehner's Spads appeared out of the darkness, rumbling to a halt amid the shouts and well wishes of the entire field and

Mitchell's dumb-founded staff. Rickenbacker too, always the gracious gentleman, offered Frank and Joe his hearty and genuine congratulations. Luke had officially scored three balloons for the day, Wehner, a plane and a balloon. Mitchell was amazed by the damage absorbed over such a brief period by both Spads. The two pursuits were total write-offs. He could only shake his head in amazement.

Luke's dusk technique would soon be adopted by the whole of the American pursuit branch as a standard method of balloon attack.

The 1st Group's total score for the day was nine aerial victories. Between them, Rickenbacker, Luke and Wehner had accounted for six of these, two-thirds of the total group score. Hartney, as Grant before him, was beginning to feel Luke and Wehner were starting to run away with the group, their high level attention overshadowing the other 124 flying officers then at Rembercourt. Something would have to be done, reins pulled in. Either way, events were beginning to spiral out of control. A crisis, he was sure, was in the offing, only its nature remained ill defined.

On Monday, the 16th, the newly arrived German jastas began to appear in large numbers. And though the number of engagements increased significantly over the following days, Rickenbacker would come up empty handed after his two voluntary patrols of the day.

Around 1830 that evening Hartney arrived with several other 1st Group fliers at a French balloon site some eight miles to the east of St. Mihiel. In his best French he suggested the crew watch those two German balloons to their east at Reville and Romagne. He informed them that at precisely 1900 hours (7:00 PM) both bags would be exploded by two of his fliers. Shaking their heads, the smiling Frenchmen looked at each other, then back at the crazy little American major. He clearly was out of his mind. Nonetheless, as the time neared they began checking their watches more often and staring into the growing darkness. The time came and passed. The Frenchmen again turned a knowing eye to the anxious American. Suddenly, a glaring flame screamed out of the gloom.

It was 1903. Within moments a second explosion joined the first. Luke would share credit for the second balloon with Joe Wehner. And Joe would further add to his own growing score of confirmed victories by taking out a third balloon five minutes later over Mangiennes. It would be the Bostonian's fourth confirmed victory, though his actual score may have been twice as many.

For Arizonan Frank Luke Jr., his credited score that evening rose to eight kills. No other 27th pilot would equal that score during the entire course of the war, Hartney himself would come closest with seven kills by war's end, and one of these remained unconfirmed. What was even more amazing, in those brief three days of successful engagements, was that Luke, from his first confirmed kill to his eighth, had bested Rickenbacker, who'd been flying at the front since April. Luke that evening had passed Rickenbacker by a single kill to become America's newest living top scorer on the Western Front and its newest Ace of Aces.

Rickenbacker learned of Luke's success when he landed at dusk that evening after his final and again fruitless voluntary patrol of the day. The intensely competitive, yet emotionally secure Rickenbacker was also rapidly becoming a team player, and as magnanimous a good sport as he was a determined champion. Upon learning of Luke's score and new title, the sport racer set about organizing a group party for Luke which came off handsomely the following evening, Tuesday, 17 September.

It was back to the war on Wednesday, 18 September. Rickenbacker would not score again for the next week. The group as a whole was having a great deal of trouble with the American-made Marlin machine guns and their incessant jamming.

For unrecorded reasons, such mechanical drawbacks seemed to have had little effect on Frank and Joe's extraordinary string of confirmed victories. But one must wonder whether the accolades of the previous evening had not gone to Frank's head, further insulating his personal paradigm of invincibility, further removing from his operational concerns the genuine perils involved in his chosen combat specialty. That evening, clearly, Frank and Joe had finally arrived. The loud, enthusiastic, alcohol-charged acclaim of their peers, led by the universally admired Eddie Rickenbacker, was a goal and accomplishment all those present perceived as having been earned with honest, hard-earned capital. In the end to be recognized by one's peers ushers forth an emotional satisfaction for most equaled by few other honors. It almost certainly had been a prime motivating factor behind the pair's remarkable accomplishments.

Mission accomplished.

Whatever the reasons, or the mindset, Frank Luke elected the following day to ignore his own proven, and marginally safer, dusk method of attack and took off with Joe Wehner around four that afternoon to down a pair of German balloons at Mars-la-Tour. The attack would be made in broad daylight. The consequences would be disastrous.

The fame generated by the team's string of recent successes had spread across both sides of the line. German balloon commanders were now hauling down their bags at the mere sound of approaching aircraft. Covering German pursuit patrols had been beefed up to slow the Allies determined efforts. In short, German response to Luke and Joe's efforts had been anything but static. If this was part of Frank's tactical considerations this fateful afternoon, there is no evidence. Rather, it would seem, the pair had fallen back on an earlier, demonstrably riskier method of attack, pursued this day without either a 1st Group squadron or a waning sun's low visibility to cover them.

Wehner took off from the field that morning without wearing his good luck ring. It was the first and, regretfully, only time he made the omission. Were it not true, it would be a fiction writer's too obvious contrivance.

It was 1640 when Luke downed the first balloon and swooped for the second balloon before it could be winched into its nest. As usual, Joe waited above, his neck on a swivel. Suddenly he spotted a flight of six Jasta 15 Fokkers diving for his friend. He fired a Very flare to offer warning and a call for help, but Frank was now intent on lining up the second balloon in his sights. Joe dove headlong for the formation. Unseen above him was a seventh German.

Within moments Joe was trapped between the German pursuits. One of Germany's youngest aces, Lieutenant Georg von Hantelmann closed on Joe's tail. Four days earlier, on 14 September, the 19-year-old German had downed three Allied planes, including that of the then American Ace of Aces, David Putnam of the 139th Pursuit Squadron. Putnam's death had cleared the way for Rickenbacker's brief one-day stint as America's new leading ace. And now, von Hantelmann was again closing on the wingman of the current American Ace of Aces. Again a chance happenstance, a chance meeting too strange to be believed - if it were not true!

Hantelmann's well-placed rounds began tearing into Joe's Spad. Wood and canvas, metal fittings and guy wires exploded on impact. Joe's fuel reserve burst into a raging inferno. As Lufbery before him, Joe was consumed. Every flier's worst nightmare, an airborne fire, which at once became his final reality and epitaph. The gallant Bostonian, the young von Hantelmann's 16th confirmed aerial victory, was no more.

Too late, Frank saw the torched Spad that held his closest friend as its black plume arched earthward. As a wild man, Luke tore into the Germans. And though he was outnumbered seven to one, flamed two of the Fokkers before escaping alone for his lines. Nearing the frontier, Luke, now on his reserve fuel supply, saw the white puffs of friendly antiaircraft fire near Verdun that announced an interloper. He spotted a Halberstadt C over Jonville being pursued by three French chasse planes. Though short on fuel, the enraged Arizonan tore through the Frenchmen and downed the German scout himself. It was his fifth confirmed aerial victory in nearly as many minutes!

Luke was shattered. He sensed more than knew his friend was gone. He cut his throttle and settled his battle-scarred Spad down in a field near an American 16-inch naval railroad gun. And there beside his mount he would spend the night trapped in his own world of grief and torment, oblivious to the scores of American soldiers milling about his torn and gun streaked Spad. Late that evening Grant and Hartney finally received word of Luke's safe

Frank Luke's flight school photo

Clearly the grim business of aerial warfare and the recent loss of close friend Joe Wehner have taken their emotional toll on Frank Luke since his flight training days.

Frank Luke shortly after the loss of his friend Joe Wehner.

return and whereabouts.

The next morning, Hartney gathered together Eddie Rickenbacker and Mrs. Welton, the group's YMCA girl, for the drive up. They found a changed man, sobered by new realities and fresh emotional wounds. Gone was the braggadocio; gone was the loud bravado.

"Wehner isn't back yet, is he, Major?"[7] Hartney nodded in the negative, but Luke had known before he asked. America's leading ace said little on the trip back. There was too much to sort out, too many conflicted emotions, too many memories pulling at him. His external world had lost its resonance amid the inner turmoil. Nonetheless, in an effort to regain some measure of his emotional equilibrium, he insisted on getting back into the air the same day. At the controls of his new Spad, probably number eight, and with grief dulling his sharp edge, Luke crashed on takeoff into the 147th gun test pit.[8]

Hartney had seen the signs before. Luke was through with flying, at least for the time being. And maybe for good. The group commander saw to it that the cowboy was sent off the field - "almost by force." Hartney tells us Luke was sent off on ten days leave to Orly and Paris. Hartney soon lost all thought of the distraught Arizonan as the demands of his group once again took hold. The St. Mihiel Offensive had been a spectacular success for Pershing's newly consolidated all-American 1st Army. But the gravest test, the battle for the Argonne Forest, lay just ahead.

September 20th to the 26th was a period of relative inactivity at the front. On Sunday, the 22nd, Rickenbacker arranged for a troupe of American entertainers to put on their show in the 94th hangar. Among the performers, Rick was particularly drawn to a young actress, Lois Meredith. Soon, the pair would be seeing each other on a regular basis, whenever the 94th ace could manage time away from his duties.

But Hartney had his own eye out as well for Rickenbacker. The 94th desperately needed a new commander. In peacetime, seniority would have dictated an officer of longer standing such as Reed Chambers - certainly not a "Mustang," a recent enlisted man such as Rick. But Rickenbacker possessed, if not seniority, certainly more relevant qualities of maturity, fighting spirit, natural leadership, as well as an engineer's thorough understanding of the new technology upon which the air arm was based. It was a daring choice, to jump this immigrant's son with the seventh grade education over the heads of so many of his more-polished peers. It was a choice that would be received with serious misgivings among many of his career superiors, particularly Colonel Billy Mitchell himself. And ultimately, perhaps, it was a decision that could only have been made by a guardsman, a citizen soldier like Hartney whose barrister client instincts were stronger than his instincts to play the career game.

As group commander, Hartney recognized that the 94th had become the weakest link in his organization. Perhaps only such a bold choice could revive the unit's former luster. Rick already had the respect of both the 94th's mechanics and fliers. Chambers took the news on the 24th of Rickenbacker's appointment as good-naturedly as did the rest of his squadron. And while Mitchell did not personally approve of Hartney's appointment, neither did he rescind it. Time, he acknowledged, would prove the best judge.

On Wednesday, 25 September, Rick's first day as the 94th's new CO, he set out early to establish a new pace for his new command. Launching out on another voluntary dawn patrol, he single-handedly took on a formation of five Fokkers escorting a pair of Halberstadt C photo planes. Crawling up the rear of the pursuit formation, Rick flamed the rearmost D.VII. And after breaking up the formation, he returned to down one of the photo planes as well.

Rick's two kills were quickly confirmed. Of the 47 enemy aircraft downed by the 94th under Rick's command, Rickenbacker ultimately will claim 20.

To celebrate his new command, Rick threw a party that evening. Lois Meredith was once again at his side. As the festivities and gaiety began to wane, the ominous rumble of sustained Allied artillery fire took hold. The softening-up process had begun for the final Meuse-Argonne Drive. At 0530 the following morning, Thursday, 26 September, the U.S. 1st Army was once again advancing all along the front.

Hartney's group was assigned the job of clearing the air below 2,000 feet. Eighty-one 1st Group Spads, all the mechanics could make airworthy, had taken off in the pre-dawn darkness. The typical fall menu of mist, rain and low-hanging clouds had settled in over the region. Fog hugged the ground, though the artillery fire spectacularly illuminated the lower cloud deck from within.

That evening Hartney was gratified that despite the marginal weather, the group had downed two enemy aircraft and six balloons for no casualties. Rickenbacker had downed another Fokker D.VII over Damvillers, his third victory in the last two days. But most surprising was the appearance of Luke's name in the daily operational report. It had been seven days since Luke had been sent to Paris. He was not due back for another three - yet there was Luke's name claiming another Fokker. It was a claim that would never be confirmed.

From the start, Luke had made it clear he wanted no part of Paris. In typical bad boy fashion, he'd stolen back to his unit and the only brand of emotional validation, grim though it was, he'd even been able to accept since his arrival in Europe.

Unbeknownst to Hartney, Luke had returned to the cockpit on the 25th and that day, with new partner Ivan Roberts in tow, had dropped candy and cigarettes into the American lines.

The 26th of September marks the beginning of a hazy, contradictory final four-day period in the life of Frank Luke Jr. That said, however, it is not suggested that the earlier events of Luke's career and life are not wholly without controversy. What is certain is that from this date the record of Frank Luke Jr's. life - and death - begins to move into that gray area canvassed under the heading of "legend."

What is documented, on this opening day of the Meuse-Argonne Offensive, was that Luke claimed another kill over a Fokker and that his new flying partner, Ivan Roberts, did not return from the engagement.

World War One aviation writer, if not a true historian, Arch Whitehouse suggested in 1966 that contrary to Hartney's own 1940 autobiography, not only was Hartney aware, within hours, if not minutes, of Luke's early return, but he insisted the Arizonan remain grounded until his leave period was concluded.[9] Such a turn of events, it would seem to this writer, was wholly contrary to Hartney's known nature - though not Grant's. Whether Luke and Roberts defied orders for the 26 September balloon-strafing sortie remains unclear. Luke's report of the subsequent action makes it clear the pair had been joined by an unnamed third flier. And rather than finding a balloon, the trio happened upon a flight of five Fokkers which they promptly attacked, Luke claiming one, for the loss of Roberts.

Norman S. Hall's early postwar account of Luke, first appearing in 1928 as a serialized story in the popular *Liberty* magazine goes further, suggesting Luke's victim that day was none other than Jasta 15 commander "Lt. J. von Ziegesar."[10] Latter day historians Franks and Bailey, however, make no mention of a "von Ziegesar" ever having commanded the jasta in question. Ultimately, Hall's undocumented exercise in hyperbolae, later appearing as a thin volume titled *The Balloon Buster*, marks the formal beginning of the Luke Legend.

And, sadly, with Hartney's own attentions slaved to the demands of his group command, we have precious little other first-person accounts to go on - and those are fragmentary at best.

And, to be sure, popular WWI aviation writer Arch Whitehouse's own later accounts of Luke appearing in his 1959 volume *The Years of the Sky Kings* and his 1966 Luke biography *Hun Killer* can be no less suspect. For as a shaky house of cards, much of Whitehouse's own later writings appear based on the unsubstantiated earlier efforts of Norman Hall.

Not surprisingly, therefore, both Hall and Whitehouse agree that upon his return to the field on the evening of the 26th, "Luke went into surly seclusion" in his tent, after venting to his armorers about more gun jams and stoppages.[11]

On 27 September, a rainy Friday, Rickenbacker's diary affirms he drove into nearby Fleury to again see Meredith. That same day, Whitehouse suggests Luke was grounded and that he "stomped about (the field) like an enraged panther."[12]   Both Hall and Whitehouse, the latter in his *Sky Kings* volume, further suggest that Luke defied authority later that day and took off on an unauthorized flight and was thoroughly chewed out by Grant upon his return.

Strangely, no mention of such a flight is made in Whitehouse's later *Hun Killer* volume.

It has also been suggested that in this period of emotional turmoil for Luke, Rickenbacker had come over to the 27th in an effort to talk the wayward flier through his trials, even to recruit him for his own new command.[13]

Early Saturday morning, around 0500, on the 28th, Rickenbacker caught, strafed and flamed a partially-inflated observation balloon in the bed of a truck near Sivry-sur-Meuse as it was being transported to a new location. It would become the ace's 12th confirmed "aerial" victory.

An hour later, at 0600, Luke downed a German balloon near Bethenville. It would be his 14th confirmed kill. Later that afternoon, at 1550, Luke scored his 15th confirmed victory downing a Hannover CL over Monthainville. Interestingly, except for his first confirmed kill on 12 September, all of Luke's daily victories were multiples.

Though Luke is officially credited with downing the Bethenville balloon around 0600 on the morning of the 28th and the Hannover later that afternoon, both Hall and Whitehouse suggest Luke was grounded that day. That he once again left the field without permission, downed a balloon at "Bantheville" and spent the night with the French Cigognes/Storks group. No mention is made of the Hannover downing. In fact, both Hall and Whitehouse, no doubt on Hall's lead, suggest Grant only learned of the balloon claim upon Luke's return the next day, on the 29th.

Hartney, in his more credible autobiography, agrees that Luke did not return that night, but suggests the Arizonan spent the evening with a decidedly less glamorous French observation balloon company, and not with the famed Storks.

According to whoever is writing the tale, Luke showed up back at Rembercourt either the afternoon, or, as Hartney recalls, the morning of the 29th.

The most dramatic, if not, perhaps, the most credible accounting of what transpired next originated with Hall and was later sec-
onded by Whitehouse. According to Hall, upon Luke's landing, he
was ushered into Grant's presence and promptly grounded. To the
squadron commander's great surprise, the Westerner gave no back-
talk, but rather offered up a smart and uncharacteristic salute,
turned on his heel, slamming the office door behind him - and
headed straight for his plane. From there he flew, again without
orders, to the advanced field near Verdun.[14]

Symptomatic of Whitehouse's "creative" approach to history,
in his 1959 *The Years of the Sky Kings* accounting of the event, he
suggests that upon Luke's defiant takeoff:

"Grant frowned, 'First, I'm recommending him for the
Distinguished Service Cross and then, by God, I'm going to court-
martial him!'"[15]

Seven years later the same writer, in his 1966 *Hun Killer*
wrote:

"Captain Grant frowned. 'First, I'm recommending him for the
Legion of Honor, and then, by God, I'm going to court-martial
him!'"[16]

The latter line is as unlikely as is an American officer's ability
to award a French decoration.

Nor do any of these accountings come close to agreeing with
Hartney's, the closest individual to the above events to have set
down his recollections or take on the tale.

Hartney did recall Grant storming into his office the morning
of the 29th as angry as a disturbed hornet's nest.

"Major," Hartney recalls Grant saying, "this man Luke is going
hog-wild…I can't handle him unless you'll back me up. He thinks
he's the whole Air Service."[17]

According to Hartney, he told Grant he'd already agreed to
send Luke up to the advanced field, which Hartney admitted he had
not in fact done. Rather than challenge Luke, Hartney, it appears in
that moment, had once again adroitly elected to channel the
Arizonan's drives toward the interests of the group.

At the Verdun field Jerry Vasconcells, the field commander, had orders from Hartney not to let Luke take off for the German balloons on the Meuse before 5:56.

Both Hall and Whitehouse suggest the time was 5:22 and that Luke, defying an earlier grounding by Grant, only got a last minute approval for the balloon strafe from Hartney himself when the latter showed up at the advance field in his unarmed Camel.

By all accounts Hartney was at the advance field that evening. And at the appointed hour, be it 5:22 or 5:56, Luke was off after his balloons.

The last sighting of Luke alive by an American unit was a balloon company, Whitehouse suggests it was the 7th at Souilly. A lone Spad circled their site near dusk and dropped a message as varied in its supposed wording as the numbers of writers retelling the event.

Hall would tell us the message said:

"Watch three Hun balloons on the Meuse. Luke."

Whitehouse in his *The Years of the Sky Kings* tells us it said:

"Watch those three Hun balloons along the Meuse. Luke."

Seven years later in his *Hun Killer* biography Whitehouse tells us it said:

"Watch for burning balloons, Luke."

The latter rendition WWI historian James J. Hudson credited in his 1968 volume *Hostile Skies, A Combat History of the American Air Service in World War I* to the official *History of the 27th Aero Squadron*.[18] The veracity of the statement, however, is no less assured.

Whatever the actual content of the message, American observers that evening witnessed the airborne fires of three separate enemy balloons. It was the last any of his countrymen ever saw of Luke alive. The widely recalled message no one then serving with the 27th disputed was the Arizonan's oft repeated vow to "never be taken alive."

And so ended a spirited, if unofficial contest of immigrant sons, of individuals from which little was expected, that in the end, would establish a record which would have no equal.

Luke left the scene with 18 confirmed kills; some historians have suggested the figure should be 21.   At the time of the Arizonan's death, Rickenbacker had 11 confirmed victories.

But, for the pragmatic warrior from Columbus, his best days still lay ahead.

Frank Luke, Jr. days before his death, captured posing with Spad XIII number 26, one of the five or more Spad XIIIs the Arizonan went through during his brief combat career with the 27th Aero Squadron.

Chapter Nine

THE CURSE: AMERICA'S "ACE OF ACES"

Enjoying near perfect weather on the morning of 15 September, Eddie Rickenbacker shot down his eighth enemy plane of his four and a half month combat career. Commandeering a car upon his return to Rembercourt, he sought to find ground confirmation for his aerial victory of the morning, as well as a signed confirmation for his single kill of the 14th. Making his way through forest and around shell-pocked roads, he finally made his way near the trench line just south of Vigneulles. There he found both his needed witnesses, as well as witnessing himself the spectacular downing of an American observation balloon.

By the afternoon, Rickenbacker had acquired the signed documents required for his sixth and seventh aerial victories of the 14th and 15th.[1]

Rick's natural competitive instincts had found gratification, yet with the honored title "America's Ace of Aces" came, as Rick himself called it, "a haunting superstition," a curse which had not treated its bearers kindly. When congratulated by Reed Chambers, his wingman, that afternoon, Rickenbacker offered his thanks, adding: "but any other fellow can have the title any time he wants it, so far as I am concerned."[2]

Within 24 hours, Rickenbacker would have his wish!

During Rickenbacker's time in France six American fliers, aside from himself, would hold the title: "America's Ace of Aces." Of these six, four would soon die in combat, and a fifth would become a wounded prisoner of war. The two wartime survivors would later have their lives cut short in postwar flying accidents.[3]

Raoul Lufbery, as we have seen, held the title upon Rickenbacker's arrival at the front, and was the first killed on 19 May 1918. And though he was flying with the 94th Aero Squadron at the time, all his 16 official victories had been acquired with N124, the famed French Lafayette Escadrille where he had been their leading ace. Among his 13 probables were two scored with the 94th.

With Lufbery's death the grim title was passed on to Lieutenant Paul Frank Baer of the US 103rd Aero Squadron, formerly the French-led Lafayette Escadrille. Lost in the fanfare surrounding the first kills of Douglas Campbell and Alan Winslow was the first aerial victory of Baer's. The latter kill, scored more than a month before Campbell and Winslow's, was the first official U.S. Air Service victory of the war, scored, as it was, by a member of the newly U.S.-commissioned 103rd Aero Squadron.[4] The Fort Wayne, Indiana native's title would be short-lived, as he was shot down and wounded four short days after the death of Lufbery on 22 May 1918. At the time, Baer's record boasted nine official victories and seven probables. He would survive the war as a POW.

Three weeks later, on 12 June, Lieutenant Frank Baylies, the son of a prominent New Bedford, Massachusetts merchant, fell to his death with the title. All 13 of his official victories at the time had been scored with his French squadron, the Cigognes of Spa Three.

Harvard alum David Endicott Putnam, late of Jamaica Plains,

Massachusetts, next held the American Ace of Aces mantle until his 12 September death at the hands of the aforementioned Jasta 15 ace Georg von Hantelmann. It was the young German aristocrat's eighth aerial victory. Putnam was flying with the Spad XIII-equipped US 139th Aero Squadron attached to the 2nd Pursuit Group. However, only the last five of Putnam's 13 official victories were acquired under U.S. colors.

The latest American Ace of Aces was buried next to the first, Raoul Lufbery.

The title next passed on to San Antonio native Edgar Gardiner Tobin, again of the 3rd Pursuit Group's 103rd Aero Squadron. As the leading American aces continued to fall before German guns, the title was passed on to ever lower scoring airmen. Tobin at the time had six victories to his credit.

Within 24-hours of Rickenbacker surpassing Tobin, Rick himself was overtaken by the phenomenal pace of Frank Luke, though the latter's reign would last but another 13 days.

By 30 September, however, Eddie Rickenbacker had more pressing concerns before him, namely the restoration of a proud squadron record. The new squadron commander and middle school dropout had little patience for paperwork and promptly delegated the odorous task to his staff. Nor did the one-time sergeant have much patience for military protocol around the field, namely saluting. If his men were doing the jobs which needed to be done, they should have no time, he felt, for such 'useless activities.'

And though at first taken aback by the practice, Colonel Mitchell soon came to appreciate its practical intent.

The Army had come into the war with a manual for every aspect of fighting on the ground, though none existed for the air. Aerial combat was on a "learn-as-you-go" basis. It was left to the often irreverent pioneers such as Mitchell, Hartney, Luke and Rickenbacker to explore and probe, and from experiment and experience to establish the guidelines for this new realm of combat. It took innovators outside the Army's mainstream to effectively build what had not existed before. Be they a British-trained guardsman and Canadian barrister, a frontier marksman or a one-time champion racecar driver and race team leader, each would leave his own unique stamp on the fledgling U.S. Air Service, each illuminating a bit more brightly than the last the road ahead.

Rickenbacker had come to the command of the 94th with the unique background of skills, both personal and technical, which soon had the squadron returned to its earlier winning ways. Rick called his officers together challenging them to a new excellence. He assured them he'd never ask them to do anything he himself would not do. But rank, he insisted, was secondary to a girded team effort. Respect would flow down as well as up. There was no small job on his team. Pilots were to listen to their ground crews, to take an active interest in maintenance issues. It was no accident that he, Rick, was getting so many more hours out of his Hisso engine between overhauls.

Rickenbacker told his ground crews, as only a former mechanic could, that should they have a better idea about how to do something he wanted to hear it, for if they didn't, by God, they surely would hear from him!

It was a message at once delivered with a firm, if open-minded hand, and received enthusiastically for the revitalizing jolt intended.

———

"October," pointed out Rickenbacker biographer Finis Farr, "was to be the most important month so far in Rick's life, the month in which his achievements would rise to such a level that he would never afterward be able to live as an ordinary man...(but rather a personage) of the world...larger than life size."[5]

Leading by example and positive force of personality, Rickenbacker never flew less than two missions a day - weather permitting. That was anywhere from four to six hours in the cockpit each day. It was a personal mandate he took on, obligating himself to fly more hours than his men.

And though Rick cleverly turned the 94th team's attention initially to overtaking the group lead from the 27th, there really was

This captured Hannover CL downed near Montfaucon, 2 October 1918. While World War One fliers each received equal and full credits for shared kills during the war, their victory totals were pared down by appropriate fractions during the U.S. Air Force's review of WWI tallies during the 1960s.

no contest. Grant's limited personality and "bulldozing" command methods had little to offer in the face of Rickenbacker's inspired leadership by example.

On the evening of Tuesday, 1 October, Rick scored his first kill since Luke's disappearance two days earlier. It was a balloon downed that evening over Puzieux. He, with Reed Chambers, had also crippled a Halberstadt photo plane and pumped some 200 rounds into a defending Fokker. Rick managed to escape the balance of the defending German pursuits by the narrowest of margins.

So close was his escape, Rickenbacker would later record in his diary, "Thought my days were ended."[6]

Despite his close call, Rick's guns got even hotter the following day when he downed a Hannover CL over Montfaucon with another assist from Reed Chambers and ten minutes later, at 1740, downed a Fokker D.VII over Vilosnes. It was Rick's 15th victory. Thursday, the third, Rickenbacker repeated his double score of the previous day, downing an LVG C over Dannevaux and a Fokker

D.VII over Clery-le-Grand that afternoon.

On Saturday, the fifth, Rick downed another Fokker D.VII north of Montfaucon for which he received no confirmation.

Seasonal storms arrived the following day and on Monday the seventh, permitting the squadron commander time off base in Bar-le-Duc with girlfriend Meredith. On Wednesday the ninth, Rick again had lunch with Meredith, returning in time to down a balloon near Dun-sur-Meuse around 1752 that evening per Luke's earlier groundbreaking example. The drachen was Rickenbacker's 18th victory. The following afternoon, the Columbus Ace of Aces surpassed Luke's score by downing another two Fokkers within minutes of each other over Clery-le-Petit.

On Friday, 11 October, the weather again soured, and again Rick headed for Paris and a few days of rest and relaxation. The gusty, wind-driven rains continued Saturday. That evening Rick had a luxuriant dinner at Maximes with Meredith. Sunday, the word circulated that Germany was sending out peace feelers.

By Tuesday, the 15th, however, it became clear the war was not yet over. Rick returned to Rembercourt, though heavy rains persisted.

A week would pass before Rickenbacker downed his next German, a Fokker D.VII over Clery-le-Petit. And, once again, his escape from the balance of the enemy formation was a close thing. This 22 October afternoon victory would officially be his 20th confirmation. The next afternoon, Rick downed another Fokker over Grande Carne Ferme. The Jasta 15 pursuit was reportedly piloted by seven-plane ace Gustav Klaudet who, though wounded, survived the engagement. It was the German's last fight of the war.

Heavy rains again curtailed flying activity on the 24th and for the next three days. And once again Rick headed for Paris. Happily, Rickenbacker's promotion to captain arrived on the 26th. And some ten days earlier, his mentor, Billy Mitchell, had finally become a general.

By the afternoon of the 27th the weather had improved sufficiently for Rickenbacker to again go aloft; and again he downed two Fokkers within minutes of each other over Bois de Money and

Grand Pre. The day's victories sent his official wartime score to 23.

On 30 October, Eddie Rickenbacker scored another two victories. Late that afternoon, he caught a red-nosed Richthofen Circus Fokker and set it aflame. With his fuel reserves running low, Rick, within five minutes of his first kill, spotted a drachen grounded in its bed near the village of Remonville. Diving to the deck, he exploded the bag on his first pass.[7] By this time Rickenbacker's fuel was nearly spent. Still behind enemy lines, with nearly empty tanks, he watched the sun set beyond the Western horizon. For one of the few times in his life "real terror" began to register as he started back for his own lines. Though his Spad had a two hour, ten minute duration under economical settings and a remarkable glide ratio from 15,000 or 20,000 feet, he'd claimed his last victim "on the deck." Had his engine quit then, he would have become a "guest" of the Germans. It was not a happy prospect given his own German roots.

The minutes passed and his engine continued to tick over. West of Verdun, he crossed the Allied lines where he was greeted by inaccurate antiaircraft fire. When he reckoned he was within ten miles of Rembercourt he fired a pair of red Very pistol flares into the darkness. As his engine began to sputter its last, a pair of thin torch lines began to delineate themselves beyond the nose of his Spad. It was his field! Unlike the graceful Nieuport before it, novice fliers were advised not to attempt power-off landings in "the Brick." Rickenbacker's silent Spad settled with a teeth-chattering, if safe thud between the kerosene lines of fire.

Though he hadn't realized it at the time, Rickenbacker's winning aerial combat days had come to an end.

His six week tenure as commander of the 94th Pursuit Squadron would prove a stellar performance by any measure. And not only had he led the 94th back into the lead as the top scoring American pursuit squadron of the war, his personal score of 26 victories would account for nearly 40% of the squadron's total of 67 wartime victories![8] The last 14 of his victories had been amassed in October, a record even Frank Luke would have admired.

In the end, Eddie V. Rickenbacker had amassed a remarkable

nine Oak Leaf clusters to his DSC.

With the first of November began the wind-down of the war. American 1st Group patrols found no enemy planes, nor would they for the next three days. Germany's ally, Turkey, withdrew from the war on the first, as Allied troops continued to advance on the crumbling German lines. Rick once again left for Paris on Saturday afternoon, 2 November. On Monday, his diary records he had a very pleasant day shopping with Meredith in the French capital, while back at the field, 1st Group fliers found "the air full of Germans." By day's end six enemy planes and balloons had been downed for no losses.

Rick returned to the field on the afternoon of the fifth, but the weather again turned foul and remained so on the eighth, though he managed to get into the air. On 9 November, serious peace negotiations began.

It was also on this day that Major Maxwell Kirby scored the 94th's last aerial victory of the war. He'd joined the 94th on 15 October.

On the evening of 10 November, with the agreed Armistice but hours away, the 1st Group began a celebration seen, no doubt as well as heard, on both sides of the lines. Large field kitchen kettles were rolled out to mix the alcoholic punch, as Rickenbacker himself led the 185th Squadron brass band around a massive gasoline-fed bondfire. Machine gun tracers and Very pistol flares illuminated the late night sky, punctuating the loud abandonment of men who knew they would see another day.

Not only had Rickenbacker's famed good fortune found the measure of the aces' curse, but he had successfully positioned himself to launch a peacetime career that would be the envy of most of his collegiate subordinates.

*Eddie Rickenbacker and his Spad XIII in the ever-present mud
of Rembercourt during the fall of 1918.*

Chapter Nine
Insert No. 1

WORLD WAR ONE'S TOP RANKING AMERICAN ACES
(Through double ace: ten or more official
aerial victories per 1914-1918 criteria.)

Of World War One's 28 top American aces (double ace or
better), it will be noted that 22 had served at least part of their
combat tours with the British. Another three of the aces had first
served with the French, and the last three had served exclusively
with the U.S. Air Service during their 1918 combat tours.

There are several reasons for the preponderance of Americans
acquiring top scores while flying with the British. First, many of
the volunteer American fliers had been in combat for nearly a
year, and some as long as two years, before the U.S. 1st Pursuit
Group got into action. Secondly, the British accounting system
included so-called 'out-of-control' victory credits, not recognized
by either the French or American Air Services. Thirdly, British
fliers routinely shared aerial victories with their rear-seat gunners.
In fact, many of prewar Colorado cowboy Fred Libby's officially
credited 14 aerial victories with the RAF are as an aerial gunner,
and before his retraining as a pilot.

By the Armistice, when aerial victories were finally tallied,
little more than a quarter of the top American aces had at least
some measure of the higher educational backgrounds earlier envisioned by Billy Mitchell and Dr. Gros as an essential requisite for
the successful combat pursuit pilot of the Great War. By war's
end it had been learned that intelligence, and, perhaps more
importantly, aggressiveness, could not alone be measured by an
Ivy League degree.

PILOT	SCORE	UNIT	COMMENT
1. Rickenbacker, E.V.	26	94 Aero	Seventh-grade dropout
2. Beaver, W.	20	20 RAF	With back-seater victories
3. Gillet, F.W.	20	79 RAF	
4. Kullberg, H.A.	19	1 RAF	Wentworth Instit., Boston
5. Lambert, W.C.	18	24 RAF	
6. Luke, F.	18	27 Aero	High school graduate
7. Iaccaci, A.T.	17	20, 48 RAF	With back-seater victories?
8. Iaccaci, P.T.	17	20 RAF	With back-seater victories?
(Brother of A.T. Iaccaci)			
9. Coler, E.S.	16	11 RAF	With back-seater victories
10. Lufbery, G.R.	16	VB106, N-124, 94 Aero	
			Ran away from home at 17
11. Rose, O.J.	16	92 RAF	
12. Springs, E.W.	16	85 RAF, 48 Aero. Princeton University	
13. Unger, K.R.	14	210 RAF	
14. Libby, F.	14	23, 11, 43, 25 RAF	As gunner, later pilot
15. Putnam, D.E.	13	Spa 94, MS156, Spa 38, 139 Aero. Harvard	
16. Vaughn, G.A.	13	84 RAF, 17 Aero. Princeton University	
17. Baylies, F.L.	12	Spa 73, 3	Moses Brown Prep. School
18. Bennett, L.	12	40 RAF	Yale Univ., downed 9 balloons
19. Kindley, F.E.	12	65 RAF, 148 Aero Inc.	
20. Landis, R.G.	12	40, 25 RAF, 4PG	
21. Lord, F.I.	12	79 RAF	
22. Pearson, J.W.	12	23 RAF	
23. Warman, C.W.	12	23 RFC	prewar civil engineer
24. Lussier, E.J.	11	73 RAF	
25. Hamilton, L.A.	10	3 RAF, 17 Aero. Harvard University	
26. Knight, D.	10	1 RAF	
27. LeBoutillier, O.C.	10	9 Naval, 209 RAF	
28. Swaab, J.M.	10	22 Aero	

Chapter Ten

LEGACY

BITTER FRUIT

By late October frontline jastas were being rationed 40 gallons of gasoline per plane, per day - when they could get it. Ammunition, as just about every other consumable necessary to field an operational squadron, was in short supply - everything, that is, except enemy planes whose numbers were now fully twice those of the German Air Service.

Jasta 4 commander and Germany's leading surviving ace, Ernest Udet, recalled his squadron landing at a German airfield en route to a newly assigned front around this time. As he was pleading with the field's commander for the fuel to get his squadron on its way again, a lone British plane chanced upon the target-rich aerodrome, overflowing with transit Fokkers. The already frustrated Udet became enraged as the allied pilot began to merrily strafe the fuel-starved assemblage. Scrambling into his cockpit and calling for the prop to be pulled through, Udet was soon airborne. With the last ten rounds remaining in his guns, so the story goes, he downed the brazen enemy before his gasoline-starved engine coughed its last and he was forced to glide back in silence to the field and the cheers of his waiting fliers.

For all their widely heralded and hard-earned skills, the incident was but a foretaste of the bitter fruit yet to come for the men of the Richthofen Circus.[1]

It was nearly noon, 9 November 1918. Jasta 11's adjutant, Lt. Karl Bodenschatz, remembered Hermann Goering's "icy" presence. The commander of Jagdgeschwader 1 (JG1) had called a meeting of his officers from Jastas 4, 6, 10 and 11. "Coldly" he reviewed the situation at the front and at home... the mutiny at Kiel... the Kaiser's abdication... the riots in Berlin. Regardless, Goering insisted, the Richthofen group was ready for the enemy - should he come. As for the crumbling Reich itself, the commander would brook no tolerance of mutineers. His officers were ordered to remain in their Tellancourt Field quarters and to wait.

The following day an order arrived, an unthinkable message that commanded, in part: "It is to be considered that the planes may be delivered to the Americans."[2]

The Americans!

Goering, in his rage, refused to acknowledge the outrageous order. Rather, he ignored it, ordering his group to Darmstadt as soon as the fog had lifted. The adjutant was to organize the 35-truck, 250-man ground echelon convoy that was to follow. They were to bring only the essentials; what could not be taken would be burned.

By noon on the 11th the Armistice was in place. Bodenschatz, as were his men, was sullen, drained and deadened by events that were spiraling beyond his control. He silently stood in the lead truck as his weary column wove its way back to Germany. They passed through the decaying rabble that had recently been the German army, but now more closely resembled a marauding, ragged uniform gang more interested in booty, personal survival - and home - than engaging the enemy. Yet, the convoy was not harmed, for scrawled in chalk across the sides of their trucks were the words: "Richthofen, the Red Combat Pilot." When the mobs saw the words, recalled Bodenschatz, "even the loudest of the rioters became quiet and turned back."

At Darmstadt, Goering again received orders to turn over his

Crashed Fokker D.VII

planes, now to the French at Strassburg. But, if someone is to carry out this order, Goering told his men, it would not be him!

Few of the jastas' Fokker D.VIIs remained flyable as they had been intentionally "pranged" upon arrival at Darmstadt. The French would find little joy in the few abused aircraft which ultimately were flown to Strassburg.

On the 19th, the day of their formal discharge, the surviving jasta officers enjoyed one last alcohol-laced evening at the Stiftskeller in Aschaffenburg. Before they went their separate ways, Goering revisited the Richthofen Squadron's remarkable record. The officers, recalled Bodenschatz, "are deeply moved. Tears well up in their eyes, whether they wish it or not... the commandant speaks... of the future... this man with his flaming oratory... promised himself, his comrades - and the Fatherland - this squadron will again come into existence!"[3] Foot-stomping applause and cheers exploded among the once weary pilots as Goering hurled his wineglass against the banquet room wall.

Goering and his fellow jasta survivors returned to a nation in chaos. Strong-armed right wing Freikorps thugs had been recruited from the ranks of the returning veterans to enforce the shaky authority of the republican government. But there remained no

The Flying Circus' last commander, Hermann Wilhelm Goering, would be instrumental in the formation of the post-WWI Nazi Party in Germany and the systematic looting of his nation's moneyed establishment. His botched command of Germany's World War Two Luftwaffe helped lead to his nation's ultimate defeat and a war crimes conviction at the post WWII Nuremberg Tribunal. Goering managed to commit suicide on 15 October 1946 before his scheduled execution.

Ernest Udet was Germany's greatest surviving WWI ace. Though instrumental in developing the Stuka dive bomber for the new Luftwaffe, his personal independent bent, and frank personality proved a poor fit as a generaloberst in the Nazi high command. He reportedly committed suicide on 17 November 1941. Udet (right) is seen here 6 September 1931 in Cleveland, Ohio presenting former 27th Aero Squadron pilot Walter B. Wanamaker, then an Akron judge, with the original canvas mounted rudder serial of his Nieuport 28 downed at the German ace's hand on 2 July 1918.

military presence to defend its existing borders. Germany had no choice but to rely on the good will of the victorious conferees at Versailles. The French had other ideas, and persuaded her Allies to agree to what one historian has correctly labeled "extortionate" terms.

Germany, now democratized, continued to have her ports blockaded well into the spring of 1919; she had neither say nor choice in the terms ultimately handed down. As early as Eddie Rickenbacker's brief immediate postwar stay in Germany, he observed that American "cigarettes and chocolate had become the medium of exchange. The inflation that ate up the value of German money and destroyed the government was already getting under-way." But hardest for Rickenbacker to accept was the blockade-driven food shortages which generated a lost generation of under-fed and starving German children with hollow "chicken faces and protruding bellies."[4]

The French had long wanted to occupy the Rhineland, to bring it permanently under its political control. Poland was given further German territory and the German-speaking people of Austria were forbidden from uniting with Germany. The German air force was abolished, its navy gutted, and its army reduced to a carefully monitored 100,000 man volunteer establishment. And the size of the material and financial reparations demanded by the French were staggering.

On 28 June 1919, the Treaty of Versailles formally brought an end to the Great War, and with it the seeds of the next war. The spiritually undefeated people of Germany called the Versailles terms an "outrage," a "crime" which could not long be tolerated.

Within this climate of social turmoil and political unrest, the German fliers came home to tragedy and unconscionable opportunity.

On 18 September 1918, Jasta 15's **Georg von Hantelmann** had been one of the Imperial German Air Service's youngest and most promising fliers. The 19-year-old ace flamed his 16th victim, Lt. Joe Wehner of the American 27th Aero Squadron on that day. As stated earlier, Wehner was the third Allied ace the German had downed in the last ten days. And though the newly arrived Hantelmann had not acquired his first aerial victory until 29 May 1918, a month after Rickenbacker had first scored, he amassed 25 victories by war's end - one short of the famed American "Ace of Aces" final score. After the war Hantelmann retired to his East Prussian estate where, six years later, on 7 September 1924, he would be murdered by Polish poachers.

Hermann Wilhelm Goering returned to fight in the postwar German revolution. In the early 1920s, after serving for several years in Denmark as a flight adviser, he returned to Germany where he soon joined Adolf Hitler in forming the Nazi party, and began the systematic looting of the moneyed establishment. As Reichsmarschal and commander of the newly formed Luftwaffe, Goering became Hitler's heir apparent. He was captured by the Americans on 9 May 1945. Goering cheated the Nuremberg Tribunal's execution order for war crimes by committing suicide on 15 October 1946.

Ernst Udet's end would prove no happier. A free-spirited adventurer at heart, Udet spent his early postwar years as a test pilot, world-traveling exhibition pilot, and even flew to modest motion picture stardom on the German big screen!

Never really admiring Goering, Udet nonetheless was persuaded by his wartime comrade to join the new Luftwaffe. Though he achieved the rank of generaloberst, Udet's independent, frank personality proved a poor fit in the Nazi high command.

Eddie Rickenbacker, now a successful businessman, returned to Europe in the fall of 1922 with Adelaide, his new bride, for a three-month traveling honeymoon. In Berlin, amid the time's ever accelerating inflation, the Rickenbackers were guests of both Goering and Udet. When Rickenbacker returned home, he warned his military contacts of his old enemies' vision for a renewed arms program to finish the work left undone three years earlier. Few, however, were willing to listen.

Rickenbacker, now the successful general manager of Eastern Airlines, returned to Germany again in the fall of 1935. He was impressed with how his flying colleagues, in their new uniforms, had risen on the social ladder since his last visit 13 years earlier. Despite the Versailles conditions, the now rotund Goering did not hesitate to share witness to the rising phoenix that was the new Luftwaffe with his old enemy. When, however, the free-spirited Udet began to openly criticize Hitler, Rickenbacker warned his friend, "You keep talking like you're talking now, Ernst, and you'll get your goddamned head shot off!"[5]

Six years later, on 17 November 1941, the German people would be told that Ernst Udet had committed suicide in Berlin.[6]

In 1965, the now retired 75-year-old Rickenbacker returned one last time to Berlin possessing the greatest gift any combat flier could hope for - old age - to pay his respects to his long fallen old foes. When he learned their gravesites rested in the eastern communist-controlled sector of the capital he did not hesitate to go. At the cemetery, he found a locked iron gate guarded by an armed soldier and his growling dog. The retired, yet still towering American CEO refused to take "no admittance" for an answer. A series of frantic phone calls finally generated the answer Rickenbacker was looking for. The put-upon guard at last forced open the long rusted padlock.

Richthofen's massive, long overgrown monument had, as its interred namesake, seen happier days.

MANY HAPPY RETURNS

More productive and happier by far would generally be the lot of those intelligent, often handsomely educated American First Pursuit Group fliers fortunate enough to have survived the war.

On the evening of 22 October 1918, the group's commander, **Lt. Col. Harold E. Hartney**, joined the organization's newly attached and Sopwith Camel-equipped 185th Aero Squadron - the only dedicated American night fighter unit of the war - for a night sortie. Hartney would end the evening giving the squadron its only wartime kill, a Gotha bomber. And though the wreckage was later found, Hartney would never put in a claim for this, his seventh kill.

After the Armistice the widely respected commander was transferred away from his beloved First Pursuit Group to A.E.F. Headquarters in Chaumont as Chief of Training and Civil Affairs. Upon his return to the United States in 1919 he served on the staff of the Air Service in Washington D.C. His passion for flying, however, got him away from his desk on a regular basis to take part in such events as the New York-to-Toronto Air Race, and the New York-to San Francisco Reliability Tests. Hartney flew a captured Fokker D.VII in the latter 1919 contest across the country and back to place first in his category.

Equally important for the future of military aviation, Hartney played an important role in General Billy Mitchell's sinking of the "unsinkable" captured German battleship *Ostfriesland* and her obsolete American counterparts, the *U.S.S. New Jersey* and *West Virginia*. Hartney would recall, "It was so easy it was child's play - when large bombs were employed."[7]

"In 1921," wrote Hartney in his 1940 biography *Up and at 'Em*, "I felt so keenly that the safety and much of the prosperity of the United States lay in the development of aviation that I resigned from the regular army and gave my whole enthusiasm to the building up of air consciousness on the part of the public."[8]

Hartney, who finally became an American citizen in 1923, would be instrumental in the creation of the National Aeronautical Association (NAA). An avid aviation supporter to the end, Hartney accurately foretold, before America's entry into World War Two, of the vast devastation strategic bombing would bring world centers and their civilian populations in what he believed was America's coming war.

He also correctly predicted the creation, in the not too distant future, of a new Department of Defense and a post for a co-equal secretary of an independent U.S. Air Force. Hartney was to see the realization of this latter prophecy on 18 September 1947 - three weeks before his 5 October death. He was 59.

Harold Hartney was survived by his widow, two daughters, and a son. Hartney's warrior son, James, had received his USAAF wings during the recent war. By the early 1960s he was flying

F-100 Super Sabre jet fighters. In late 1966 Jim Hartney, call sign: "White Fang," entered the Wild Weasel training program with good friend, Capt. Chuck Horner - later Lieutenant General Horner, commander of Allied air operations during 1991's Desert Storm.

In 1967, Jim Hartney and his Wild Weasel detachment joined the 357th Tactical Fighter Squadron of the 355 TFW at Takhli in Thailand. It was the Wild Weasels' extremely hazardous job to find and kill North Vietnamese surface-to-air (SAM) antiaircraft missile sites. On 5 January 1968, Major Hartney and his backseat Electronics Weapons Officer (EWO), Captain Sam Fantle III, were on an Iron Hand mission to Hanoi in their F-105F, s/n 63-8356, when they were shot down over North Vietnam by a North Vietnamese MiG-17. Tragically, the younger Hartney was stoned to death by local villagers. "He and his EWO," explained Horner, "were picked up by the Army and told to run for it across a field. If they were fast enough, the Army would protect them from the villagers. Fantle was fast enough to make it across the field. But White Fang was older than the rest of the Weasels…and didn't make it. He had a wife and a son. His wife died years later of cancer."[9]

Among the balance of the officers of the First Pursuit Group's cast of supporting characters, the 27th Squadron's later commander, **Alfred "Ack" Grant**, would end the war with three official aerial victories. Despite his strict West Point view of military discipline, he would be the first to recommend "bad boy" Frank Luke for the Medal of Honor. Alfred Grant would later return to civilian life, becoming a successful Los Angeles businessman.

Eddie Rickenbacker's regular flying partner and seven-plane ace, **Reed McKinley Chambers** would take command of the 94th Aero Squadron in Germany when Rick returned to the United States in 1919. Leaving the military, Chambers became a test pilot and in 1925 joined his old friend Rickenbacker in the formation of the short-lived Florida Airways. Chambers later formed the groundbreaking American Insurance Group to provide insurance coverage for fellow aviators. In 1968, the 72-year-old ace took over the controls of a two-seat F-106B Delta Dart jet interceptor long enough to break the sound barrier. He died on 16 January 1972.

The diminutive **Jerry Vasconcells**, the 27th's perennial peacemaker, ended the war with six official victories. In November 1918 he had taken command of the 185th night fighting pursuit squadron. He was promoted to major on 21 March 1919, and promoted to First Pursuit Group commander for the last month and a half before his return to the United States in April 1919. Vasconcells soon returned to civilian life and his native Denver, Colorado, to continue his successful investment career. He died of a heart attack at the early age of 58 on 17 April 1950.

Harvard's **Douglas Campbell**, who with Alan Winslow was credited with the 94th's first two victories, ended the war with six official kills. By 1939 Campbell was vice president of Pan American Airways; by 1948 he was its General Manager. After serving 24 years with PanAm, the father of six retired in 1963 Cos Cob and later Greenwich, Connecticut, where he died at the lofty age of 94 on 16 December 1990.

Another 94th ace, Cornell University graduate **Jimmy Meissner**, was given command of the First Group's 147th Aero Squadron on 24 July 1918. He had eight official victories by war's end. In 1930 he helped form the Alabama National Guard, which he later commanded. Meissner died at the young age of 39 on 16 January 1936.

Upon his release from German captivity the 103rd and 94TH flier, **James Norman Hall**, returned to the United States to continue his literary pursuits. With wartime friend Charles Nordhoff, Hall moved to the French Island of Tahiti in January 1920, where in 1925 he married a sea captain's daughter. With Nordhoff, he wrote a two-volume history of the *Lafayette Flying Corps* and *Falcons of France*, a novel about the corps for teenagers; but the pairing's most famous book was the classic *Mutiny on the Bounty*. Hall had 15 books published, many about the South Seas, before his death on 5 July 1951. He was 64.

New pilot and prewar champion University of Southern California athlete **Corliss C. "CC"/"Mose" Moseley** had joined the 27th Aero Squadron on Sunday, 29 September 1918 - the day Frank Luke went missing in action.[10] Was Moseley a field-side witness to Luke's dramatic unauthorized takeoff, this opening final chapter on a brilliant, all too brief career? One would like to think so.

As for Moseley himself, he would receive credit for downing one German two-seater near Witanville on 8 November 1918 - three days before the Armistice.[11] He remained in the Air Service for a period after the war serving as a test pilot. He won the Pulitzer International Air Race in 1920.[12] Moseley at one time had been in command of Air Service training and in 1924-25 founded the first air unit of the California National Guard, the 115th Observation Squadron based at Griffith Park.

Leaving the service with the rank of major, Moseley went on to become a legend in Southern California aviation, first co-founding and becoming first pilot for Western Air Express, later Western Airlines. By 1929 he was head of all Curtiss-Wright corporate operations on the West Coast, and as such became manager of their new Grand Central Air Terminal in Glendale, California that year. In 1944 Moseley would buy the air complex outright for himself. "He quickly became the dominant personality at Grand Central," wrote air historian John Underwood, "and would remain so for nearly four decades."[13]

Decades later, with the encroachment of suburbia, Moseley would be instrumental in converting the field into a prosperous industrial park.

With the approach of World War Two, Moseley opened a series of privately-owned primary flight and mechanics schools for the Air Corps at Glendale, Oxnard, Santa Ana, Lancaster and Cal-Aero Field in Ontario (today Chino Airport, Chino - by the year 2000 the facility was a major West coast site for "warbird" restoration and operations).[14] By the end of World War Two, Moseley's schools had graduated more than 25,000 pilots and 5,000 aircraft mechanics.

In his later years, Major Moseley became more interested in the breeding of his thoroughbred racehorses and cattle on his Wyoming ranch. He would die at the age of 79 on 17 June 1974 in Beverly Hills.

Corliss C. "CC"/ "Mose" Mosely had joined the 27th Pursuit Squadron that Sunday, the 29th of September 1918 - the day Frank Luke went missing. During his brief stay with the squadron, Mosely earned one official aerial victory. Mosely (in the business suit) is pictured here standing with the senior cadet and USAAF commanding General "Hap" Arnold on an inspection tour of flight training facility at Glendale, ca late 1941. Photo courtesy John Underwood

The officers of the First Pursuit Group had come home in 1919 with their fellow victors to the welcoming accolades of their grateful countrymen. Most of the fliers, often well-educated, intelligent, and industrious, went on to enjoy the rich fruits of a prospering nation, helping to shape its future through a myriad of divergent, and generally successful, even grand pursuits.

None, however, would surpass those of one determined seventh-grade dropout.

EDWARD V. RICKENBACKER

On 13 December 1918 Captain Edward V. Rickenbacker and Laurence Le Tourelle Driggs took rooms at the finest German hotel Coblenz had to offer. On 17 November, Rick, with a mind to his future, had contracted Driggs, the newspaper correspondent, to assist in the writing of his wartime memoirs, eventually to be titled "Fighting the Flying Circus." Within a week of their arrival in Germany, Rick, dictating his recollections to a busily writing Driggs, felt he had covered the material. By 30 December the famed wartime ace and racecar driver was negotiating the newspaper serial rights with the New York World.

Though the order of German occupation duty for the 94th Aero Squadron had been an honor, the assignment exposed its famed commander to unforeseen hazards. In Germany, Rick learned he was the most hated of the American fliers - the product, in large part, of the Kaiser's propaganda machine. Rickenbacker, so the wartime story line went, had served in the German Army and turned against the Fatherland to fight with the Americans.

Not wanting to further endanger a national hero, the War Department ordered Rickenbacker on 26 December to return to the United States. He arrived in New York to a hero's welcome on 1 February 1919, receiving his discharge a week later.

Not long after his return, Rick was approached by the B.P. Pond Lyceum bureau to give a series of Eastern and Midwestern lectures. Rickenbacker agreed, typically though, not before making thorough preparations. He engaged famed Hearst reporter

Damon Runyon, whom he'd first met in France, to write his speech.
Rick then turned to well known voice and elocution coach, Madam
Amanda to help with his delivery. He even made a point of study-
ing Emily Post's book on etiquette.

By the middle of April 1919, audience turnouts for Rick's
speeches were beginning to noticeably drop. By the end of May,
he'd delivered his last series lecture. "The emotional sustenance of
living on military glory after the war," Rickenbacker later confid-
ed, "is like living on cream. When the cream gives out, one must
start to live on skimmed milk."[15]

In June, Rickenbacker turned down what he felt would have
been an unseemly film about his recent combat days. By the second week of October he decided to return to his automobile roots,
seeking financing to found the Rickenbacker Motor Car Company
and create a line of cars built to his demanding tastes. The line's
famous, if immodest promotional line had come to Rick in a dream:
"Rickenbacker, a car worthy of its name."

But while the financial backing and design slowly began to
coalesce, Rick went to work for General Motors in late 1920 as the
sales chief for the Sheridan line of cars in California. Rick would
be the first sales executive to cover his territory by plane, a leased
Bellanca.

Photo courtesy Phil Jelinek

During the first week of September 1922 the slim, low-slung
lines of the new Rickenbacker car made a hit when it was first
introduced to the public at the New York Automobile Show. The
car, which now carried the 94[th's] old hat-in-the-ring insignia as its

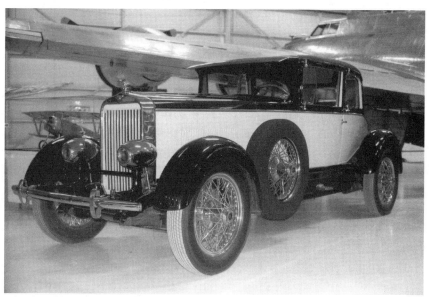

This handsome, mid-priced 1925 Rickenbacker Super Sport boat-tail is powered by an inline eight cylinder, 4.4 liter engine generating 105 hp. The Rickenbacker line was the first to incorporate four-wheel drum brakes on a mass-produced passenger car. Note the Eddie Rickenbacker- appropriated Hat-in-the-Ring logo very much in evidence, now as a corporate logo, on the automobile's radiator face and taillight displays. This beautifully restored and decidedly rare automobile is part of the extensive R. J. Pond auto and aircraft collection and was, in the spring of 2003, on public display at Pond's magnificent Palm Spring's Air Museum in Southern California. Author's photographs.

own, would register brisk and mounting sales for the next three years. The mid-priced line ranged from $1,485 to $1,985. By March of 1923, Rickenbacker Motors was producing 1040 cars a month.[16]

Riding the crest of his newfound success, Rick married divorcee Adelaid Durant on 16 September 1922 and headed off to Europe for a luxuriant three month honeymoon. In 1925 the couple adopted two sons, David and William.

Rickenbacker, the veteran racecar driver, knowing the inherent safety afforded by the system, broke new automotive ground for passenger cars by introducing four-wheel brakes on his 1924 models. Threatened by the engineering advance, and with a year's inventory of two-wheel brake cars yet to sell, the established auto industry, led by Studebaker, began a rumor-mill smear campaign suggesting the new braking system was dangerous. It forced the Rickenbacker Motor Company into bankruptcy by 1927. Rickenbacker himself shouldered $250,000 of the company debt.

After the demise of his company, Rickenbacker returned to General Motors to assist in the sales of the new Cadillac line, La Salle. Despite Rickenbacker's personal debt, his name, growing business aplomb and reputation proved sufficient to acquire the financing to purchase the Indianapolis Speedway on 1 November 1927. Within a season Rick had turned the Indianapolis 500 Race into a profitable national event with the introduction of an annual live NBC Radio broadcast of the race. He would finally sell the raceway in 1946.

Not many months after the raceway acquisition, Rickenbacker acquired the Allison Engineering Company, an aircraft engine concern, and promptly resold it to General Motors for a handsome profit.[17] Rickenbacker finally retired his debt by the acquisition and resale of the Pioneer Instrument Company, which eventually became the Bendix Aviation Corporation.

So impressed was GM Executive vice president Charles E. Wilson with the handling of the Allison sale that he invited Rickenbacker to become involved in their newly acquired Fokker Aircraft Corporation of America, selling their F-10 trimotor transport plane.

On 6 November 1930 in ceremonies at Bolling Field near Washington D.C., President Herbert Hoover presented the 40-year-old ace with a belated Medal of Honor for his actions of 25 September 1918. The bill had earlier been pushed through Congress by Congressman Robert H. Clancy.

When Fokker was merged under the General Aviation Manufacturing Corporation name and moved to Baltimore in December 1931, Rickenbacker, now a dyed-in-the-wool New Yorker, refused to move. In the midst of a worsening Depression, Rick was again without a job - but not for long. Within a month he was vice president of American Airways, and in February 1933 vice president of North American, a GM-controlled aviation holding company. And, for a while, Rick owned Sperry Gyroscope Company - which he would long regret selling.

Among North American's holdings in 1934 was a red-ink company called Eastern Air Transport. Its name was changed to Eastern Airlines later that year. The company would lose $1.5 million in 1934, but Rickenbacker believed he could turn the airline around, if he could give the challenge his undivided attention. General Motors agreed and made him general manager of Eastern Airlines in December 1934.

By the end of 1935, Rickenbacker's first full year in office, the airline showed a modest $38,000 profit. Rickenbacker was a tireless, hands on boss, personally learning every job in the company from baggage handler to ticket clerk. He understood profit margins and useless overhead when he saw it. His was a 14-hour day, seven days-a-week job; but the returns for the effort were promising. In 1936 Eastern showed a $168,602 profit, in 1937 there was $197,000 of black ink and in 1938 a truly impressive annual profit of $354,000 was amassed. When in 1938 he got wind of GM's intentions to sell the airline out from under him to Yellow Cab's John Hertz for $3 million, Rickenbacker adroitly arranged the financing to acquire Eastern for himself for $3.5 million.

And though Eastern Airlines' profits continued to mount, $884,000 in 1939, Rickenbacker placed his personal annual income at a modest $25,000 - the lowest salaried CEO of any railroad or airline then in the U.S. In 1940 Eastern netted $1,575,000.

Then on 26 February 1941, Rickenbacker was a passenger onboard one of his airlines' DC-3s when it became lost in fog on approach to the Atlanta Airport and crashed into a pine thicket near Jonesboro, some ten miles south of the state capital.

Initially, Rickenbacker's body was placed with the other dead crash victims - Eastern's first fatalities - upon arrival at Piedmont Hospital. And no wonder, he had a caved in chest with 12 broken ribs, a broken nose and dented forehead, a dislocated (externally hanging) eyeball, wrenched left knee, broken left elbow and broken hip. Movement, however, was finally detected. And in one of the world's many strange turns, Rickenbacker was attended to by Dr. Floyd W. McRae - the same Dr. McRae who'd operated on Rick's infected mastoid bone in Paris during the war.

The nation waited as Rickenbacker's condition remained touch and go for the next week. As Rickenbacker himself later liked to tell the story, when he heard the voice of commentator Walter Winchell announcing to the country that the famed WWI ace was dying, he tore apart his oxygen tent and lofted a nearby pitcher at the hospital room's radio - scoring a direct hit. It was then, Rickenbacker declared, he started fighting back. Recovery remained a long and arduous task. He would remain in the hospital for the next four months and continue to mend at a Candlewood Lake cottage in Connecticut with his family for many more additional months.

Then came the Japanese attack on Pearl Harbor and America's entry into World War Two. In March 1942, Rick, at USAAF chief Hap Arnold's request, made a 32-day inspection of stateside Air Corps' flying facilities, equipment and personnel. For the arduous flying trip, Rickenbacker was accompanied by a personal osteopath and masseur.

Upon his return, Arnold asked Rick to make arrangements with the other domestic airlines for the transfer of half their fleet and crews directly to military service, the foundation of the Air Transport Command.

At Long Beach Municipal Airport in So. California during the spring of 1942, Rickenbacker heralds the return of the 94th Fighter Squadron's long absent Hat-in-the-Ring insignia, appropriated years earlier for his long defunct automobile company. The 94th, then operating the new P-38 twin-engine fighter, began its deployment across the Atlantic within weeks of the presentation.

In September, Secretary of War Stimson asked Rick to inspect new U.S. air bases in England. On 13 October 1942, Rickenbacker returned with glowing reports of an experimental installation of a British Merlin aircraft engine in the airframe of an American P-51 Mustang. Rickenbacker urged immediate mass production.

So impressed was Stimson with Rickenbacker's insightful report that he asked the WWI ace-turned-airline executive to head to the Southwestern Pacific on a similar tour. On 13 October 1942, Rick's USAAF B-17D became lost looking for its refueling stop at Canton Island and ditched at sea. The world waited to learn of his fate. The Rickenbacker luck held again when after 21 days he and the crew were sighted by an OS2U floatplane pilot. His 1943 book, *Seven Came Through*, and subsequent 1945 motion picture, *Captain Eddie*, recount the ordeal.

After finishing the balance of his tour, Rickenbacker returned to the United States as "The Great Indestructible," more popular than ever. Even the Republican Party, with an eye on the 1944 presidential race, encouraged Rickenbacker to throw in his fedora. But he declined, well aware that his well known and negative views of labor unions foredoomed a campaign.

During the first week of April 1943 Stimson asked Rickenbacker to see if he could unlock the closed society of Russia. His international fame and reputation would open doors closed to all but a handful of trusted Russian party members. Rickenbacker returned to the United States with the Russian order of battle for the defense of Moscow!

By war's end, the battered and limping Rickenbacker had traveled more than 55,000 miles to fronts around the world for the Air Force and War Department. His reports had offered valuable information of the most sensitive kind.

He had once again served his country above and beyond the call, while at home his busy airline, with 6,700 employed by 1946, was showing 1945 profits of $2,126,000. Though Eastern had a reputation for operating on the cheap, with often run-down interior cabins, it nonetheless offered reasonable rates and "Eastern's double dependability...to get where [the passengers] were going safely and on time."[18]

On 17 April 1950, Rickenbacker made the cover of *Time Magazine*. He was called "One of America's most famous and successful men...an intimate of rulers, and a self-made captain of industry." The accompanying article went on to say "Rick... was the only living human soul who had ever been able to wring consistent profits from the debt-ridden peacock of modern transport, the airline industry."[19] In 1949 Eastern's net was again flirting with the $2 million mark - its 15th consecutive year of profitability.

Rickenbacker brought Eastern into the jet age in 1957 by placing $25 million worth of orders for an upgraded, turbine-powered fleet. In 1958 Eastern took delivery of 40 new turboprop Lockheed Electras. On 9 September 1959 the 70-year-old WWI ace retired from active management of Eastern. The airline's profit for the year was $11,403,000. It would be its last year of profit for many years.

On 1 December 1963, Rickenbacker finally retired from Eastern's board of directors. Rickenbacker and his wife indulged in travel ranging from Berlin to Africa. He retained an office in fashionable Rockefeller Center and in 1965 began dictating his

A senior Rickenbacker, with his ever present fedora, poses by a Spad at one of an endless list of public appearances he took joy in attending throughout his remarkable and long life.

final autobiography. He enjoyed television's *Bonanza*, as he had earlier radio's *Lone Ranger*. He disapproved of the government's handling of the Vietnam War - "don't let the enemy lay down the rules of the fight," and believed birth control was the key to world progress. He also believed "Utopias will not be realized until the good Lord permits a change in the basic structure of human nature."[20]

Around 1970, Rickenbacker and his wife finally gave up their beloved uptown New York for Coral Gables, Florida. On 12 October 1972 he suffered a massive stroke, but amazed doctors with his fighting spirit. In June 1973 he decided he wanted to make one last trip to retrace his ancestral roots. He was in Zurich, Switzerland, when doctors discovered his irregular heartbeat. Returning to the United States, Rickenbacker's 82-year-old heart finally gave out on 23 July 1973.

Upon committal of his ashes, next to those of his parents at Green Lawn Cemetery in Columbus, Ohio, a finger-four formation of 94th Fighter Squadron jets hove into view. Their leader steeply climbing his camouflaged F-4E Phantom II out of position as the jets roared over the mourners' heads.

David Rickenbacker, the World War One Ace's son, would remember the effect of the missing leader formation as "shattering."[21]

Rickenbacker will be remembered for his energy and his honesty; his orderly, analytical mind; his courage in both combat and corporate affairs, as well as his survival instincts. He had no love for unions, military commanders comfortably behind the front, or government interference. Nor did he have a high opinion of the French, Jews or African-Americans. But love him or hate him, as did President Franklin D. Roosevelt, Rickenbacker's word remained his bond until the day he died.

Today, the most tangible reminder of the Rickenbacker family is his childhood home that during the spring of 1999 was to become part of the *Motts Military Museum* display in Groveport, Ohio.

FRANK LUKE

As Rickenbacker began negotiations with the *New York World* for the newspaper serial rights to his forthcoming, ghosted wartime autobiography and prepared for his imminent and triumphal return to the Big Apple, a Graves Registration officer had come upon the burial site of an unidentified American flier. The site was located on 3 January 1919, in the small French village of Murvaux, situated some 20 miles North of Verdun in a shallow valley just east of the Meuse River. More interesting than the site itself for the investigating American officer, a Capt. McCormick of the 301st Graves Registration Station, were the extraordinary tales of the dead flier's last moments related by the local villagers.

During the second week of January, Colonel Harold Hartney received a transmission, dated 7 January, from Captain Merian C. Cooper, late of the 20th Aero Squadron (Bombardment),[22] detailing McCormick's findings. It read, in part:

"Subject…Unidentified Aviator:

"This officer was killed at Murvaux (5 kilometers east of Dun-sur-Meuse) on Sunday, September 29, 1918. The Germans stripped him of all identification, but Capt. McCormick was so interested in the story told by the French people of Murvaux that he exhumed the body and stated that it was that of a man of medium height, heavy set and with light hair. On his wrist he found an Elgin watch #20225566,[23] which was under the sleeve of his combination and which the Germans who stripped him of all papers and identification marks had evidently missed. The village people of Murvaux told Captain McCormick that the aviator first shot down three German balloons and two German planes,[24] then descended low over the ground and killed eleven Germans with either hand bombs or machine gun bullets. While flying low his plane was hit from the ground and he himself was apparently wounded. He made a successful landing, got out of his plane and when the Germans called on him to surrender he replied by drawing his automatic and opening fire, thus standing he continued to defend himself until killed. The description of this aviator by Captain McCormick and the fact that Lieut. Frank Luke dropped a note to a balloon company that day stating he was going to shoot down the balloons which were shot down make it almost certain that this officer was 2nd Lieut. Frank Luke."[25]

Following up on Cooper's later suggestion, an Air Service investigative team was sent to Murvaux, where on 15 January a signed affidavit was obtained from village witnesses. The latter statement adds the specific locations of two of the downed balloons as being at Briers Farm and Milly. And now, after being wounded while attacking the balloons, the affidavit states he flew back over Murvaux where he strafed and "killed six" (not eleven) "German soldiers and wounded as many more."

Upon landing, the American flier was seen to have gone some 50 yards down to the stream when he saw German soldiers advancing on him. He "still had the strength to draw his revolver to defend himself. A moment after he fell dead following a serious wound received in the chest."[26]

Among the 17 villager signatures were those of Cortine Delbart and Voliner Nicholas who placed the aviator's body on a

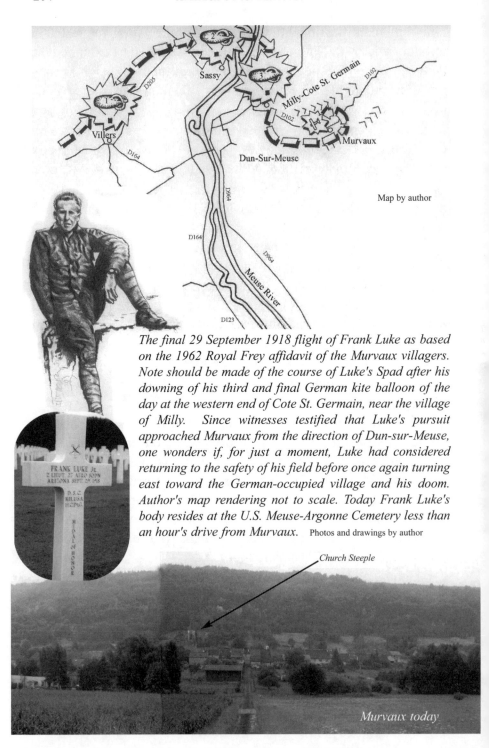

Map by author

The final 29 September 1918 flight of Frank Luke as based on the 1962 Royal Frey affidavit of the Murvaux villagers. Note should be made of the course of Luke's Spad after his downing of his third and final German kite balloon of the day at the western end of Cote St. Germain, near the village of Milly. Since witnesses testified that Luke's pursuit approached Murvaux from the direction of Dun-sur-Meuse, one wonders if, for just a moment, Luke had considered returning to the safety of his field before once again turning east toward the German-occupied village and his doom. Author's map rendering not to scale. Today Frank Luke's body resides at the U.S. Meuse-Argonne Cemetery less than an hour's drive from Murvaux. Photos and drawings by author

Church Steeple

Murvaux today

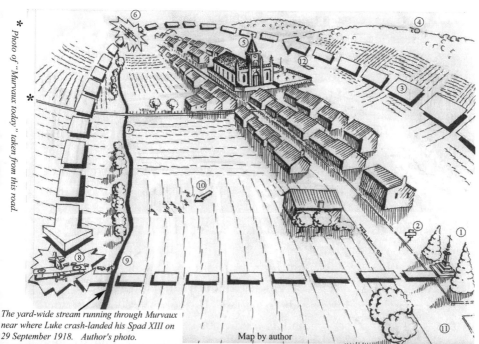

The yard-wide stream running through Murvaux near where Luke crash-landed his Spad XIII on 29 September 1918. Author's photo.

Map by author

The final moments of Frank Luke's last flight over the French village of Murvaux as outlined in Frey's 1962 affidavit. The author's out-of-scale rendering offers only a general approximation of the village as it appears today. (1) Nestled between a pair of trees is the Luke Monument in Murvaux today. (2) The sign marking the western boundary of the Village of Murvaux today. (3) The arrows mark the final moments of Luke's last flight. (4) A single German revolver cannon of 20mm or 37mm was located on the south hills overlooking the village. Another two similar guns were located in the hills to the north. (5) Luke's Spad reportedly flew past the village's church steeple near its top elevation. (6) Luke was reportedly struck by small arms fire upon turning back onto a westerly heading. (7) The creek. (8) Luke's Spad made a crash landing some 75 meters north of the creek. (9) Luke, fatally wounded, crawls down to the creek where he dies. (10) German soldiers run toward the sound of a single report from Luke's service automatic. (11) The beautifully maintained two-lane country road which runs through the heart of Murvaux today is D-102. (12) Frank Luke's body was initially buried, at the command of the Germans, in a shallow unmarked grave outside the walled cemetery of the village church.

horse cart and carried it to the cemetery.

When air historian Royal D. Frey visited Murvaux in July 1962 he interviewed three of the original signatories. For the first time, they were shown a photo of Frank Luke, which they confirmed was indeed the flier who came down in their village that long ago Sunday. The statement then acquired by Frey from the surviving witnesses in Murvaux proceeds to flesh out Luke's final flight in more detail. The specifics, as recalled in 1962, though, are at some variance with the earlier affidavit, its tone taking on a decidedly somber turn away from Cooper's initial 7 January report.

"Now I hate to change fact to fable," Frey later wrote, "but whenever you read that Luke fired at the German troops and they returned the fire, killing him, remember that it is not true. According to the French people to whom I talked in 1962, three of whom had signed the affidavit of 1919, Luke stumbled or crawled to a spot near the creek and as the troops came toward him he was apparently lying on the ground. He raised himself on one arm and fired at the Germans with the service automatic, and BEFORE (Frey's emphasis) the Germans could locate the source of the gunshot and shoot at it, Luke fell back on the ground, dead."[27]

According to the recollections of the resident-witnesses still residing in Murvaux in 1962, Luke's Spad approached the village from the west, from a region to the west of Milly-Cote Germain where the Arizona flier had just downed his third enemy balloon of the evening. Headed east toward Murvaux the American pursuit plane was reported by witnesses as flying at 50 meters, or some 150 feet off the deck. Three so-called "revolving cannon" of 20 or perhaps 37mm caliber, two located in the over-looking hills north of Murvaux and another at the crest of the hill to the south of the village church, peppered away at the Spad - along with every German rifleman within range. Because of his minimal altitude below the tops of the surrounding hills, it is unlikely Luke was downed by the heavier caliber guns.

Luke's Spad was said to be flying at the height of Murvaux's church steeple as it passed south of the church, between the church

The Luke family in 1930 on the occasion of the dedication of the World War One/Frank Luke memorial on the Phoenix Capital grounds in Arizona. Frank Luke, Sr. and his wife are seen at the center, back row. Photo courtesy R. G. Schipf

and the south-facing range of hills. At the east-end of the village
Luke banked to the north, or left around the church, apparently
intending to retrace his course back to the Meuse River and home.
It was at this point, as he rolled out of his turn at the northern edge
of Murvaux, again westbound, that he was hit - most likely by small
arms fire. At no time, the villagers now reported, did Luke fire at
anyone in Murvaux. Altering his course a bit to the right the Spad
was seen to make a power-on descent, setting down just west of the
village, and some 75 meters north of the meter-wide creek which
parallels what is now known as Highway D-102, yet another 200
meters to the south. German soldiers closing in on the landing site
from both Murvaux and the region of Milly reportedly reached the
abandoned Spad within ten minutes and followed a trail of blood
south heading toward the stream. Luke, who had been hit in the
right breast, the shell exiting near his left shoulder blade, had apparently crawled to the stream. Hearing the sound of the approaching
enemy, the Spad pilot apparently drew his automatic revolver and
fired once into the gathering darkness before dropping dead of his
airborne wound. The searching German soldiers, who had no target, were drawn to the revolver's report and found Luke already
dead.

According to Frey's 1962 affidavit, the local German commandant, arriving on the scene, reportedly commented, upon finding Luke's body, "Well, it was about time we got him."

Luke's exposed body was transported up the main street of
Murvaux in a villager's two-wheeled horse-drawn wagon. Some
50 feet beyond the church's south-facing graveyard wall, the body
was unceremoniously deposited in a shallow grave recently vacated by a German war dead removed for re-interment in his homeland. No funeral rites were performed or permitted. The Germans
loaded Luke's damaged Spad No. 26 on a truck for removal from
the village. The plane was never seen again.[28]

Despite ample evidence to the contrary, Arch Whitehouse,
always the dramatist, could not resist speculating about a more glo-
rious passing in his 1966 Luke biography *Hun Killer*.

"Some say," wrote Whitehouse, "he clambered over the crumbling stone wall of the churchyard and stumbled among the ancient headstones... German voices ordered his surrender... He watched them deploy, bracing himself against the monument. They fired, and he fired back, and his aim was deadly..."[29]

For those who have actually visited Murvaux, it is quickly grasped just what a fanciful impossibility such a heroically lauded scenario truly is. The church in Murvaux is a good quarter mile to the south of the stream and the walled graveyard still further beyond that. It was and remains an impossibly long trek for someone reportedly so gravely wounded.

According to Luke biographer Norman S. Hall, when Captain Grant heard the details of Luke's last flight and the subsequent ground fire fight, as related by Cooper and the villagers in their original 1919 affidavit, he immediately petitioned Hartney, recommending Luke for the Medal of Honor. "Grant was opposed to Luke's conduct from the standpoint of discipline, but he was the first to urge America's highest award for bravery for the flier he had ordered under arrest."[30]

In fact, suggests fellow Luke biographer Arch Whitehouse, such a recommendation, at Grant's hand, may have been in the works as early as 3 November 1918 - based on the sum total of the Arizona flier's known accomplishments to date. Grant's November recommendation reads, in part: "On many occasions, Luke had shown marked gallantry and courage during many combats with the enemy on the Chateau-Thierry, St. Mihiel and Verdun sectors...

By the year 2000 all that remained of Frank Luke's Phoenix home at 2200 West Monroe St. is the front concrete walk. Local television newscasts during the 1980s reportedly aired tales of the abandoned Luke homestead being haunted. The structure was gutted by fire and finally torn down during the early 1990s. Since 1999 much of the site has been walled in and converted to an auto repair compound run by Fair Exchange Auto Sales. Author's photo

As late as the year 2000 the Luke family continued to hold a place of prominence in the sprawling Phoenix community. Frank's youngest brother Bill's massive five-star Bill Luke Chrysler-Plymouth/Jeep-Eagle dealership at 2425 W. Camelback Rd. continues to do land-office business at the hands of Bill's son, and WWI ace Frank Luke, Jr's. nephew Don Luke. Author's photos

Lt. Luke probably made the most wonderful record in any army during the war ... for the length of time he was at the front." [31]

After the details of Luke's last combat came to light - as they were then known - Grant's recommendation was soon signed off by Hartney, who'd earlier recommended Luke for the Distinguished Service Cross. The nation's highest award became a reality when it was finally approved, on 14 April 1919, by the Commanding General, AEF, John J. Pershing. In ceremonies taking place at the Arizona State Capital not long after that, Frank Luke Sr. accepted the medal on behalf of his son.

The Luke family would return to the Capital steps 11 years later for the 1930 dedication of the towering Luke statue which today continues to grace the Capital grounds.

Nor is the Luke name today ever far from the minds or television screens of Phoenix residents. Aside from nearby Luke Air Force Base, the family-owned five-star, multi-block Luke Chrysler-

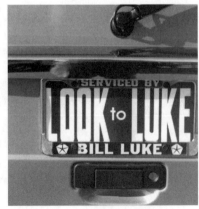

Plymouth/Jeep-Eagle auto dealership, founded by Frank's youngest brother Bill in the 1920s and by the year 2000 headed up by Bill's son Don, remains a major staple of Phoenix life at 2425 W. Camelback Road.

As for Frank Luke's old homestead at 2200 West Monroe Street in Phoenix, nothing remained in 1998 but a concrete walk-way on a bare sandlot and a handful of aging palm trees. By the year 2000 much of the former Luke homestead had been buried under a fresh layer of asphalt - the property employed by the neigh-boring Fair Exchange Auto Sales used car dealership for auto main-tenance. Located a scant quarter mile west of the modern, beauti-fully kept State Capital grounds complex, the former Luke lot resides amid the often rundown dishevelment of small area busi-nesses, aging commercial litter and poor, immigrant occupied 800-square foot adobe residences astride their barren sandlots.

The Luke home was reportedly torn down in the early 1990s - but not before making the local Phoenix television newscasts. After being gutted by fire sometime during the previous decade, the cinder ruins had become the site of teen gatherings and eyewitness tales of a haunting by the image of a young man with light hair.

In the spring of 1919 Frank Luke's body was re-interred at the military cemetery at Romague-sous-Montfaucon.

In the late 1920s, when Norman S. Hall asked Frank's father why he agreed to leave his son in France, Luke Sr. responded: "You see, when they took him to Romague where those thousands of other boys are, it seemed right to leave him there. He would have wanted it, I know that, and I wanted to do the thing that would have pleased him most. But sometimes, when I'm alone... he was such a darn lively kid!"[32]

Dick Day's beautiful replica Spad XIII at the Champlin Museum in Mesa Arizona. Number 26 was one of the five or more Spad XIIIs that Frank Luke went through during his brief combat career with the 27th Aero Squadron. The Blue cowling nose ring denotes a 27th Squadron aircraft.   Author's photo

Chapter Eleven

MILITARY HERITAGE

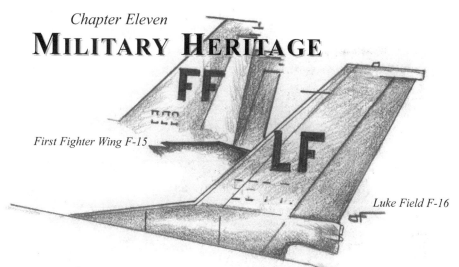

First Fighter Wing F-15

Luke Field F-16

T hey were the undereducated sons of poor working-class
immigrant families. Their impact on American society
should, by all reasonable estimates, have been calculated as negligible at best. Yet the native gifts of these two men, Rickenbacker
and Luke, represented a remarkable and rare confluence of certain
physiological gifts, principally in the areas of eyesight and hand-
eye coordination. These skills, coupled with a native intelligence,
particularly in the area of situational awareness, were aligned with
an extraordinary personal, and sociological-based drive to excel -
call it aggressiveness. These accumulated factors were then set
loose to a truly extraordinary degree within a wartime context by a
liberating brand of dismissive courage.

There remained, however, differences. What the city boy
Rickenbacker may have lacked in the kind of long practiced marksmanship and rough-hewn courage employed by "country cousin"
Luke, he more than made up for in his mature, carefully-weighed
practice of the calculated risk. Rickenbacker's long-practiced habit
of finding the tactical advantage to insure success today, as well as
his assuring another opportunity for tomorrow has become legendary within the fighter pilot community.

This unanticipated confluence of attributes within a pair of
blue-collar soldiers, each successful in his own way, and in turn

their timely arrival at the same place and same formative moment in the history of modern warfare, can have a long-term ripple effect on those individuals' respective military organizations. For the best of these skills continue to serve as an example and inspiration to those who follow.

SQUADRON HISTORIES

By December of 1969 the Air Defense Command's First Fighter Wing bore but a passing resemblance to its famed founding World War One unit, the First Pursuit Group. The Wing's three F-106 squadrons, the 94th, 27th and 71st, were spread across Maine, Michigan and Montana providing teeth for the U.S./Canadian radar Distant Early Warning (DEW) Line net guarding the northern approaches from the Soviet Union.

Worse, the air defense wing was facing imminent deactivation. General William W. "Spike" Momyer, the Tactical Air Command's commander, however, had other plans. In late 1970 he issued an edict to "retain illustrious designators for the active tactical forces."[1]

The recently retired and historically charged designators would be assigned to an F-4 Replacement Unit (RTU) then based at Florida's MacDill AFB. But which of the operational Phantom squadrons, then identified as the 45th, 46th and 47th, would receive which of the First Fighter's historic identities?

The 94th, America's first bloodied fighter squadron and the top scoring pursuit unit by the end of the Great War, led at war's end by the famed Captain Eddie Rickenbacker, carried more historic weight than say the 27th. And the 94th's record loomed mightily over that of the relatively new 71st which wasn't constituted until 14 December 1940.[2]

The solution came easily enough for the American commanders; there would be a modern rendition of an old fashioned Western shoot-out. The inter-squadron gunnery contest was held on 14 May 1971 at the Avon Park Gunnery Range. The 47th's commander, Lt.

By the late 1960s the U.S. Air Defense Command's First Fighter Wing's 94th, 27th and 71st Squadrons were spread across Maine, Michigan and Montana providing teeth for the U.S./Canadian Distant Early Warning (DEW) Line radar net guarding the northern

approaches from the Soviet Union. Both the 94th and 27th began receiving their first F-106s, such as the 94th's new 58-779 pictured here, in 1960.

Photo courtesy David Menard

Col. Donald W. Martin, scored a 113 of a possible 126 points to come in with the highest squadron C.O. score. Not surprisingly, he picked Rickenbacker's old 94th "Hat-in-the-Ring" unit number - and history - for his own. The second place unit, the 46th, acquired the 27th designator, while the 71st identity went to the third-place shooter.[3]

Two years later it would be a flight of four F-4E Phantom II's from the newly designated 94th Squadron that was called upon to perform the "missing leader" formation above the Columbus, Ohio funeral service on the occasion of the passing of the unit's famed WWI leader, Captain Eddie Rickenbacker.

THE POST-WWI "HAT-IN-THE-RING" SQUADRON

Seldom has a squadron commander made such an impact on a squadron or gained the notoriety that Rickenbacker had during his brief three months as the head of the 94th. By the end of December 1918, Rickenbacker, who had only taken command of the unit the previous 25 September, was gone - states-bound for a brilliant postwar business career. His place had been taken by his old fly-ing partner, now Captain, Reed Chambers.

On 17 November 1918 the 94th, which had ended the war with 67 official victories, had been detached from the First and assigned

This postwar 95th Pursuit Squadron Spad was just one of a wide variety of foreign and domestic types, ranging from the British SE-5 and German Fokker D.VII through the Orenco D, PW-5s and Thomas Morse MB-3 Scouts that equipped the Selfridge Field-based 1st Pursuit Group during the early 1920s.

First Pursuit Group P-1s airborne over Texas in their bogus German 'makeup' during the fall of 1926/spring of 1927 for their screen role in the silent air film classic Wings.

to the Fifth Pursuit Group for German occupation duty. The 94th's famed, much-photographed and outrageously flashy postwar aircraft paint schemes began to appear that December at Reed's command. It was an effort to relieve the unit's growing restlessness, as well as in anticipation of an April 1919 Banner Day celebration fly-by over the French capital, which in the end did not come to pass.

With the 13th Aero Squadron taking over their brightly-marked Spads that month, the war-weary men of the 94th had returned to the United States by the end of May 1919 where they were demobilized on 1 June.

In August 1919 a new First Pursuit Group became one of the three group-level flying establishments to make up what was soon to be called the U.S. Army Air Corps. Remarkably, the postwar Air Corps would remain a diminutive three-group organization for much of the next decade.

The group's first postwar commander of note would be Major Carl Spaatz, the former Issoudun training field commander and later head of WWII's famed Eighth Air Force. Once again the group was comprised of the 94th, 95th, 147th and the 27th Squadrons, the latter having ended WWI with 56 official victories and second only to the group's 94th in total aerial kills. As was true of Rickenbacker's later efforts, Luke's brief 18-day score represented a remarkable one-third of the squadron's total war-end record of aerial victories.

FALLING BY THE WAYSIDE

The Ninety-fifth "Kicking Mule" Pursuit Squadron, which ended WWI with 47 aerial victories, remained a part of the First Pursuit Group until June 1927 when it was assigned to the Air Corps Training Center, and on 1 June 1928 it was attached to the 7th Bombardment Group. Its mission had long since changed to that of a bombing squadron by World War Two. Fully a third of the eighteen B-25s launched from the U.S. aircraft carrier Hornet in April 1942 for the Doolittle Raid on Japan were manned by volunteer

95th crews from the 17th Bombardment Group. Among them was 95th Mitchell pilot Lt. Ted Lawson, author of the classic autobiography *Thirty Seconds over Tokyo*.[4] Re-equipping with Martin B-26s later in 1942, the 95th saw combat in North Africa and Europe - escorted on occasion by P-38s of its WWI companion squadrons, the 27th and 94th! The Douglas A-26 later served as the unit's light bomber/intruder mount during the Korean conflict. By 1 October 1958, when the unit was deactivated, the squadron had been flying the B-66 medium jet bomber for two years.[5]

A new 95th Fighter Squadron, historically unrelated to its WWI designator, was activated in February of 1942. The squadron's P-38s were soon assigned to the 82nd Fighter Group and covered much the same combat territory during World War Two as the First Fighter Group, fighting its way through North Africa and Italy. Deactivated and reactivated a number of times during its post-WWII history, the 95th FS was most recently reactivated in September of 1974. The new 95th was, and remains, based at Tyndall AFB in Florida where it has long since turned in its

This Curtiss P-36, along with the Seversky P-35, represented the first of the U.S. Air Corps' so-called "modern pursuits," with their enclosed cockpits, all-metal semi-monocoque construction, monowing design with semi-retractable landing gear. The 27th Curtiss P-36 is clothed in a temporary experimental camouflage scheme used during the 1939 Carolina War Games at Fort Bragg. The P-35 and P-36 entered operational squadrons during 1937 and 1938 respectively.

Vietnam-era F-4s for F-15 Eagles. The Squadron gained nation-wide, if brief, notoriety early in 2002 when it was featured in the CBS Television network eight-part reality mini-series *AFP/American Fighter Pilot*. Unfortunately, the series was can-celed after the airing of the second episode. "Mister Bones," its present skeletal squadron insignia, traces its roots directly back to its separate World War Two origins.

Less fortunate was the designator for the First Group's 147th Squadron. The unit ended WWI under the command of former 94th ace Capt. J. A. "Jimmy" Meissner, with a total of 28 aerial victo-ries to its credit. On 14 March 1921 the squadron was redesignat-ed the 17th Squadron. The latter had been a WWI American pur-suit unit that had served with the RAF during WWI. The wartime squadron, equipped with Sopwith Camels, had amassed 53 kills and 11 more "out of controls." It was a total score, when recog-nized, second only to the 94th. Their squadron emblem was the winged snow owl.

Earlier still, the First Group's pioneering night fighting 185th, with Hartney's lone unofficial victory to its credit, had been per-manently deactivated during the spring of 1919.

Lost along the way was the 94th Squadron's famed Hat-in-the-Ring insignia which the War Department and squadron felt, the lat-ter reportedly with some bitterness, it was forced to drop in the mid-1920s when the unit's former wartime commander appropriat-ed the logo for his new line of automobiles, the Rickenbackers.[6] So, too, did the Schwinn Bicycle Company later acquire the Hat-in-the-Ring as its licensed trademark. In September of 1924 the squadron adopted the Indian head insignia of the newly consolidat-ed 103rd Squadron, which had earlier served with the French as the famed Lafayette Escadrille.

Perhaps less traumatic was the postwar adoption, approved 4 March 1924, by the 27th of a winged and diving falcon in place of its original wartime diving eagle. This, in an effort to distance the squadron's prized emblem, as originally drawn by the late 27th pilot Malcolm Gunn, from its commercial inspiration and roots - that of the Anhauser-Bush beer company's winged eagle logo.[7]

Between The Wars

For more than a decade the 1st was the only pursuit group in the postwar U.S. Army Air Corps. As such, it was solely responsible for what pursuit training and experimentation was carried out in the name of new fighter tactics and equipment. It would also provide the fodder for a major Hollywood motion picture.

Much of the First Pursuit Group's inter-war years were spent at Selfridge Field in Michigan. The initial postwar mounts of the unit's 17th, 27th, 94th, and 95th Squadrons included the British Royal Aircraft Factory's sleek SE-5, though Spad X111s, Fokker D.VIIs, JN-4s, JN-6s, DH-4s, Orenco Ds and PW-5s were counted in their eclectic inventory. In 1922 Thomas Morse MB-3 scouts were added to the mix. PW-8s were introduced in 1924, the first P-1s were on hand by early 1926, and PW-9s began appearing on the group rolls by 1930.

In September 1926, significant elements of the 1st Group, along with dozens of their group aircraft, principally the new Curtiss P-1s, were assigned temporary duty at Kelly Field in Texas for the filming of veteran WWI flier-turned-director William "Wild Bill" Wellman's classic silent feature film *Wings*. Once in the Lone Star state, the P-1s donned a coat of "bad guy" black and large white theatric, historically incorrect Maltese crosses to portray a sleeker rendition of the German Fokker. The 1st Group pursuits appeared opposite the Thomas Morse MB-3s of the 10th School Group's 43rd School Squadron serving the U.S. Army Air Corps Advanced Flying School at the field. The latter aircraft type repre-sented Allied Spads in the film. A handful of original Spad VIIs and Fokker D.VIIs were sprinkled through the production's airfield and flying sequences to lend an air of authenticity to the feature.

The temporary stay, however, stretched into more than half a year of mostly stand-by duty on location waiting for cooperative weather and technical problems to be ironed out. Among the 1st

Pursuit Group fliers on hand were Lieutenants Clarence "Bill" Irvine, a gifted engineer, and Bill Taylor who worked closely with lead cameraman Harry Perry to develop the remote-controlled cameras used to film the flying lead actors in the air.[8]

Despite the enthusiastic box office reception of *Wings*, widespread "good press" for the young air service and receipt of the Motion Picture Academy's first ever Best Picture Award in 1928, the Air Corps had had enough of Hollywood for the moment. Though the film's success generated a flood of filmland requests for further 1st Group cooperation, the service politely, but emphatically demurred for the balance of the decade.

The group continued to evaluate and troubleshoot a wide variety of new aircraft types into the 1930s beginning with the classic and well received Curtiss P-12, along with a host of less popular types, including the P-2, P-3, P-5, P-6, and P-16. In 1933, the famed and popular, if obsolescent P-26 "Pea Shooter," with open-cockpit, fixed-gear and externally-braced mono-wing, was introduced and flourished within the unit.

Less well received was the ill-conceived and tragic assignment of the ill-equipped and trained Air Corps to temporarily fly the U.S. Mails between February and June of 1934. The 1st PG lost two pilots and ten aircraft during this sad, politically inspired chapter of early American military aviation history.

Still newer aircraft types were introduced into group service as the decade progressed. Certainly problematical was the P-30 (PB-2) flown by the squadron during the 1934-38 period until the introduction of Seversky's demanding P-35 and more popular Curtiss P-36 in 1937 and 1938. These were followed the next year by the upgraded P-43 and P-40B.

The decade proved a challenge to morale on a number of fronts. The field testing of new aircraft types saw greater losses of men and machines than desired by a peacetime organization. So, too, did the Air Corps turn to the veteran 1st in 1932 for men and equipment to seed the new 20th and 8th Pursuit Groups.

DARK HORIZONS

As tensions increased in October 1940 on the Pacific Rim, the 1st Group's 17th Pursuit Squadron was detached for service in the Philippines where it would endure the full brunt of the opening Japanese assault a year later. In January of 1941 the 71st Pursuit Squadron (the "17" designator cleverly and intentionally reversed) was activated at Selfridge as the 1st's new third squadron, its initial presence seeded with more veteran 94th and 27th personnel and equipment. And as the 1st's original two parent squadrons pressed ahead with training to get the new 71st up to speed, morale again became a factor as further personnel were drained away that year, first to seed the new 51st Group. The 1st was bled once again in April 1942, for the new 82nd Group.

A NEW MOUNT

In July 1941 the 27th, now officially the 27th Pursuit Squadron (Interceptor) became the first squadron of the group to receive the new P-38 twin-engined, high-altitude fighters. The Lockheed Lightnings were a quantum leap beyond the relatively simple "Pea Shooters" of just four years earlier, with wingspans, speeds, altitude, range and certainly operational and maintenance complexities near to, or far exceeding, twice those of the P-26.

It would be several more weeks before the 94th began receiving their own Lightnings, their older types of aircraft, as well as those of the 27th being passed down to the new 71st.

On 7 December the air echelon of the 94th, some 20 P-38s strong, found itself at El Paso en route to California's March Field for a 90-day temporary duty assignment when it learned of the Pearl Harbor attack. By the 10th, the 94TH had been joined at their newly assigned San Diego locale by the balance of the First Pursuit Group's P-38 Lightnings from the 27th along with the 71st's

Republic P-43 Lancers.

During the first three months of 1942, ranks of the Lightning-pioneering 1st were tapped again and again for the experienced personnel needed to jump-start the Air Corps' rapidly expanding wartime fighter units. Ninety-fourth and 1st Group members provided the "seed material" for the newly formed 80th and 82nd Pursuit Groups.

In March of 1942 Air Corps chief, Henry "Hap" Arnold asked Eddie Rickenbacker to go on a nationwide fact-finding and morale boosting tour of USAAF units. In Southern California, the World War One ace ran into his old 94th outfit, then assigned to coastal defense patrol duty and temporarily based at the Long Beach Municipal Airport.[9] At his old squadron's request and with Arnold's hearty approval, Rickenbacker saw to it that the unit's original Hat-in-the-Ring insignia was returned to the P-38 outfit.

In late June, the recently redesignated 94th Fighter Squadron and First Fighter Group took part in Operation Bolero, the overseas deployment of bomber and fighter units directly by air to Europe in staged hops across the North Atlantic. By the end of July both the air and ground elements of the 94th and 71st Squadrons were in place with the new Eighth Air Force in England. The 27th had been left in Reykjavik, Iceland, on temporary air defense duty and would not rejoin the group until August.

The 94th and 27th were transferred in November 1942 to North Africa with the group. Now serving with the Twelfth Air Force, it operated from a series of bases through Algeria, Tunisia and Libya. Initial escort and fighter-bomber sweeps flown by the green American airmen generated less than spectacular results. Nor were commanders convinced of the heavy twin-engined P-38's suitability to combat with Germany's more agile Bf-109. Growing experience bore welcome fruit on 5 April 1943 when the group caught a formation of escorted Junker transports evacuating German troops out of North Africa. The final score was 11 JU-52s, a Bf-109 and Fiesler F-156 Storch.

In late August 1943, between the close of the fighting in Sicily and the Allied landings in Italy proper at Salerno, the 1st FG saw some of its most intense fighting of the Second World War. On 25 August 1943 in a low-level strike, with the 82nd Fighter Group, the 1st FG caught the large complex of enemy airfields around Foggia in central Italy completely by surprise. The 1st Group received its first highly coveted Presidential Unit Citation (PUC). For the action the 1st alone accounted for 43 JU-88 bombers, a JU-52 transport and an enemy fighter destroyed on the ground, with another JU-52 caught and destroyed in the air. Another 13 enemy planes and a locomotive were also damaged for the loss of two P-38s and their pilots. The 82nd accounted for another 21 enemy aircraft destroyed and 43 damaged for the loss of three P-38s and crews.

Five short days later on 30 August, the 1st earned its second PUC for the gallant defensive battle against superior numbers of enemy aircraft while escorting two groups of Martin B-26s to the Italian marshalling yards at Aversa. During a running battle with three successive waves of German fighters, the outnumbered 1st FG Lightnings destroyed eight of the enemy, with another three probables and three damaged for the loss of 13 of their own fighters. The citation called the action "a brilliant defensive aerial battle" for not a bomber was lost in the contest.[10]

By the second week of December, the group was operating from Gioia del Colle in the heel of the Italian boot. During the spring of 1944, as a member of the newly formed 15th Air Force, the 1st FG began receiving its first P-38Js. The group continued its bomber escort duties and occasional fighter sweeps, as well as fighter-bomber missions helping to cut the German's lines of supply and escape. But perhaps the unit's most famous missions occurred on 18 May 1944 when they successfully escorted a formation of heavy bombers out of the famed Ploesti oil fields in Romania, downing 15 of the enemy in the process. The action earned the 1st Group its third Presidential Unit Citation of the war.

Moving that August to the Island of Corsica, the group provided much needed air support for the successful invasion of Southern France. On 16 October 1945, after 36 years of near continuous service, the group and its squadrons were deactivated at Caserta Field near Naples, Italy.

The group's World War Two score of 440 aerial victories was more than double the 1st Pursuit Group's Great War total of 201. Also changed was the relative rankings of the 27th and 94th Squadrons as based on their aerial kill totals. While the 94th Fighter Squadron had amassed 136.66 official victories by war's end, the 27th led the group with 187 World War Two aerial kills and served as home to the group's two top wartime aces, Tom Maloney and Philip Tovrea, each with eight victories. Despite the continuing fame and notoriety of the Hat-in-the-Ring 94th and its last Great War commander, the 27th remains the USAF's oldest squadron and what is now the First Fighter Wing's historic top scoring unit.

THE JET AGE

On 3 July 1946 the First Fighter Group was reactivated to once again serve as a pioneering agency for the new technology of the post-WWII era - the turbine-powered fighter: the jet. Again the 27th and 71st Fighter Squadrons joined the 94th at California's March Field. But once again it was the 94th that would steal the lion's share of the group's thunder. Whether it was the squadron's handsomely-painted F-80 Shooting Stars, with their prominent Hat-in-the-Ring fuselage emblems, splashed nationally across the cover of a 1948 *FLYING* magazine, or, a year later, the unit's new swept-wing F-86A Sabres featured in the Hollywood and Howard Hughes air epic *Jet Pilot* - the 94th was THE USAF jet squadron of the immediate post-WWII era. In fact, few air buffs then or today who recall the F-86A flight demonstration team of the "Sabre Dancers" remember the popular air show team was a product of the 27th FS and not the 94th.

In May 1949, the 1st Group was transferred to the Strategic Air Command. As the group had earlier done in 1942, and would again do during the Vietnam era, the unit provided trained flight crews for

There was little doubt in the post-WWII public and mass media's mind. The First Fight Group, and particularly the 94th Fighter Squadron, were the premiere units of the new USAF, be the Hat-in-the-Ring emblem found gracing the cover of a national magazine or its aircraft featured in such Hollywood air epics as Jet Pilot. Shown here is the December 9, 1946 issue of Life magazine and the February 1948 issue of Flying magazine. Author's collection.

Sergeant Richard Abbott with P-38J-15, s/n 43-28746, "Maloney's Pony" at Salsola, Italy in September 1944. The Lightning was named in honor of the 27th's wounded top ace Tom Maloney. It is a tradition which continues to this day with Langley AFB's 1st Fighter Wing.
Photo courtesy John D. Mullins

The 27th's top World War Two ace Tom Maloney in 1993 in the cockpit of a 1st Fighter Wing F-15 named in his honor, "Maloney's Pony." Photo courtesy John D. Mullins

the new war zone in Korea. Returned to the Continental Air Command on 1 July, 1950, the group was transferred from March to Victorville (later George) AFB in California's Mojave Desert.

The group became part of the Air Defense Command on 1 January 1951. In an effort to cover all the probable northern approaches into the United States by the Soviets, air defense squadrons were widely dispersed, for the most part, across the northern regions of the nation. By 1955 the 94th was again based at Selfridge Field, while the 71st had moved on to Pittsburgh and the 27th on to Griffiss AFB, New York, and by October of 1959 to Loring AFB in Maine. Each squadron was assigned to a new air defense wing.

Changes also were being made in the equipment flown. The 94th transitioned on to the radar-equipped F-86D "Dog Sabre" in early 1953, and, in 1956, upgraded to the F-86L variant in 1956. Meantime, the 27th transitioned on to Northrop's F-89 Scorpion in 1952 and on to the Lockheed F-94C in 1954, and again transitioned three years later onto the F-102. In 1960 both the 94th and 27th acquired Convair's spectacular performing F-106A Delta Dart.

After the Korean War in 1955, the First Fighter Group (Air Defense) was again activated, though only the 94th and the 71st were assigned to the Selfridge Field organization. By January 1967, with air crews being assigned to Vietnam-bound units, the 94th was the only flying unit assigned to the increasingly fragmented 1st Fighter Wing (Air Defense).

By August 1990 and after General Momyer's "illustrious designator" program, the F-15C/D-equipped, Langley Field, Virginia-based 1st Fighter Wing - with the 94th, 27th and the 71st Squadrons on board - had once again arguably become the USAF's premiere fighter organization. As such, it would be the first to be fingered for duty during the Operation Desert Shield/Gulf War buildup. Though only the 27th and the 71st would initially be deployed, the wing would be credited with one of the first shoot-downs of the conflict.

The 94th and 27th have had a virtually unbroken 80-plus year record of service. Today, the 27th remains the USAF's oldest operational fighter squadron, while the 94th was the first American pursuit squadron to claim an aerial victory and, by the end of WWI, was the nation's top scoring pursuit outfit. Their record, their heritage, and their fame was seeded and seasoned by the sweat and blood of a pair of poor immigrant sons who wanted nothing more than to succeed in their adopted homeland.

AIR BASES

In 1917, shortly after the United States' entry into World War One, the U.S. Army purchased Ford Island in the middle of Pearl Harbor's East Loch, on Oahu in the Pacific's Hawaiian Island chain. The price for the one and a quarter by a half-mile wide landmass was $236,000. The island had been known in earlier times to the original Hawaiians as Mokuumeume or the "Island of Strife." Later it had been called "Rabbit Island," "Marin's Island" and still later "Little Goats Island" - until 1886 when Dr. Seth Porter Ford married the island's then owner, Ms. Carolina Jackson. During World War One, when the Army moved onto what was then known as Ford Island, they displaced the Oahu Sugar Company to build a military airfield on the island's western side.[11]

The Army airfield became operational with the wartime arrival of the 6th Aero Squadron on 25 September 1918. Between 1918 and 1920, the squadron operated Curtiss N-9 seaplane trainers, R-6s, Curtiss HS2L flying-boats and JN-6 and DH-4s from the site. It was around 1919 that the name of the Ford Island Army Air Field was officially changed to Luke Field in honor of the World War One air ace and Medal of Honor recipient Frank Luke.

On 1 January 1923 the navy took up residence on the east end of Ford Island with its Pacific Air Detachment led by Commander John Perry Rodgers, Naval Aviator Number Two. By 1936, Naval Air Station Pearl Harbor, also known as NAS Ford Island, had grown to overflowing. Consequently, Luke Field was closed, its hangars and associated army structures turned over to the navy.

The army, in turn, moved its operation a stone's throw south to the newly completed Hickam Field complex. As part of a complex swap of airfields between the services that year, the navy also took over the army's North Island, San Diego site where Luke had received his primary flight instruction 18 years earlier.

And so Luke disappeared from the army's list of base names until construction began in 1941 on a new advanced and operational air training facility outside of Frank Luke's home town of Phoenix. Officially opening in 1942, Luke Field had graduated over 12,000 fighter pilots by the end of World War Two and become the largest fighter training base in the U.S. Army Air Forces.

And though talk of a feature dramatization about the remarkable wartime flier has continued to circulate through the Hollywood community since the late 1920s, it would be his namesake that would first and repeatedly actually make it to the big screen. Luke Field first went before the Hollywood second unit cameras for the basic training flight sequences featured in the 1943 MGM air classic *A Guy Named Joe*. In 1945 a Luke auxiliary field stood in for an American Volunteer Group (AVG) field in China for the Flying Tiger/Colonel Bob Scott air epic *God Is My Co-Pilot*. Prominently featured were the field's own 544th Single Engine Flight Training Squadron P-40E/Fs, and Luke or nearby Williams Field AT-6s - the latter serving as the ubiquitous "Hollywood Zero." Additionally, eighteen 952nd B-25 Transition Group B-25Gs (principally) were flown in for the filming from Sacramento's Mather Field.[12]

Luke Field was deactivated in 1946, but was reopened in 1950 at the onset of the Korean War. The base's resident 127th Pilot Training Wing provided flight instruction for fliers from countless friendly nations, including France, Belgium, Italy, the Philippines, Pakistan, South Korea, Iran, Free China, and the United Kingdom.

In November 1952 the 127th became the 3600th Combat Crew Training Wing, Fighter (CCTW). By 1958 the 3600th CCTW was instructing principally on the F-84F and newer F-100. It was in this year that Hollywood again returned to Luke for the epic Twentieth

A March Field-based 94th FS F-86A, c1950. This aircraft, s/n 48-130, took part in the Howard Hughes production of Jet Pilot. Photo courtesy David Menard

The 27th Fighter Interceptor Squadron operated the F-94C Starfire from 1954 through 1960. Photo courtesy David Menard

Saturday, 18 May 1974, 45,000 visitors were present for the official renaming and dedication of Ohio's Lockbourne Air Force Base as Rickenbacker AFB in honor of the recently deceased World War One ace. On display for the occasion was one of Rickenbacker's original racecars and a Spad in his famous-number "1" markings.

Century-Fox wide-screen color feature *The Hunters*. The Korean air war drama starred Robert Mitchum and Robert Wagner and featured the 3600's F-84Fs, repainted a drab gray for their role as communist MiGs, opposite the F-86F Sabres from nearby Williams AFB's 3525th CCTW. Hollywood craftsmen turned the remarkably barren Luke Auxiliary One into a thoroughly authentic Korean Sabre base for the film's fictional "54th Fighter Group."[13]

In 1958 the 3600th became the 4510th CCTW. By the 1960s, in addition to the operational training of F-100 pilots, the base became host to a long line of West German Luftwaffe pilots training on the unforgiving, Mach-Two F-104 Starfighter. Hollywood again turned to Luke and the Luftwaffe when they needed a pair of German-owned/USAF-marked F-104s from the 58th TFTW for 1983's *The Right Stuff*.

By the 1990's Luke AFB had become the largest fighter training base in the Western World and home to principally the 58th and 405th Tactical Fighter Training Wings, training both USAF and foreign pilots on the F-5, F-16 and F-15. Base operations were supported by 5,543 military and 1450 civilian personnel. The field's massive acreage includes 4,197 acres at the main site, as well as another 2,700,000 acres at its Gila Bend bombing/gunnery range.[14] A decade later, Luke became home to the largest fighter wing in the USAF inventory, the 56th TFTW (formerly the 58th TFTW), redesignated after WWII's famed 56th Fighter Group, which is dedicated exclusively to the training of F-16 Fighting Falcon pilots.[15]

RICKENBACKER: A LATE BLOOMER

On Saturday, 18 May 1974, with 45,000 visitors present for an Armed Forces Day open house, Ohio's Lockbourne Air Force Base was officially renamed Rickenbacker AFB in honor of America's World War One "Ace of Aces," Captain Edward V. Rickenbacker. The dedication ceremony, which took place some ten months after the great ace's 23 July 1973 passing, was attended by Rickenbacker's two sons, David and William. Speeches were offered by master-of-ceremonies and noted radio/television personality and air power supporter Arthur Godfrey, along with General John C. Meyer, Commander in Chief of the Strategic Air Command and Under Secretary of the Air Force, James W. Plummer.

Among the exhibits on hand were a Spad fighter in Rickenbacker's famed Number One markings - all but lost in the shadow of its ramp mate: a new F-15 Eagle. Also on display was the white 1914 Dusenberg with which Rickenbacker sped to a 10th place finish in that year's Indianapolis 500 Race.

As had Phoenix's Luke Field - Lockbourne, so named for the nearby town, had opened for business in 1942. Initially a glider pilot training school, by October of that year the field had become a four-engine pilot training school - which it would remain until war's end.

In 1946, the field became home to the all-Black 447th Composite Group. In 1949 the field was occupied by the Ohio National Guard. In April 1951 Lockbourne AFB was transferred

By the year 2000 Arizona's Luke Air Force Base, established in 1941 outside of Phoenix, had become the largest fighter training base in the Western world with more than 200 F-16s assigned to the massive facility.

from the Eastern Air Defense Command to the Strategic Air Command. The field was soon home to the RB-47s of the 801st Air Division, the 91st Reconnaissance Wing arriving that September, and the 26th SRW arriving the following May. The B-47s of the 301st Bombardment Wing, Medium arrived at the field in April 1958.

In 1964, Lockbourne became home to the 840th Air Division and the C-130s of the 317th Tactical Airlift Wing, replaced by those of the 302nd TAW in August 1971.[16] The year 1964 also saw the redesignation of the 301st to that of an air refueling wing and re-equipped with KC-135 jet tankers.

In April of 1980 SAC turned the base over to the Ohio Air National Guard. By 1990 the base was home to the Ohio Air National Guard's 166th TFS, operating A-7D/Ks and 145th Air Refueling Squadron, operating KC-135s. The Air Force Reserve also made its presence felt with the 356th Tactical Airlift Squadron, operating C-130As.[17] By the end of the decade the base was home to the KC-10s of the 121st Air Refueling Wing. In 1997 Hollywood would call on the unit for a brief sequence in Columbia-Tristar's *Air Force One*. By 1990, the base's 1,836 military and 406 civilian personnel operated from the base's some 2,016 acres of operational real estate.

By 1999, the Air National Guard base was but a modest portion of a field that had become a rapidly growing commercial enterprise, known today as Rickenbacker Airport. The field, now home to Federal Express, ranks 47th in size of the nation's 140 air-cargo airports, the neighboring foreign-trade zone complex is home to 50 growing companies, 12 of these, Fortune 500 money-makers. The Rickenbacker Port Authority, which manages the airport, has projected revenues approaching $3.9 billion by the year 2003.[18] They are figures to warm the heart of an old Eastern Airlines CEO and field namesake.

Luke Air Force Base F-16

First Fighter Wing F-15s

Chapter Eleven
Insert No. 1

A MATTER OF PRIDE

World War Two P-38 pilot Frank Lawson, fresh out of flight training, recalls his first day with the 27th Fighter Squadron in North Africa:

"8/23/43: First impressions are usually lasting and as one of six new pilots assigned this date, that memory is still quite clear. The squadron was based on a dry lakebed (dry until the rains began) just outside the little town of Mateur, about 40 miles inland from the port city of Bizerte, Tunisia. Everyone was reasonably friendly, but there was a 'no nonsense' attitude which made it clear that the drills, training and such were a thing of the past. Before we even had a place to unroll our gear, Lt. Butler, the operations officer, sat us down in the intelligence tent and had us read a copy of the squadron history. The 27th was and still is the oldest fighter squadron in the Air Force, dating back to May 1917. Pride in the squadron ran deep and we were expected to 'measure up.'"[19]

Col. Francis Robert "Frank" Lawson, USAF (Ret.)

Chapter Eleven
Insert No. 2

THE 27th: ANOTHER WAR, ANOTHER ACE OF ACES

One of the 27th Fighter Squadron's top scoring World War Two aces, Oklahoma son Tom Maloney, understands where Eddie Rickenbacker, Frank Luke, Joe Wehner and their similarly humble brethren had come from. As a matter of fact, his clear-eyed appraisal of that earlier group of 1st Pursuit Group fliers pretty much sums up in a couple of sentences one of the major thrusts of this volume!

"Back in 1918, Billy Mitchell naturally turned to the colleges for some men with smarts. But what he didn't take into consideration was that, at the time, for someone to go to college he almost had to come from a silver spoon family. A lot of these guys had never had to hustle a day in their lives. And a lot of the World War One aces, the big scorers, were from relatively poor families, and they had had to hustle and scrounge like a dog for everything they ever got. That's where they got the edge on those boys from Harvard and Yale.

"That's the first, most important element of any fighter pilot worth his salt: aggressiveness. It was as true then as it is today. But, of course, it's hard to blame those guys because their folks had always provided them with everything they needed. They didn't need to be aggressive. Personally, I think that had a lot to do with it."

Today Tom recalls that, as during the First World War, the 1st Fighter Group entered World War Two uniformly staffed with pilots required to have two or more years of college behind them. That would not still be the case when he joined the group some two years later. The educational barriers had already begun to fall in the face of the accelerated Air Corps expansion program as it moved into high gear even before the December 1941 attack on Pearl Harbor. And with a wartime casualty attrition rate running around a third of the unit's pilots, the demand for a high volume of replacements remained high throughout the Second World War.

Today, the Depression-reared Tom Maloney recalls:

"I was 19 years old when I entered the Air Corps. I had one semester at Northwestern Missouri State Teachers' College. I was so poor I had to drop out because I had a basketball scholarship, but absolutely no money; and I found out you can't live with absolutely zero money. So, I dropped out and joined the service on Friday, the 13th of June 1941."

The severely wounded veteran today comments with a touch of bemused irony, "Friday the 13th - I should have known better, but I didn't."

Tom Maloney joined the U.S. 12th Air Force's 1st Fighter Group and their 27th Squadron in North Africa on 18 October 1943. The activities of the P-38 group were then divided between occasional tactical air-to-ground work and, more often, the escort of relatively small bomber formations, most often Martin B-26s. The latter assignment became the unit's principal occupation when they joined the new 15th Air Force in Italy during 1944.

"What few people appreciate," adds Maloney, "is that when the 15th Air Force was formed we had two to three times as many heavy bombers as fighters to escort them. Consequently, we didn't have enough fighters to cover all the various wings of bombers. So the Germans would often merely fly down the bomber formations until they found an unescorted bomber wing and go in for the attack.

"The 1st Fighter Group in Italy flew under strict restrictions to always stay with their assigned bomber wing. The only time we ever, ever got into a fight was when the German fighters were persistent in trying to attack us. On the escort missions the Germans always seemed to appear two to four thousand feet above us. They had an excellent radar system in place and always knew our altitude. If they started to attack the wing of bombers we were escorting, we, of course, would engage, turn into them, but the Germans would almost never mix it up with us. When we met their attack they would simply turn on their backs and dive away, and we, per standing orders, stayed with our assigned bombers.

"The newer (15th AF) fighter groups were allowed to go ahead and attack the Germans, but in the 1st Fighter Group we seldom were. While I was there, the 1st Fighter Group's score reflects the kind of defensive aerial war we were ordered to fight.

"All the victories I got, with a couple of exceptions, were made in breaking into the German fighters and getting to them quickly before they could dive away."

And unlike the brand of free-for-all aerial engagements of Luke and Rickenbacker's earlier war, the lion's share of Maloney's opportunities would only come after he had paid his dues and moved up the more structured finger-four formation ladder from wingman to element and then flight lead. And while Rickenbacker and Luke were permitted to amass their relatively large bags of aerial victories during an unending series of two-hour voluntary patrols, that was certainly not the case in 1944 Italy where assigned missions could run an exhausting six hours at high altitude. Unlike the problematic, back-biting Spads and Nieuports of that earlier era Maloney doesn't hesitate to call his twin-engined Lockheed mount "The Cadillac of Airplanes." The Germans aside, the 27th ace found the P-38 also vastly superior to the P-47 Thunderbolt and even marginally superior "in the right hands," he adds, to the vaunted P-51 Mustang.

By 19 August 1944, Captain Maloney was the 27th's operations officer and the squadron's leading ace with eight aerial victories to his credit. It remains a 27th tally equaled by Philip Tovrea, but never surpassed before the war's end. That day, however, Tom Maloney would begin a new, grimmer war that would test his resolve and courage as had no other contest before.

Leading an element of a flight of 27th P-38's on a low-level air-to-ground strike over Southern France, the quartet exploded what turned out to be an ammunition train. The resulting series of extremely violent explosions damaged all the Lightning fighters in the vicinity, including, fatally so, both of the engines on Maloney's fighter. Successfully ditching off the French coast, Tom eventually made his way to shore where he stepped on a land mine some fifty feet inland from the surf line. Underground partisans got Maloney out of Nazi-occupied territory and eventually to a stateside hospital. And along the way the 27th ace tenaciously engaged in the fight of his life, even enlisting, at one point, the support of his group commander in his war to stop the doctors from amputating both of his shattered legs.

Finally released from the hospital in October 1947, Maloney used the GI Bill to get the college education denied him before the war. On graduation in 1951 the steel-willed ace dove headlong into the dog-eat-dog world of the Oklahoma oil business where he soon had his own long-thriving drilling company.

Today, Langley Air Force Base's 1st Fighter Wing and their 27th Squadron continue to maintain an F-15C Eagle fighter with the legend and art work of Maloney's Pony on its nose, in honor of a P-38 from an earlier war and the man for whom it was named.[20]

Chapter Eleven
Insert No. 3

A QUESTION OF AGGRESSIVENESS

The following is a discussion with Major General Frederic C. "Boots" Blesse, USAF (Ret.), an Army doctor's son who grew up wanting to follow in the footsteps of his childhood hero, Captain Eddie Rickenbacker. His classic treatise on air combat maneuvering (ACM) - or dogfighting - *No Guts, No Glory*, would have a profound effect on fighter tactics during the latter phases of the Vietnam War. Earlier during his formative years as a fighter pilot, Blesse had flown F-86 Sabres with Rickenbacker's old 94th Squadron at George Air Force Base in the Southern California desert. He would subsequently return from Korea in late 1952 as America's leading jet ace with ten official victories to his credit.

AUTHOR: Given superior piloting skills and the requisite situational awareness assets, what additional factors go into the make-up of a superior fighter pilot?

GENERAL BLESSE: "I think that the one single quality that all of them possess, and that must be possessed, is aggressiveness. It's that aggressiveness that leads someone to try different things; it leads him to investigate and study. It's a prime asset. Without it you really don't have very much."

AUTHOR: With the history of Frank Luke in mind, is it sometimes an awkward fit for such an aggressive person within the constraints of a military organization?

GENERAL BLESSE: "No, I don't think so. Just because you have an aggressive nature, it doesn't mean you have to be obnoxious with it. You display that aggressiveness in the interests you take up. For instance, if you're a fighter pilot you're going to want to study. If you have the aggressiveness to be a fighter pilot and want to be a good one, you're going to study different things and read different things that other people are going to pass over.

"It doesn't mean you're walking around bumping into people all day long. That's not the kind of aggressiveness I'm talking about. The aggressiveness I'm talking about leads to inquisitiveness; it leads to greater learning. It leads to attempting to do the right thing at the right time and if you fail you try it again. And if you fail then you try it a third time. You keep trying it until you get it right. The person that's not too aggressive, he'll try it once, maybe even twice and then if it doesn't work - to hell with it. That's it.

"Another person, a more aggressive one, will make it work."

AUTHOR: You flew with both Ralph Parr and Joe McConnell at George AFB before they became such outstanding aces in Korea. Some have even likened elements of McConnell's nature to that of Frank Luke. Tell me about Joe McConnell.

GENERAL BLESSE: "Joe was a very competent pilot who operated right at the edge all the time. A wingman who was not quite as capable would probably have had a very difficult time with him. He and Parr and I were in the 94th Squadron in 1951 and in early 1952 at George.

"We did a lot of air-to-air fighting. Parr and I and McConnell probably did more of it than anybody else. It really paid off, because when we all got to Korea we got some 37 MiGs between the three of us. Parr and I both had had air-to-ground combat tours. His was in F-80s and mine was in P-51s and F-80s. When we all got to George and we started to do this (practice dogfighting) we were doing it with a purpose. We felt we were making ourselves better fighter pilots. We wanted to get into the air-to-air war with the MiGs.

"McConnell was extremely aggressive. He did things...if a

younger kid followed him around and said, 'Okay, I watched Joe do this, this is the way you do it,' he'd probably get himself into a lot of trouble. The better you are, the closer you can operate your airplane to its limits. Mac could do that."

AUTHOR: You called McConnell "extremely aggressive." Could this have played a part in his losing his life later in the F-86H test flight at Edwards Air Force Base?

GENERAL BLESSE: "Well, I think it borders on that. If my memory serves me correctly, he had a hydraulic failure in an earlier F-86, I'm not sure, out there at Edwards and he landed it successfully. He thought because of that he could do it again. The second time he tried, it just wasn't possible. The failures apparently were not identical, and by the time he got down to the point where he could see that they weren't identical it was too late. He was below bailout altitude and the plane was out of control and he lost it right there."[21]

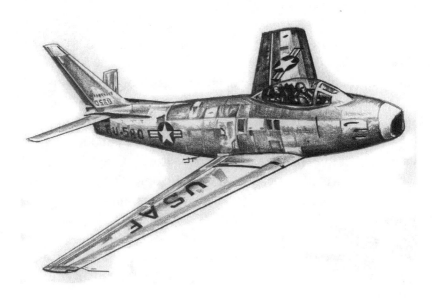

Final Chapter

FRANCE TODAY

Photo by Art Ronnie

The Author - James Farmer

It had been a quarter century since this writer had last seen France. The unseasonably wet weather during the late summer of 2002 did little to dampen the enthusiasm of the return. The people were no less warm, the cities no less vibrant, as only European cities know how to be, the countryside no less wholesome, nor, certainly, any less green.

Rather, quite the opposite was true. And though the roads, particularly those in the country, remain rather narrow by American standards, their upkeep and surface quality are second to none! The so-called "round-about" intersections, on the other hand, still take some getting used to for the neophytes among us — though speed limits beyond city and village limits are nonexistent.

In short, France today has an excellent infrastructure, ideally suited for the exploration of World War One and World War Two battle sites and bases. Further, the recent introduction of the "Euro" into Western Europe with a virtual one-for-one exchange rate with the U.S. dollar (as of 2002) has considerably simplified overseas travel in the region.

Though time constraints limited the number of sites this writer could visit in a two-week period, some small 'flavor' of the wide array of meaningful and historic locales offered by a personal visit to France may be gleaned from this brief, if decidedly personal, narrative.

This writer's 1,900-mile (3000-plus kilometer) journey in search of World War One-period sites, during the summer of 2002, began, not surprisingly, in Paris. Sitting that first evening in late July at a trendy outdoor café on the tree-lined Avenue des Champs Elysees, virtually in the shadow of the Arc de Triomphe, we thought of Luke. Had he aimlessly wandered down this kinetic street of forced wartime gaiety during that final leave of September 1918?

What, indeed, had been flowing through his dazed mind? Had he wandered along the Seine, perhaps made his way into the musty environs of the grand Notre Dame cathedral or viewed the Eiffel tower one last time? What is certain, the charms of the French capital were viewed in an entirely different light by the emotionally more mature, life-affirming Eddie Rickenbacker.

For those who wish to seek out some point of recognition for the origins of American involvement in the airwar of 1914-1918 there is the impressive **Lafayette Escadrille Monument** on the western outskirts of Paris in the picturesque forest in Saint Cloud. The massive iron gates with their cast Indian head insignia are found on Raymond Poincare Boulevard near the cross street of Rue Pasteur.

A brief drive down a tree-lined dirt path brings one to an informal parking area. A short walk across a small bridge opens onto a large expanse of lawns, reflection pond and beautifully kept floral gardens, all fronting the massive monument itself. Once in the monument, stairs lead down to the underground vaults where a number of the original fliers are interred, reportedly among them Raoul Lufbery.

Today, more than 80 years after the Great War, the monument itself is all but ignored by local families who prefer the nearby woods and water to walk their dogs and watch their children play. And this, too, is somehow fitting.

Heading south out of Paris for central France, we came across the sizeable town of **Issoudun** with signs clearly marked, showing us the way through the vast, level plains of golden grain fields, some nine kilometers out of downtown proper to the "aerodrome."

The gates' Indian Head plaques in Saint Cloud, on Raymond Poincare Boulevard, clearly mark the wooded entrance to the "Memorial de l'Escadrille LA FAYETTE." The monument is but a short ride to the western outskirts of downtown Paris.
Author's photo.

The imposing front of the Lafayette Escadrille Memorial and its facing reflection pond, had been built during the mid-1920s. A number of the famed squadron's fliers are interred here, among them, reportedly, Raoul Lufbery. Author's photo.

The former massive American flight-training center in central France at Issoudun is today a pleasant, up-to-date civilian aerodrome for small private aircraft and gliders. The field, located some nine kilometers outside of downtown Issoudun, also has extensive camping grounds for visiting families. Author's photo.

(In France today, a "sizeable town" was always confirmed by the presence of at least one McDonald's fast-food restaurant.)

A look at the World War One-period pictures on the civilian airport's lounge walls and a few questions confirm this is indeed the site of the once massive American aviation instructional center. Today the small, beautifully maintained civilian aerodrome is home to a sizeable host of privately owned gliders and small single-engined aircraft. The field's one large metal hangar and lounge/office are sided on their left by a large expanse of well-kept, enclosed lawn area for children to play in. Many are the offspring of the countless SUV campers who come to the attractive field for their vacation.

Setting out again on back roads through France's rolling farm-land, we drive toward the northeast, seeking out **Saints**. Nearing the village, we happen upon the small civilian airfield known as Aerodrome De Chaubuisson. What had originally caught our eye was the massive bulk of an old four-engined Breguet 763 Deux-Ponts airliner, which, as it turns out, has been converted into a pop-ular local aviation-restaurant. Though the airport has a vintage green quonset-type military aircraft hangar, the civilian aerodrome itself had not come into existence until the 1960's.

In the lounge, this writer again asked if anyone spoke English. We wanted to know if an airfield existed today near the town of Saints. A middle-aged gentleman volunteered that there was indeed a civilian airfield near Saints today, though he had no idea whether its origins could be traced back to World War One. He then graciously added, "Would like me to fly you over there?"

Though the weather remained marginal, as it was for our entire trip, we climbed into his small two-place Jodel homebuilt and headed for Saints! The pilot and this author's generous host was Andre Donzeau, a lieutenant colonel in the French Army Reserve - a specialist in Soviet and Russian military affairs. Flying in and out of small rain cells we made our way over the aerodrome at Saints, a small L-shaped arrangement of hangars and a single grass-cov-ered runway.

More interesting today was our overflight, on the return leg,

The author near the out-skirts of Saints. Note the area's typical rolling farmland. Art Ronnie photo.

The author (left) at Aerodrome de Chaubuisson with pilot Andre Donzeau preparing to climb into his small two-place Jodel home-built plane for the short flight to Saints. Art Ronnie photo.

An aerial view of the small civilian aerodrome at Saints today. Author's photo.

over the former World War Two German fighter base at
Coulommiers. There several concrete oval racetrack-style taxi
rings with their associated hardstands were still clearly visible from
the air.

It took little effort imagining how the squadrons of
Messerschmitt Bf-109s and Focke-Wulf FW-190s employed this
typically efficient German airfield layout to scramble after the
miles-long streams of American B-17s and B-24s flying into the
country, en route to their targets in France and later Germany.

As the European war wound down, the field was used as an
advanced base for American Ninth Air Force P-47s and P-51s, and
still later as a home field, in late 1944-45, for the A-20G light attack
bombers of the 410th Bombardment Group. Today, only a small
portion of the field remains in use as a civilian operation.

Before this early August day was over we had driven into
Touquin and found the handsomely maintained chateau Major
Hartney was so proud of requisitioning for his squadron during late
June-July 1918. Some 25 miles later we settled in for the night in
famed **Chateau-Thierry**. This latter resort town on the Marne
River had just been host to the Tour de France long-distance bicy-
cling tournament, again won that year by American Lance

*The chateau at Touquin where Hartney briefly housed
his pilots during late June-July 1918.* Author's photo.

Armstrong. Chateau-Thierry itself is a small, beautifully up-to-date city, home to a thriving tourist industry. And, yes, there is a McDonald's here!

The next day we made our way to the small village of **Rembercourt**. Typical of such small farming villages it was almost impossible to find anyone about. Yet, once again, when we pulled up in front of the village's surprisingly large church, a set of second-story shutters swung open and a villager offered to open the church for our visit.

Walking through the musty, gray, high-vaulted interior, one wondered if Frank Luke's Catholic traditions had beckoned him to this holy place during his last weeks of life. Did he make the brief journey from his nearby airfield on motorbike to offer up a prayer for his recently lost partner, Joe Wehner?

Soon, we were heading east out of town on the two-lane D 902 highway. Driving through vast rolling fields of golden grain crops it was not hard to imagine where the Rembercourt Aerodrome must have been located. For there, but a few kilometers outside of town, off the right shoulder of the road was the only handful of level acres for miles around. There was, however, no marker to confirm our suspicions.

Waking the next morning at our beautiful hotel in **Verdun** on the picturesque shores of the Meuse River, we headed for the well preserved battlefield sites, museums and vast cemeteries associated with the horrific bloodletting which took place there nearly 90 years ago. Among the first sights to greet us was the enormous vertical monolith at the **Douaumont Ossuary**. While, it is said, simple statistics tend to dehumanize war's personal toll - this is not always the case. For the expansive grounds of this Verdun cemetery alone house the remains of 130,000 *unknown* soldiers.

As we neared famed Fort Douaumont, a moonscape of sorts began to make its presence known on the road's shoulders. In 1916 this French fort had been bombarded *daily* with between 800 and 1,400 German artillery shells until its capture. The shell craters remain very much in evidence today, covered with a soothing green mantle of low grasses and a forest of young trees.

War-scarred Verdun

Nortre-Dame Cathedral

Beautifully restored Verdun today, looking across the Meuse River with the London quay (by the water fountain on the left) and the famed twin-medieval towers of Porte Chaussee by the bridge on the right. Author's photo.

The author at the Ossuary and National Cemetery at Douaumont near Verdun, the final resting place of 130,000 unknown soldiers.

Art Ronnie photo.

All that is evident of the fort above ground from the enemy's front of advance are rolling hills, punctuated at regular intervals with circular concrete foundations supporting black, steel-domed artillery and machine gun turrets. To venture forth into the seeping, perpetually wet underground galleries evokes strong feelings of uneasiness, of the closeness of death, feelings of almost being buried alive.

Heading north out of Verdun, we made our way to Highway D 998 and eventually to the **Meuse-Argonne American Cemetery** at Romagne. Covering more than 130 acres, this is the largest American cemetery in Europe, the final resting place of 14,246 combat dead.

The cemetery is also the final resting-place of Frank Luke. His specific gravesite location and those of the other eight Medal of Honor recipients there, are prominently displayed on the entry wall of the cemetery's reception center. Frank Luke's stone white cross, located in Block A, Row 26, gravesite 13 (A-26-13), has been made more prominent by the additional star and gold-coloring inlay of the cross's engravings denoting his Medal of Honor status.

Setting out again some 12 kilometers to the east and north across the Meuse River we passed through **Milly-St. Germain**, continuing on the two-lane Highway of D 102 before shortly entering the small farming village of **Murvaux**. The steady light rain this August day seemed to well set the mood for the site of Frank Luke's final minutes of life. It was all there, the overlooking, parallel line of hills on either side of the village that had once been occupied by German infantry and antiaircraft units, and the small creek to the north of the church and highway.

One could almost imagine Luke's Spad XIII flashing by just to the south of the church at steeple height. The American's reputation had preceded him; the glare from his final downed balloon still illuminated dusk's gathering gloom but two kilometers to the west, near Milly.

German occupation troops had rushed into Murvaux's streets and fields. Was this the American balloon buster they had heard so much about - and sought for so long? The muzzle flashes and rapid

The Verdun Battle Memorial/ Museum houses, among its numerous military displays, an early French Nieuport pursuit plane, as well as a German Fokker Eindecker.
Author's photo.

The author atop one of the numerous gun turrets at Fort Douaumont on the Verdun line. A tour of the fort's damp underground galleries is not recommended for the claustrophobic! Art Ronnie photo.

The author at the American Meuse-Argonne Cemetery at Romagne, the final resting place of Medal of Honor flier Frank Luke, Jr. Luke's grave is located in Block A, Row 26, gravesite 13 (A-26-13).

Art Ronnie photo.

report of their bolt-action rifles resounded through the village and surrounding foothills.

Standing on the northern slope overlooking Murvaux, one could almost see his small pursuit plane as it ran the gauntlet, it's wings smartly and suddenly dipping into a left bank just east of the church, headed toward us, making for a reciprocal course home. And then it happened. He was hit. The Spad had noticeably convulsed in protest of the violation.

And there up the slope, not 200 meters to the south of our parked car was that dark, inviting creek, which today is marked with a long line of trees. It was between that meter-wide rush of water and this writer that Luke had sat his Spad down for the final time. There, perhaps, sweating profusely, gasping for air, choking on his own fluids, with blood flowing freely from his gaping chest wound, the Arizonan had left a grizzly trail as he stumbled and crawled that last 75 meters to the water's edge - there to die.

As for those fanciful pulp tales of the critically wounded American having a final OK-Corral-style shoot-out with German infantry in the walled-in church graveyard — located more than a quarter mile to the south — it simply did not happen!

One piece of business remained in Murvaux. Where was the **Luke Monument**? Typical of such small villages, there was no one about, but then, too, it was raining lightly. Driving up and down the few streets in town, we came across an open garage and a local resident at the trunk of his large black Citroen automobile. Stopping to ask about the monument, we found resident Bruno Alberti spoke about as much English as this writer spoke French. But in time, repeating the mutually-understood word "monument," a glimmer of understanding began to reach his eyes. "Monument? Frank Luke? Aviateur Americain? Luke? Que! Que!"

His hand gestures began pointing back up D-102. We thanked him and finally found the modest 15-foot tall stone and metal monument some one hundred feet beyond the village's western exit sign on Highway D-102. We'd already driven past the structure at least once, as it was buried within several trees by the roadside.

The modest, recently restored Frank Luke Monument in Murvaux, off highway D-102 at the village's western boundary. Author's photo

A new plaque dedicated in the year 2000 declared both in English and French:

> "MEMORY OF LT. FRANK LUKE,
> UNITED STATES AIR SERVICE,
> BALLOON BUSTING ACE OF W.W.I
> CRITICALLY WOUNDED
> LANDED HIS SPAD 700 YARDS NORTH AND
> WAS KILLED BY GERMAN SMALL ARMS FIRE
> 29 SEPTEMBER 1918."

The final line obviously based on the original 1919 affidavit of the Murvaux villagers.

As this writer was taking pictures of the monument, Mr. Alberti drove up and invited us back to his home where he and his wife kindly related through photos and newspaper clippings the story of the monument's recent restoration. Mr. Alberti, it turns

A rather soggy author with Murvaux resident and Luke Monument committee associate Bruno Alberti on the steps of the recently restored Luke Monument at the western boundary of Murvaux on Highway D-102. Art Ronnie photo.

out, had himself been associated with the committee of Frenchmen and Americans headed by Stephane Skinner, who had restored and rededicated the monument only two years earlier, in 2000. The new plaque replaces one which had been placed on the monument in 1957 and which had long since disappeared.

Headed westbound for the Normandy beaches, we stopped in **Compiegne**. There in the forest resides for public viewing Marshall Foch's famed rail car, the site for the signing of the Armistice which ended the First World War, as well as the site of French capitulation in 1940 to Hitler's conquering Nazi armies.

The **American Cemetery at Normandy** overlooking World War Two's famed Omaha Beach was the site for the opening and closing moments of director Steven Spielberg's 1998 war film classic *Saving Private Ryan*. Today the cemetery's more than 172 acres contains the graves of 9,387 American war dead.

Among those residing above Omaha Beach is President Teddy Roosevelt's son, Brig. Gen. Teddy Roosevelt, Jr., who gained fame and the Medal of Honor for his commanding role in the 1944 D-Day landings at and inland from Utah Beach. The general's gravesite (D-28-45) resides next to that of his brother and World

War One 95th Pursuit Squadron pilot **Quentin Roosevelt** (D-28-46).

Should a balanced perspective of war's terrible toll be sought, this writer suggests visiting one of the numerous and well kept, if decidedly more somber, cemeteries of German war dead. Particularly moving was the relatively new circular cemetery for Germany's World War II dead at **Mont-de-Huisnes/Frankreich**, overlooking the famed French abbey of Mont St. Michel in the English Channel.

This German cemetery was opened in 1963 with the re-interred remains of 11,956 known and unknown soldiers from throughout the French region. Unlike so many of the World War One resting places, this cemetery of World War Two dead was well attended by middle aged and middle class families and their children — quite Western in every sense, including their German dialects.

BIBLIOGRAPHY

Books

Andrade, John M. *U.S. Military Aircraft Designations and Serials since 1909.* England: Midland Counties Pub., 1979.

Archibald, Norman *Heaven High, Hell Below*, New York: Albert and Charles Boni, 1935.

Barrett, William E. *The First War Planes, abridged edition.* Greenwich, Connecticut: Fawcett, 1964.

Blesse, Frederick C., M/Gen. USAF (Ret.), Check Six: *A Fighter Pilot Looks Back.* Mesa, Arizona: Champlin Fighter Museum Press, 1987.

Bowen, Ezra, et al. *Knights of the Air:* The Epic of Flight series, Virginia: Time-Life, 1980.

Boyne, Walter J. *Beyond the Wild Blue: A History of the U.S. Air Force.* New York: St. Martin's Griffin, 1997

A Brief History of Luke AFB and the 56th Fighter Wing. Arizona: Office of History, HQ 56th Fighter Wing, 1995.

Clancy, Tom and Horner, Chuck. *Every Man a Tiger.* New York: G.P. Putnam, 1999.

Chessman, E.F., ed. *Fighter Aircraft of the 1914-1918 War.* Herts, England: Harleyford, 1960.

_____, ed. *Reconnaissance and Bomber Aircraft of the 1914-1918 War.* Warwick, England: Warwick, 1962.

Cohen, Stan. *East Wind Rain: A Pictorial History of the Pearl Harbor Attack.* Missoula, Montana: Pictorial Histories Publishing, 1981.

Connors, John F. *Albatros, Fighters in Action series*. Texas: Squadron/Signal, 1981.

_____ *Spad Fighters in Action*. Texas: Squadron/Signal, 1989.

Cooksley, Peter. *Nieuport Fighters in Action*. Texas: Squadron/Signal, 1997.

De Tocqueville, Alexis, *Democracy in America*. New York: Mentor edition, 1997.
Dunning, John. *On the Air - The Encyclopedia of Old-Time Radio*. New York: Oxford University Press, 1998.

Edwards, Betty. *Drawing on the Right Side of the Brain*. New York: Jeremy P. Tarcher/Putnam, 1989.

Everett, Susanne. *World War I: An Illustrated History*. New York: Exeter, 1987.

Farmer, James H. *Celluloid Wings:The Impact of Movies on Aviation*. Blue Ridge Summit, Pennsylvania: TAB, 1984.

Farr, Finis. *Rickenbacker's Luck:An American Life*. Houghton Mifflin, 1979.

Faust, Albert Bernhardt. *The German Element in the United States*, volumes one and two. New York: The Steuben Society of America, 1927.

Franks, Norman L.R., Bailey, Frank W. and Guest, Russell. *Above the Lines: A Complete Record of the Fighter Aces of the German Air Service, Naval Air Service and Flanders Marine Corps, 1914-1918*. London: Grub Street, 1993

_____, _____. *Over the Front: a Complete Record of the Fighter Aces and Units of the United States and French Air Services, 1914-1918*. London: Grub Street, 1992.

Glines, Carrol V. *The Doolittle Raid: America's Daring First Strike against Japan*. New York: Orion Books, 1988.

Goldner, Orville and Turner, George E. *The Making of King Kong*. New York: A.S. Barnes, 1975.

Gordon, Dennis. *Lafayette Escadrille Pilot Biographies*. Missoula, Montana: The Doughboy Historical Society, 1991.

Green, William and Swanborough, Gordon. *The World's Great Fighter Aircraft: The inside story of 100 Classics in the Evolution of Fighter Aircraft.* New York: Crescent, 1981.

Hall, Norman S. *The Balloon Buster.* Garden City, New York: Doubleday, Doran, 1928.

Hartney, Harold E. and Sutton, George W. Jr. *Up and at 'Em: The War Memoirs of an American Ace.* Harrisburg, Pennsylvania: Stack Pole Sons, 1940.

Historical Statistics of United States: Colonial Times to 1970: Bicentennial Edition, Part 1. Washington D.C.: U.S. Dept. of Commerce, Bureau of Census, 1975.

Hudson, James J. Hostile Skies: *A Combat History of the American Air Service in World War I.* New York: Syracuse University, 1968.

Jablonski, Edward. *Outraged Skies: Airwar, Vol. 3.* New York: Doubleday, 1971.

Jackson, Robert. *Fighter Pilots of World War I.* New York: St. Martin,1977.

Jerram, Michael F. *Antiques of the Air.* Basinghall Books Ltd., 1980.

Korn, Jerry, editor. *This Fabulous Century, Volume II, 1910-1920.* New York: Time-Life Books, 1969.

Lawson, Frank, Col. USAF (Ret.). *War Diary, 27th Fighter Squadron.* Baltimore, Maryland: Gateway Press, 1997.

Levine, Isaac Don. Mitchell: **Pioneer of Air Power**. New York: Duell, Sloan and Pearce, 1943.

Maurer, Maurer, ed. *Combat Squadrons of the Air Force, World War II* Washington D.C.: USAF Historical Division, Air University, Department of the Air Force, 1969..

May, Ernest R. *The Life History of the United States, Volume 9, The Progressive Era, 1901-1917.* New York: Time-Life Books, 1964.

Mullins, John D. *An Escort of P-38s: The 1st Fighter Group in World War II.* St. Paul, Minnesota: Phalanx, 1995.

Ravenstein, Charles A. *Air Force Combat Wings*, Lineage and Honors Histories,

1947-1977. Washington D.C.: Office of Air Force History, 1984.

Renehan, Edward J., Jr. *The Lion's Pride: Theodore Roosevelt and His Family in Peace and War*. New York: Oxford, 1998.

_____, ed. *The U.S. Air Service in World War I, Vol. 1 and 2*. Washington D.C.: Office of Air Force History, Headquarters USAF, 1978.

Rickenbacker, Eddie V. *Fighting the Flying Circus*. New York: Doubleday, 1919.

_____. *Rickenbacker, an Autobiography*. New Jersey: Prentice-Hall, 1967.

_____. *Seven Came Through*. New York: Doubleday, 1943.

Roberts, Michael. *The Illustrated Directory of the United States Air Force*. Crescent Books Pub., 1989.

Robertson, Bruce. *Air Aces of the 1914-1918 War*. Los Angeles: Aero, 1959.

Shettle, M.L. *United States Naval Air Stations of World War II, Volume 2 - Western States*. Bowersville, Georgia: Schaertel Pub., 1997.

Sloan, James J., Jr. *Wings of Honor: American Airmen in World War I*. Pennsylvania: Schiffer,1994.

Slotkin, Richard. *Gunfighter Nation: The Myth of the Frontier in Twentieth-Century America*. New York: Atheneum, 1992.

Strahan, Hew, ed. *World War I: A History.* New York: Oxford University, 1998.

Swanborough, Gordon and Bowers, Peter M. *United States Naval Aircraft since 1911*. New York: Funk and Wagnalls, 1968.

Thayer, Lucien H. *America's First Eagles.* San Jose, California and Mesa, Arizona: R. James Bender and Champlin Fighter Museum, 1983.

Underwood, John. *Madcaps, Millionaires and "Mose": The Chronicle of an Exciting Era when the Airways led to Glendale. Glendale, California*: Heritage, 1984.

United States Presidents, The: Their Lives, Families and Great Decisions as Told by The Saturday Evening Post. Indianapolis, Indiana: Curtis. 1980.

Whitehouse, Arch. *Hun Killer*. New York: Award, 1966.

_____. *The Years of the Sky Kings*. New York: Doubleday, 1959.

Winter, Denis. *The First of the Few: Fighter Pilots of the First World War*. Georgia: University of Georgia, 1982.

Yeager, Chuck and Janos, Leo. *Yeager, an Autobiography*. New York: Bantam, 1985.

Periodicals

Bodenschatz, Karl. *"Final Days of Jasta 11."* Cross and Cockade Journal, Vol.5/No.1/Spring 1964.

Bowers, Peter M. *"The Rotary: Rough on Fighter Pilots."* Air Trails Military Aircraft, 1970.

Cadwaller, Bruce. *"Rickenbacker Growth to Bring Windfall, Study Shows."* Dispatch County Offices Reporter, 2 March 1999.

Catlin, Russ. *"The Rickenbacker Saga."* Speed Age, May 1955.

Christy, Joe. *"Super Ace from Arizona."* Air Progress, February 1968.

Craig, James. *"Garland-Lincoln Nieuports."* WWI Aero, August 2000.

Door, Robert F. *"94th Fighter Squadron."* Wings of Fame, Vol. 4/1996.

"Famed Aviation Hero Eddie Rickenbacker Dies at 82." Cross and Cockade Journal, Vol.14/No.3/Autumn 1973.

Farmer, James H. *"The Hunters."* Air Classics Magazine, June 1988.

"Frank Luke's Elgin at the U.S. Air Force Museum." American Aviation Historical Society Journal, Spring 1985.

Franzi, Emil and Luke, Terri Solty. *"WWI Ace Frank Luke: An Enigmatic American Hero."* Arizona Highways, February 1998.

Frey, Royal D. *"A.E.F. Combat Airfields and Monuments in France, WWI."* American Aviation Historical Society Journal, Fall 1972.

Glines, C.V. *"Charmed Life of Captain Eddie Rickenbacker."* Aviation History Magazine, January 1999.

Gordon, Dennis. *"The Ordeal of Alan Winslow."* Over the Front, Vol.1/No.1/Spring 1986.

Gose, Ben. *"Gore's Controversial Priorities for Higher Education."* The Chronicle of Higher Education, September 15, 2000.

Grosz, Peter M., et al. *"Gone West."* Obituary column. Cross and Cockade Journal, Vol.15/No.4/Winter 1974.

Guttman, Jon, *"Balloon Buster."* Aviation Heritage .

Hackett, Dr. Thomas. *"Profile of a Successful American Great War Pilot."* World War I Aeroplanes, July, 1983.

Hays, Peter, *"Flying the Spad VII."* WWI Aero, The Journal of the Early Aeroplane, February 2001.

Houchin, Roy F., Jr. *"The Technical Problems of the Nieuport 28C-1 1918."* WWI Aero, April 1988.

Kimes, Beverly Rae. *"The Rickenbacker."* Automobile Quarterly, Vol.13/No.4/Winter 1975.

Morris, Michael J. *"Combat Success in American Aviation: 1918."* Over the Front, Fall 1997.

Patin, Jacques. *"The History of a Volunteer: The American Ace - Gervais Raoul Lufbery."* Cross and Cockade, Autumn 1991.

Peddrick, Wendy Alexis. *"Mustangs."* Air Force Magazine, March 1998.

Robertson, Bruce. *"Drachen!"* Windsock International, Vol.3/No.2/Summer 1987.

"Slayer of Lieut. Quentin Roosevelt." Los Angeles Times, 7 January 1919.

Stair, Ian. *"Bessonneau Hangar File."* Windsock. No date available.

Swearinger, Ed. *"Kuster Und Der Drachen."* Cross and Cockade Journal, Vol.5/No.2/Autumn 1964.

Tillman, Barrett. *"The U.S.A.S. Ace Race of 1918."* American Fighter Aces and Friends Bulletin, Vol.8/No.1/Spring 1991.

"Heroes: Durable Man." Time Magazine, April 17, 1950.

Urwin, Gregory J.W. *"The Balloon Buster: The Story of Second Lieutenant Frank Luke, Jr."* Air Classics, December 1978.

Vittali, Paul. *"Balloon Commander."* Over the Front, Vol.6/No.3/Fall 1991.

Williams, Walter S. *"The Diary of Cpl. Walter S. Williams, Twenty-Seventh Aero Squadron U.S.A.S., A.E.F."* Journal, American Aviation Historical Society, Summer 1992.

Wynne, H. Hugh. *"A Brief History of the 27th Aero Squadron - A.E.F."* Cross and Cockade Journal, Vol.1/No.2/Summer, 1960.

Chapter Notes and References

Chapter One: "A Gentleman's Game?"

1. On 23 April 1960 Art Ronnie, at the time a newspaper columnist, stole a few hours away from a field assignment to interview former Lafayette Escadrille flier Edward F. Hinkle at his New Mexico home. An edited rendition of this interview was later published in 1964 in the Volume Five, Number One issue of *Cross and Cockade* magazine. Mister Hinkle, however, requested that certain aspects of the discussion related to the darker side of Norman Prince's habits not be printed. It seems, as Ronnie has related to this writer, that Prince had been known among his fellow fliers as "The Snowbird" because of his ongoing addiction to cocaine. The general consensus among the squadron's fliers at the time was that Prince was under the influence when his fragile Nieuport crashed into power lines while he was attempting a landing on 12 October 1916. He died of his injuries three days later. This, however, is strictly hearsay information as Hinkle did not join the squadron until 1 March 1917.
2. Winter, *The First of the Few: Fighter Pilots of the First World War,* 19.
3. Ibid.
4. Hudson, *Hostile Skies: A Combat History of the American Air Service in World War I,* 12
5. Ibid., 26.
6. As a point of reference, in the year 2000, 36 percent of the American population between the ages of 25 and 29 have an Associate in Arts (two-year) or Bachelors (four-year) degree.
7. Levine, *Mitchell: Pioneer of Air Power,* 88.

Chapter Two: "Blue Collar Cadets"

1. Winter, The First of the Few: Fighter Pilots of the First World War, 24.
2. Farr, Rickenbacker's Luck, An American Life, 6.
3. See: Edwards, Drawing on the Right Side of the Brain.
4. Rickenbacker, Rickenbacker: An Autobiography, 17.
5. Ibid., 92.
6. Hall, The Balloon Buster, 4.
7. Carrying on the family flying tradition, Luke's first cousin once removed, Bob Schipf, was going through Naval flight training at NAS Pensacola at the end of WWII and received his wings in 1946 as an enlisted Aviation

Pilot First Class, graduating to the command of a Kingfisher floatplane. Schipf served a number of decades as a Naval Reserve officer, while a professor of library science at the University of Montana.

8. Haiber and Haiber, Frank Luke: The September Rampage, 157-159.
9. De Tocqueville, Democracy in America, 282.
10. African-Americans, who were separated out of this 1910 accounting as part of the "colored population," numbered just short of ten million; Indians registered a quarter million; and Chinese and Japanese each numbered some 72,000. The latter were, unfortunately, more amenable to internment than was the vastly larger German population. During World War Two a reported 110,000 Japanese were interned, while just some 10,000 German-Americans shared in their loss of wartime freedom.
11. Faust, The German Element in the United States, Vol. 1, 590.

Chapter Three: "Birth of America's First Pursuit Group."

1. Sloan, Wings of Honor,164.
2. Maurer, U.S. Air Service in World War I, Vol., 97.
3. Jackson, Fighter Pilots of World War I, 113.
4. Dorr, "94th Fighter Squadron," Wings of Fame, Vol. 4, 20.
5. The operative word here is "official" as Raoul Lufbery led Rickenbacker and Douglas Campbell, in their still unarmed Nieuports, over the front lines as early as 6 March 1918.
6. Rickenbacker, Fighting the Flying Circus, 37.
7. Ibid., 41.
8. Ibid., 54.
9. Strangely, though Sloan lists Lt. Oscar J. Gude as having joined the 94th on 1 March 1918, three days before Rickenbacker, Rickenbacker tells us this was the pilot's "first actual combat." Perhaps his poor showing on this occasion suggests the reason.
10. "Knock-out" blow was a popular term, no doubt of wishful thinking, used by ever more desperate German military planners of the period.
11. Everett, World War I, 210.
12. Rickenbacker

Chapter Four. "What Price Glory?"

1. Hartney and Sutton, Up and At 'Em (Stackpole Sons, 1940), 152.
2. Ibid., 167.
3. Ibid., 174.
4. Archibald, Heaven High, Hell Deep, 103-104.

5. Ibid., 106.
6. Stair, "Bessonneau Hangar File," Windsock International, Vol. 11, No. 1, 17-20.
7. Winter, The First of the Few, Fighter Pilots of the First World War, 86.
8. Ibid., 87.
9. Rickenbacker, Fighting the Flying Circus, 121,144.
10. Hartney, 195-196.
11. Rickenbacker, 195.
12. Cheesman, Fighter Aircraft of the 1914-1918 War, 98.
13. So short were the Americans of Vickers that many Nieuports never flew with more than one gun before they were phased out in favor of the Spad.
14. Bowers, "The Rotary: Rough On Fighter Pilots," Air Trails Military Aircraft, 27.
15. Houchin, Jr., "The Technical Problems of the Nieuport 28C-1: 1918," WWI Aero, April 1988, 16.
16. Archibald, 186-188.
17. Jerram, Antiques of the Air, 60.
18. The details of Hartney's recounting of the 16 August 1918 mission vary depending upon which section of his 1940 autobiography one is reading at the time. Compare pages 198 to 256.
19. Hartney, 256.
20. Sloan, Wings of Honor, 287.
21. Ibid.

Chapter Five: "Hartney's Gang."

1. DeTocqueville, Democracy in America, 274.
2. Winter, The First of the Few, Fighter Pilots of the First World War, 19.
3. Ibid., 20
4. Ibid., 22
5. Hartney and Sutton, Up and at 'Em, 107.
6. DeTocqueville, 281, 282
7. Ibid., 282
8. Hartney, 108
9. Farr, Rickenbacker's Luck, An American Life, 56
10. Williams, "The Diary of Cpl. Walter S. Williams, Twenty-Seventh Aero Squadron, U.S.A.S., A.E.F., Journal of the American Aviation Historical Society, Summer 1992, 90.
11. Hartney, 163-164.
12. Farr, 59
13. Sloan, Jr., Wings of Honor, American Airmen in World War I, 113.
14. Renehan, The Lion's Pride, Theodore Roosevelt and his Family in Peace

and War, 193
15. There has long been some conjecture as to just who brought Roosevelt
down. Rickenbacker, in his first autobiography, Fighting the Flying
Circus (p. 184) suggested it was then 24-plane ace "Sergeant K. Thom of
the Richthofen Circus." Yet, Franks, Bailey and Guest's recent, authoritative Above the Lines (p. 215) lists Karl Thom as flying with Jasta 21, not
a "Circus"/JGI unit; nor is Thom credited with a 14 July 1918 kill. *Wings
of Honor* author James J. "John" Sloan suggested that the credit for
Roosevelt's downing rests with an "Adj. Donhouser of Jasta 11." Indeed,
a 7 January 1919 article in the Los Angeles Times seems to confirm that
Christian Donhouser, at 94 pounds, called the "smallest aviator in the
Kaiser's army," did down the president's son. The article goes on to say
that Donhauser hoped to soon become a U.S. citizen. *Above the Lines* (p.
99) states, however, that Donhauser, credited with 19 aerial victories, was
killed in Koblenz in a 1919 crash. Their carefully assembled list of aerial
kills shows that the German ace, recovering from earlier combat wounds,
was officially credited with no aerial victories between 18 May and 20
August 1918. Nor was his Jasta 17 unit a member of the Flying Circus!
What is clear, the news devastated the outspoken former president, who'd
actively advocated U.S. involvement in the European conflict as early as
1915. A rapid decline in health followed, with death coming on 6
January 1919 less than two months after the Armistice. The former president died the day before the Donhauser article appeared in the L.A.
Times.
16. Hartney, 183
17. Ibid., 187
18. Ibid.
19. Hartney claimed nine losses for the period, though Sloan's later research
shows only eight.
20. Once again the numbers do not add up. Hartney claims he received nine
replacement pilots between the 23 July and 25 July arrivals. Sloan lists,
by name, the arrival of ten replacement pilots for the 27th over the same
period of time.
21. The author had the pleasure of casually visiting with Grandville Woodard
at a Southern California Cross and Cockade meeting some three decades
ago. The aviator's recollections of Frank Luke's bad boy escapades
remained vivid, perhaps overly so, as such larger-than-life characters
often must be seen to be believed!
22. Archibald, Heaven High, Hell Deep. 101-102.
23. Hartney, 189.

Chapter Six: "A Cowboy Despised"

1. Rickenbacker, Fighting the Flying Circus, 231.
2. Hartney and Sutton, Up and at 'Em, 251.
3. Archibald, Heaven High, Hell Deep, 123.
4. Hartney, 116.
5. Jablonski, Outraged Skies, 48.
6. The number of Spads on the protection patrol just as easily could have been nine or even 15! Hartney has generated tremendous confusion with his conflicting and separate accounts of the 16 August mission - or, more properly, missions. On page 198 of his Up and at 'Em autobiography he seems to suggest Luke took off an hour late, due to mechanical problems, after Hartney had led a patrol of 11 planes aloft at 9:10 a.m. Here Hartney intimates Luke made his first claim that morning. Hartney then, incidentally, mentions he led another patrol of nine planes at 5:05 that evening by way of telling us new pilot Nevius was killed shortly there-after in an operational accident. No further mention is made of Luke at this point. But, later, on page 256, the 16 August, 5:05 PM evening mis-sion is revisited. This time, However, Hartney tells us he led 15 Spads, 12 from the 27th and three from the 94th, on the flight. After losing the entire formation of Spads to aborts, save that of Luke's, the Arizonan shot an enemy plane off the tail of his squadron C.O.
7. Hartney, 257.
8. Further adding to the confusion, Luke's 16 August combat report makes no mention of ever finding Hartney's formation, let alone shooting a German pursuit off his C.O.'s tail. Rather, Luke specifically reports he saw no other Allied aircraft during this engagement!
9. Hartney, 214
10. De Tocqueville, Democracy in America, 24.
11. Williams, "The Diary of Cpl. Walter S. Williams, Twenty-Seventh Aero Squadron U.S.A.S., A.E.F.," Journal, American Aviation Historical Society, 92.
12. Hartney, 213.
13. Sloan, Jr., Wings of Honor, American Airmen in World War I, 310-312.
14. Hartney, 213-214. More than one historian, among them James J. Hudson in his "Hostile Skies," basing his source solely on Hartney's written word, misreported the 1st Pursuit Group's move up to Rembercourt as taking place on the night of 22 August 1918. The actual 1 September move is confirmed by Walter Williams' diary, as well as that of Maurer's official USAF history of Combat Squadrons of the Air Force, World War II.
15. It was Arch Whitehouse, in his 1959 WWI history: The Years of the Sky Kings (Doubleday), p.283 and in his 1966 Luke biography Hun Killer (Award Books), p.26, who tells us of Luke's time as squadron engineering officer.

16. In his autobiography, Fighting the Flying Circus, Rickenbacker tells us he arrived at Rembercourt on the evening of 11 September, yet Finis Farr's authoritative Rickenbacker's Luck, based in large part on the flier's personal diaries, lists the date of arrival as "Monday, September 9."

17. Frank Luke's Combat Report for 12 September 1918: "Saw 3 EA near Lavigneulle and gave chase following them directly east towards Metz. Saw enemy balloon at Marieville. Destroyed it after three passes at it, each within a few yards of the balloon. The third pass was made when the balloon was very near the ground. Both guns stopped so pulled off to one side. Fixed left gun and turned about to make one final effort to burn it, but saw it had started. The next instant it burst into great flames and dropped on the winch, destroying it. The observer, Joseph M. Fox, who saw the burning said he thought several were killed when it burst into flames so near the ground. There was a good field near our balloons so landed for confirmation. Left field and started back when my motor began cutting out. Returned to same field, and there found out my motor could not be fixed, so returned by motorcycle. Attached you will find confirmation from Lt. Fox and Lt. Smith. Both saw burning."

18. Haiber and Haiber, Frank Luke: The September Rampage, 210-211.

19. Ibid.

20. Hartney, 260.

21. Korn, This Fabulous Century, Volume II (1910-1920), 235.

22. Ibid., 238

23. Ibid., 236.

24. Ibid., 238.

Chapter 7: The Enemy

1. Franks, Bailey and Guest, Above the Lines, 15.

2. Barrett, The First War Planes, 74.

3. Franks, Bailey and Guest, 17.

4. Swearinger, "Kuster Und Der Drachen," Cross and Cockade Journal, Vol.5/No. 2, 246.

5. Ibid., 248.

6. Ibid., 250.

Chapter 8: The Contest

1. Hartney and Sutton, Up and at 'Em (Stackpole Sons, 1940), 116.

2. Ibid., 260

3. Ibid., 261

4. Ibid., 262
5. Ibid., 265-266
6. Ibid., 268
7. Ibid., 277
8. Williams, "The Diary of Cpl. Walter S. Williams: Twenty-Seventh Aero Squadron, U.S.A.S, A.E.F.," Journal, American Aviation Historical Society, Summer 1992, 92.
9. Whitehouse, Hun Killer, 166.
10. Hall, The Balloon Buster, 107.
11. Whitehouse, The Years of the Sky Kings, 288.
12. Whitehouse, Hun Killer, 171.
13. Bowen and the editors of Time-Life, Knights of the Air, The Epic of Flight series, 171.
14. Hall, 108.
15. Whitehouse, The Years of the Sky Kings, 288.
16. Whitehouse, Hun Killer, 173.
17. Hartney, 282.
18. Hudson, Hostile Skies, A Combat History of the American Air Service in World War I, 297, footnote

Chapter 9: The Curse: America's Ace of Aces

1. Rickenbacker's second aerial kill on 7 May 1918 would not be confirmed until 1960.
2. Rickenbacker, Fighting the Flying Circus, 227.
3. Paul Frank Baer lost his life when his plane crashed into Hong Kong Harbor on 9 December 1930. Edgar Gardiner Tobin was killed on 10 January 1954 when his Grumman Mallard amphibian crashed into Lake Wallace near Shreveport, Louisiana. He was 58.
4. The 103rd had officially joined the US Air Service on 18 February 1918.
5. Farr, Rickenbacker's Luck, An American Life, 66
6. Ibid., 68.
7. See Franks and Bailey's Over the Front, p.68, which, contrary to Rickenbacker's autobiography, lists the day's two kills as both balloons.
8. Farr listed the squadron count as "68." See Farr, p.73.

Chapter 10: Legacy

1. Bowen, Knights of the Air (volume from Time-Life series The Epic of Flight), 169-170.
2. Doerflinger translation, "Final Days of Jasta 11," excerpted from the book

272AMERICA'S PIONEER ACES

Jagd in Flanders Himmel by Karl Bodenschatz, Cross and Cockade
Journal, Vol.5/No.1, 77.
3. Ibid., 79.
4. Farr, Rickenbacker's Luck, An American Life, 78.
5. Ibid., 181.
6. Despite reports of Udet's death by gunshot, Rickenbacker would continue to
believe that Udet was actually killed testing an airplane sabotaged by the
Gestapo. Indeed, just such a scenario was dramatized in the 1954 West
German and Curt Juergens feature film "The Devil's General."
7. Hartney and Sutton, Up and at 'Em, 312
8. Ibid., 310
9. Clancy with Horner, Every Man a Tiger, 107.
10. Sloan, Wings of Honor, American Airmen in World War I, 134.
11. Wynne, "A Brief History of the 27th Aero Squadron - A.E.F.," Cross and
Cockade Journal, Vol.1/No.2, 29: C.C. Moseley's 8 November 1918 combat report.
12. Grosz, "Gone West" obituary column, Cross and Cockade Journal,
Vol.15/No.4, 381.
13. Underwood, Madcaps, Millionaires and 'Mose,' p.45. So much a part of
the Southern California social fabric of the time was he that it was no surprise to hear "Major Moseley" referred to in the Grand Central Air
Terminal set, 1934 Shirley Temple feature "Bright Eyes." [Farmer]
14. The latter field, first commanded by Robert "God Is My Co-Pilot" Scott,
was the location for the 1941 Abbott and Costello farce "Keep 'Em
Flying," the opening and latter sequences of "Best Years of Our
Lives"(1946) and the 1964-67 ABC Television series "12 O'Clock High,"
among numerous other Hollywood productions.
15. Farr, 86.
16. Kimes, "The Rickenbacker," Automobile Quarterly, Vol.13/No.4, 422,
426.
17. During World War Two, Allison aircraft engines would power the P-38,
P-40 and early models of the P-51 Mustang fighter plane.
18. Farr, 295-296.
19. Ibid., 300.
20. Ibid., 334.
21. Ibid., 344.
22. Merian C. "Coop" Cooper, whose life motto was "The Three D's: keep it
Distant, Difficult and Dangerous," was another one of those extraordinary
WWI American flying veterans who was to fully pack four lifetimes within his lone remarkable span. The high-spirited Jacksonville, Florida native
and expelled Annapolis cadet flew DH-4s with the 20th Aero Squadron.
He was shot down and captured on 26 September 1918 - three days
before Luke's final flight. He later commanded an air squadron for the

Polish Army fighting the Bolshevists. By the mid-1920s Cooper was an established Hollywood film producer. His between-the-war credits include "Grass" (1925), "Chang" (1927), "King Kong" (1933) - in which he appears as a rear-seat Naval aerial gunner peppering away at the giant ape, and "The Last Days of Pompeii" (1935). There is some speculation that Cooper may have proposed a film biography of Frank Luke during the mid-1930s, but this remains unconfirmed. By 1940 Cooper's wander-lust had again gotten the better of him, sending him off to war-torn China with Claire Chennault, commander of the American Volunteer Group - the famed Flying Tigers. Cooper would return in 1946, a 14th Air Force vet-eran and soon retired USAAF brigadier general, to produce, with Admiral John Ford, USNR, some of the finest postwar Westerns Hollywood would screen. Titles included: "She Wore A Yellow Ribbon" (1949), "The Quiet Man" (1952), and "The Searchers" (1956). Merian Cooper would pass away on 21 April 1973, within hours of his longtime friend and "King Kong" star Robert Armstrong - and two months before the death of Eddie Rickenbacker. Cooper was 81.

23. The Elgin in question was actually a small pocket watch, now displayed in the U.S. Air Force Museum's World War One Medal of Honor case. See: Journal, American Aviation Historical Society, Spring 1985, p. 23.
24. Luke never received credit for these two planes.
25. Hartney, 285-286
26. Ibid., 286-287
27. Frey, "A.E.F. Combat Airfields and Monuments in France, WWI," Journal, American Aviation Historical Society, Vol.13/No.3, 198.
28. Haiber, Frank Luke, The September Rampage. See: Royal Frey's 27 July 1962 Murvaux affidavit, 201-203
29. Whitehouse, Hun Killer, 178-179
30. Hall, The Balloon Buster, 118.
31. Whitehouse, Hun Killer, 192-193.
32. Hall, 121.

Chapter 11: "Military Heritage."

1. Dorr, "94th Fighter Squadron," Wings of Fame, The Journal of Classic Combat, Vol. 4, 36.
2. Maurer, Combat Squadrons of the Air Force, World War II (USAF Historical Division, 261-262.
3. Mullins, An Escort of P-38s, 160.
4. Ted Lawson, an aeronautical engineer by training, went on to work for North American Aviation Company after WWII where one of his first jobs was the writing of the flight manual for the new F-86A Sabre, which

then was first service field tested by the 1st FG.

5. Maurer, 317.
6. Per author's discussion with 94th and 1st FG historian John D. Mullins, 11 Nov. 2000.
7. Ibid.
8. This is the same Bill Irvine who, in later years, was so instrumental in the development of the Second World War's B-29 program. In 1951 Irvine became the commander of the Strategic Air Command's Eighth Air Force, and, as a Lieutenant General, served in the late 1950s as the Deputy Commander of the USAF's Air Materiel Command.
9. Dorr's excellent account suggests the 94th was then stationed at March Field, while Maurer's authoritative Air Force squadron histories suggest the unit was then based at the Municipal Airport at Long Beach, California, the latter position confirmed by 94th and 1st FG historian John D. Mullins.
10. Mullins, 82.
11. Cohen, East Wind Rain: A Pictorial History of the Pearl Harbor Attack (Pictorial Histories, 1981), 20.
12. Farmer, Celluloid Wings, The Impact of Movies on Aviation, 197, 219-225.
13. Farmer, "The Hunters," Air Classics, June 1988, 20-27, 80.
14. Roberts, The Illustrated Directory of the United States Air Force, 134.
15. A Brief History of Luke AFB and the 56th Fighter Wing, 6.
16. Ravenstein, Air Force Combat Wings, Lineage and Honors Histories, 1947-1977, 148.
17. Roberts, 162.
18. Cadwaller, "Rickenbacker Growth To Bring Windfall, Study Shows" Dispatch County Offices Reporter, 2 March 1999.
19. Lawson, War Diary, 27th Fighter Squadron, 4-5.
20. Author's interview with Tom Maloney, 1 Nov. 2000.
21. Author's interview with M/Gen. Frederic C. "Boots" Blesse, USAF (Ret.), 1 Nov. 2000.

INDEX